SACRED
PLUNDER

SACRED PLUNDER

VENICE AND THE AFTERMATH OF THE FOURTH CRUSADE

DAVID M. PERRY

THE PENNSYLVANIA STATE UNIVERSITY PRESS

UNIVERSITY PARK, PENNSYLVANIA

Library of Congress Cataloging-in-Publication Data

Perry, David M., 1973–
Sacred plunder : Venice and the aftermath of the
Fourth Crusade / David M. Perry.
pages   cm
Includes bibliographical references and index.
Summary: "Explores the emergence of a body of texts
about relics transported from Constantinople to the
West as a after the Fourth Crusade, and the role of
these texts in the development of Venice's civic identity
in the thirteenth century"— Provided by publisher.
ISBN 978-0-271-06507-6 (cloth : alk. paper)
ISBN 978-0-271-06508-3 (pbk : alk. paper)
1. Venice (Italy)—History—697–1508.
2. Group identity—Italy—Venice—History—To 1500.
3. Crusades—Fourth, 1202–1204—Historiography.
4. Crusades—Fourth, 1202–1204—Sources.
5. Crusades in literature.
6. Relics in literature.
I. Title.

DG677.6.P47   2015
945'.304—dc23
2014033309

FOR *Lewis and Elisabeth Israels Perry*

CONTENTS

ILLUSTRATIONS

ACKNOWLEDGMENTS

The authors of medieval *translatio* narratives wrote with a profound sense of the community in which they were operating. The community provided these authors with inspiration, audience, guidance, and even funding. As I bring my work on this book to a close, I find myself deeply aware of the debts that I owe to my family, friends, colleagues, mentors, and institutions.

The project owes much to the comments and advice from Alfred Andrea, Bernard Bachrach, Cecilia Gaposchkin, Michael Lower, Susan Noakes, Thomas Madden, Kathryn Reyerson, Jay Rubenstein, Susanna Throop, John Watkins, Brett Whalen, and Diana Wright. I am deeply grateful to the anonymous readers for the Pennsylvania State University Press, as well as to my editor, Ellie Goodman, and to my copyeditor, Julie Schoelles, for their many useful suggestions. In the final stages of compiling the manuscript, I benefited from the assistance of an extraordinarily competent research assistant, Breeanna Watral. Special thanks go to my parents, Lewis and Elisabeth Israels Perry, who by now have become quite expert in medieval Venetian studies.

Funding for research trips to Italy and elsewhere was provided by the Gladys Krieble Delmas Foundation, the Center for Early Modern History at the University of Minnesota, the History Department at the University of Minnesota, and the Faculty Development Committee at Dominican University. The provost's office and the Department of History at Dominican University provided support for image rights, maps, and indexing.

I am exceptionally grateful to Kathleen Rhoades, the interlibrary loan librarian at Dominican University, who made it possible for me to access books from libraries across North America and Europe. I am also grateful to the staffs at the Biblioteca Nazionale Marciana, the Archivio di Stato di Venezia, the Biblioteca Nazionale Braidese in Milan, and the Dumbarton Oaks Byzantine Photograph and Fieldwork Archives for their assistance. The Procuratoria of the Basilica of San Marco, the Patriarchate of Venice, and the Ecumenical Patriarchate of Constantinople all opened many doors for me along the way and periodically allowed me to photograph sacred objects.

Last, I would like to thank my family. The research and writing of this book has overlapped with my marriage to Shannon Leslie and the birth of my two children, Nicholas and Elisabeth. Miracles fill the medieval narratives that I study, but none seem as amazing as my family's enduring love and support.

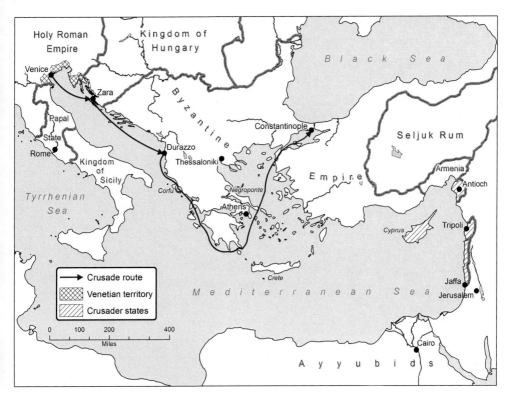

The Fourth Crusade (1202–4). Map by Slaviša Mijatović.

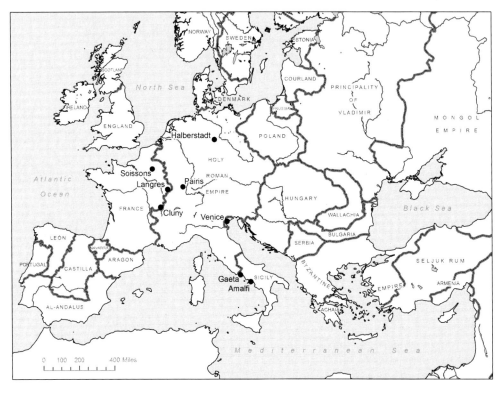

Europe as of 1270 with sites of Fourth Crusade translatio narrative production.
Map by Slaviša Mijatović.

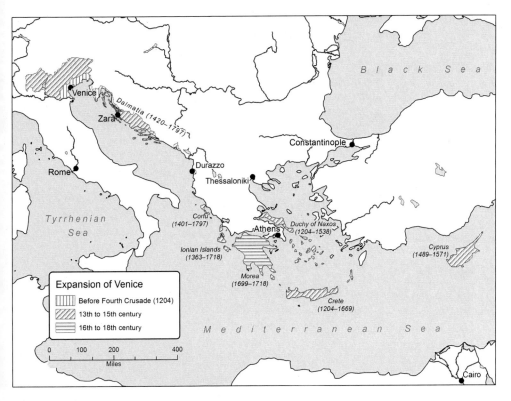

The world of the Venetian empire (1204–1797). Map by Slaviša Mijatović.

Introduction

On April 12, 1204, around midday, a Venetian sailor leaped from the assault bridge of a massive ship called the *Paradiso*. He grasped the top of a tower on the seawall of Constantinople, where the blades of the Varangians and Byzantines made short work of him. His name is unknown. But as the waves drove the *Paradiso* against the walls a second time, a French knight, André d'Ureboise, clambered atop the tower. Managing to unsheathe his sword, he cleared a small space for his comrades as they climbed onto the battlements and claimed several towers. Inspired by this success, men from other ships emulated their heroic actions and surged atop the great walls. "Holy Sepulcher!" they cried.

Even with this foothold, the army of Latin-speaking soldiers had not yet won the day; hordes of Greeks still remained in battle dress at the foot of the great walls. But when an armed priest and crusader, Aleaumes of Clari, emerged from a small gate and brandished his sword, the Greek defenders at the scene fled. Soon, other units of the poorly trained Greek army abandoned the defense, followed by their emperor, Alexius V Doukas Mourtzouphlos. The next day, the Latins prepared to subdue the civilian population but instead found Greek citizens lining the streets, ready to welcome a new Latin emperor. The crusaders, however, had not yet chosen one, and without an emperor no single leader could keep the army in check. The troops overran the gathered citizens and the sack of Constantinople began.[1]

The battle of April 12 and the coronation of Count Baldwin of Flanders as the first Latin emperor of Constantinople on May 16, 1204, closed the long, complex saga of the Fourth Crusade. This book concerns itself with the contest over memory and meaning that followed.

Here, I trace the ways in which that contest shaped the emergence, development, and cultural influence of a distinct body of hagiographical texts known as *translatio* narratives. These texts all describe the movement of relics from the East to the West in the aftermath of the Fourth Crusade. I argue that as the new Latin Empire failed to cohere, critics of the crusade, especially Pope Innocent III, blamed the failures on the loss of God's favor and fixated on the looting of churches as the cause of this loss. Meanwhile, sacred plunder began arriving in the West, and the medieval traditions of translatio required beneficiaries of relics to craft valorizing counternarratives that placed these objects within local sacred geographies. In most cases, these beneficiaries, or the mostly anonymous hagiographers they commissioned, labored to memorialize their newly acquired relics so as to exempt them from broader scrutiny or criticism. In other cases, particularly within Venice and its expanding empire, the translatio narratives served broader cultural purposes. These relic-focused counternarratives and the interpretative modes they revealed played a key role in reshaping Venetian cultural development over the thirteenth century and beyond.

Going to Constantinople, let alone conquering it, was never part of the original plan for the crusade. In fact, the leaders of the crusade had commissioned a massive fleet from Venice in order to launch an amphibious assault upon Egypt. The crusaders and their sponsors hoped that the wealth of Egypt would sustain a campaign in the Holy Land and provide the means for regular resupply and reinforcement. But controversy and unanticipated challenges had dogged the enterprise since nearly the beginning. Despite innovative attempts to organize leadership, transportation, and financing so as to avoid problems of past crusades, the crusaders found themselves in debt, stuck in Venice, and commanded by a sometimes disorderly committee. Constantinople's wealth eventually lured the crusaders into a Byzantine dynastic struggle that left them in little better financial condition, far from their original destination, and excommunicated by the pope. As emperor after emperor fell to internal pressures and Greek and Latin antipathy intensified, the crusaders decided to launch a last-ditch assault on the city. Much to everyone's surprise, it succeeded.

Initially, the Latins who conquered Constantinople, supporters back home, and even some critics of the crusaders were extremely optimistic in the wake of the conquest. This feeling did not last. Although Rome tried, Constantinople's Greek citizens did not convert to the Latin rite in large numbers. The empire was immediately beset by various Greek pretenders to the throne as well as outside invaders. The first Latin emperor soon died in battle. Moreover, despite carefully laid plans concerning the division of plunder that were meant to forestall conflict, the victors argued among themselves over the spoils and then argued collectively with papal legates who came to assert authority over the churches of Constantinople and their vast possessions.

Meanwhile, narratives about the conquest proliferated in diverse genres, with varying degrees of relationship to the events themselves and largely in isolation from one another. And yet, in an act of surprising unanimity, both those most critical of the crusade and those who directly benefitted from it fixated on the looting of the city and its churches. For critics, faced with the inarguable signs of divine favor in the successful assault, blasphemous looting provided a new set of sinful acts to explain why God had subsequently turned his face from the new empire. Pope Innocent III numbered chief among these critics of postconquest sacrilege, but even the crusader-chroniclers Robert of Clari and Geoffrey of Villehardouin identified looting-related impropriety as having caused the loss of divine favor.

Writers within religious institutions newly enriched by sacred objects and saintly patrons from Constantinople faced a distinct set of issues. As sacred relics of all degrees and stature arrived in the West in a great holy diaspora, their presence created the potential for both fiscal enrichment and rise in stature for the Western churches and monasteries. Mere possession of a new relic, however, was not sufficient to transform potentiality into actuality. For that, a relic needed a story.

This book explores the widespread hagiographical memorialization of the Fourth Crusade that took place roughly in the decade following the conquest of Constantinople. Translatio narratives, a subgenre of hagiography that focuses on the movement, or "translation," of relics, are a peculiar group of texts. Their erratic relationship to actual events in the East renders them unreliable as military or political sources. In number and content, they are unusual in the history of crusade memorialization as well. Relic discovery and translation occur throughout the history of the crusades to the Holy Land, but translatio narratives are rare at best. And yet, after 1204, diverse religious houses with no known points of contact with one another responded to their sacred plunder by generating new hagiographical narratives. The circumstances of the composition, content, and cultural impact of this unique intersection of hagiography and memory in the wake of 1204 make up the core of this book.

These texts exist as a body to be studied en masse thanks to the work of a nineteenth-century French historian named Count Paul Èdouard Didier Riant (Comte de Riant). On October 14, 1874, Riant first presented his work on the spoliation of relics from Constantinople in the thirteenth century to the Société Nationale des Antiquaires de France at the Louvre. His report, which took another six meetings to complete, was eventually published in the memoirs of the society as "Dépouilles religieuses à Constantinople au XIIIe siècle."[2] The next year, Riant founded the Société de l'Orient Latin in Paris. In 1877, he published the first volume of his extraordinary *Exuviae sacrae Constantinopolitanae* and began the process of establishing the scale and extant source base for the translation of relics from the East to the West after 1204.[3] Scholars have since located a few additional sources, and Alfred Andrea, in particular, produced superior editions of select texts, essays on the authors and important figures, and a number of extremely useful translations and commentaries. It was the *Exuviae*, however, that defined the hagiographical accounts of the aftermath of 1204 as a corpus.[4] That said, my book benefits from over a century of new scholarship on the crusade itself and new approaches to the study of medieval texts and culture. Riant sought to understand the truth behind the narratives and locate both the origin of specific objects and their destinations in the West. Andrea's scholarship focuses on single texts and figures, explicating each one as fully as possible. Yet, while no work on the relics of 1204 can occur without reference to Riant or reliance on the critical editions and detailed commentaries of Andrea, this book asks new questions about the intertwining of memory and narrative.

Part I, "Contexts," establishes two different types of context for the hagiographies of 1204. Chapter 1 places each act of relic acquisition in a chronological moment and conceptual framework. Rather than conflating all types of acquisition as theft or looting, the framework distinguishes between authorized and unauthorized acts, as well as between early and late moments of acquisition. Chapter 2 explores the creation of normative Latin discourse on the crusade. Pope Innocent III fixated on the looting and disseminated his understanding of events throughout the Latin world; other voices followed his lead. The hagiographers, all beneficiaries of the stripping of Constantinople's sacred resources, sought a way to situate their new possessions in their own locales without directly contradicting papal interpretation.

Part II, "Texts," turns to the hagiographies themselves. Chapter 3 lays out the whole of the corpus (from complete texts to fragments), stories from later centuries, and evidence of *perdita* (lost texts). Chapter 4 turns from content to method. It compares the techniques that hagiographers used to create didactic spaces in the midst of their tales. For some, these didactic moments drew attention away from the relic theft and the troubles with the crusade, while others operated more fully in the medieval mode of pious thievery, a tradition dubbed *furta sacra* by Patrick Geary.[5] For the latter, the logic of pious theft enabled a full-throated defense of the Fourth Crusade as providential, including the looting of churches.

Part III, "Outcomes," turns to Venice. In ways distinct from other sites that received relics from Constantinople, the hagiographies of 1204 took root in Venice's culture and flourished. Chapter 5 links these texts to themes and mythographic practices extant in Venice both before and after 1204. The Venetian translatio texts, perhaps written without knowledge of competing interpretations from Rome or France, embrace the principles of sacred thievery in order to make broader claims about Venetian destiny. Chapter 6 traces the cultural aftermath of the Venetian hagiographies of the Fourth Crusade from the 1230s to the last centuries of the Middle Ages. In the later stages, Venetian mythographers shifted from pinpointing recent temporal origins for Venetian greatness, such as the Fourth Crusade, to claiming an ancient grandeur for the city.

Four topics require a brief overview to contextualize the work that follows: the Fourth Crusade itself, the medieval practice of translatio and hagiographical memorialization, the concept of commemoration and memory as used within this book, and the relationship between translatio and the Crusades before 1204. The last is simple; there is almost none. The relative explosion of translatio narratives after 1204 stands out as a singular event of narrative innovation in part because of the absence of such textual creations during the twelfth century. True, the looting of Constantinople's churches produced relics and the potential for forged relics on a scale unprecedented in Christian history. Relics had played a pivotal role, however, in the First Crusade, particularly during the saga of the Holy Lance and the use of the True Cross.[6] The *inventio* of relics of various sorts shaped the Catholicization of the newly conquered territory during that period.[7] Throughout the twelfth century, crusaders acquired Holy Land relics and installed them in their home churches in the West, but only one contemporary translatio narrative of the style employed in the thirteenth century is known to exist. This lone text relates the translation of the arm of St. George to Flanders, along with other relics, by Count Robert "of Jerusalem."[8] To this source, we might add Venetian translatio narratives that at least tangentially touch on the crusades, discussed in chapter 5. Otherwise, the post-1204 hagiographical writing stands on its own with little medieval precedent.

Nevertheless, narrative had long been central to the practice of relic veneration in Western Christendom. Mere possession offered little benefit without a story to promote the fact of possession. When the relic was already wrapped in stories from other sites or eras, narrative generation became paramount. Narrative controlled meaning. Cynthia Hahn, in her recent study of reliquaries, writes that "the real content of a treasury" is "the power and combination of narratives and 'conversations'" among the sacred objects.[9] For Hahn, the reliquaries themselves often speak. But when meaning becomes contested, more explicit forms of memorialization must support visual programs and speaking objects. Two hagiographical subgenres—*inventio* for "found" relics and *translatio* for transported relics—provided explicit narratives for placing a new relic in its locality.[10] Relocated reliquaries did not, and perhaps could not, simply carry old meanings along with the objects themselves.[11] Rather, movement created the possibility for innovation and the establishment of new patterns of imaginative memory, sometimes in direct opposition to previous meanings.[12] The hagiographies of the Fourth Crusade reveal how a set of thirteenth-century voices responded to such a moment of narrative possibility through distinct commemorative acts.

Memory, as a concept, stretches along a continuum from event into perpetuity, guided by conscious and unconscious choices of communities and those who shape communal memory. Mary Carruthers was among the first to introduce memory as a field of study for medieval scholars. In her work on mnemonic systems and the ways in which medieval people engaged with and interpreted the past, Carruthers emphasized diverse interpretive modes of recollection.[13] James Fentress and Chris Wickham focused on the relationship of "the social function of the past to its narrative structures" in their chapter on historians who wrote during the Middle Ages.[14] These pioneering works and the many that followed have generally examined the shaping of historical memories over time as we expand our understanding of medieval people and their perceptions of the past.[15] Some engage retrospectively, starting with memorializing acts produced at some chronological remove from the time that they consider.[16] Others, such as the essay "The Venetian Version of the Fourth Crusade" by Thomas Madden, work forward, starting at the event in question and tracing the development of ideas about it over time. My book, on the other hand, focuses on commemorative translatio narratives produced while the objects concerned were still trapped within a kind of cultural gravitational well formed by the conquest of Constantinople.[17] These texts represent early reactions in a contentious environment, yet the mostly anonymous hagiographers had to think about posterity in order to craft a usable narrative that could accompany the relic into the treasury or below the altar, as well as into liturgical traditions and depictions in sacred art.

As for the crusade itself, the publication of *The Fourth Crusade* by Donald Queller, later revised with the help of Thomas Madden, has shifted scholarly debate away from an endless argument about blame and diversion. There is wide scholarly agreement about the basic facts of the crusade. Neither papal, military, nor Venetian leaders intended the crusaders to become badly indebted or to be diverted to Constantinople, but rather designed what seemed to be a reasonable plan to fund an amphibious assault on Egypt. Plans went awry and various actors took advantage of the situation. When the crusaders turned toward Constantinople, they still expected to set sail for Egypt in the near future. No one expected Constantinople to fall to the Latin forces—not even the Latins.

But outside the narrow constraints of crusade and Mediterranean scholarship, the memory and meaning of the Fourth Crusade remain contested ground to this day, a contest that can still fixate on relics and narrative. On November 27, 2004—950 years since mutual excommunications officially began the great schism between Catholicism and Orthodoxy and 800 years after the Fourth Crusade—Pope John Paul II presented two relics to the Orthodox patriarch Bartholomew I of Istanbul in Rome. The relics were the bones of St. John Chrysostom and St. Gregory Nazianzus, both fourth-century prelates who played pivotal roles in the formation of normative Christianity. The plan was that these relics would be placed in new reliquaries of crystal, given to the patriarch on the twenty-seventh, and reinstalled in Istanbul on November 30, the feast of St. Andrew, patron saint of Istanbul.

A week before the handover, disputes between the patriarchal staff in Istanbul and the curia had soured the mood of reconciliation. On Sunday,

November 20, the patriarch gave a sermon in which he praised the pope for his apologetic gesture. Bartholomew said, "For 800 years these relics have been in exile, although in a Christian country, not of their own will, but as a result of the infamous Fourth Crusade, which sacked this city in the year of our Lord 1204. . . . This gesture differentiates them [John Paul and his curia] from the deeds of their predecessors eight centuries ago, who accepted the spiritual and material treasures that had been taken from our city and our Church."[18] The patriarch concluded that the return of the relics was a "warning to all those who arbitrarily possess and retain treasures of the faith, piety, civilisation of others."[19] Note how Bartholomew invoked the concepts of the living saints, held imprisoned against their will in a wicked Rome. Such language would not have been out of place in an anti-Latin tract from medieval Byzantium.

A Vatican spokesman, Joaquín Navarro-Valls, retorted that although "'certain media' had portrayed the pontiff's gesture as a reparation and a means for the Pope to 'beg pardon'. . . this interpretation . . . was 'historically inexact.' The handover was a 'return, not a restitution.'" Furthermore, although the patriarchate maintained that both relics had come to Rome through looting after 1204, the Vatican was not so sure. Navarro-Valls claimed that Greek nuns had translated St. Gregory's bones to Rome in the eighth century in order to protect them from Greek iconoclasts. Thus, instead of being a piece of war booty, these relics went to Rome in search of protection, brought by those least warlike of beings—nuns. The Vatican gave little ground on the relics of St. John as well, admitting only that the translation had probably occurred "at the time of the Latin empire of Constantinople."[20] Rome's rhetoric tried to shape the exchange as a translatio, not a reparation after an act of relic theft. Although John Paul apologized for the Fourth Crusade (and other wars between Latins and Greeks) in 2001, he was not apologizing for having received the relics. How could the Church apologize for the translation of relics, an act only possible if the saint wanted to be moved? The relics were translated, and now they were being translated back —God wills it.

The exchange still took place, as planned, on November 27, but the episode shows that in 2004, as in 1204, mere possession of a relic was not enough. In order to control the meaning of possession, one also had to write a compelling narrative explaining why, and how, the saint wanted a new home. It takes a story to situate the translation of any relic in both its immediate and historical context.

A study of the hagiographers and their texts will not soothe modern conflicts between Orthodoxy and Catholicism, nor reveal mysteries about what really happened to all the relics. Instead, this study examines the shaping choices of the creators and manipulators of institutional and civic memory, the challenges of contested meaning, and the transformative potentiality of relics and their stories.

PART I

CONTEXTS

1

Constantinople's Relics, 1204–1261

In March 1204, the secular leaders of the crusading army optimistically drew up an agreement about what to do with Constantinople if they were lucky enough to seize it. All parties swore sacred oaths to adhere to the terms of the treaty, which became known as the "March Pact." The pact governed nearly every aspect of the division of Constantinople's wealth. It mandated that all plunder be brought to one of three central locations so that it could be doled out appropriately. It stated that the Franks would pay off their debt to the Venetians before all parties split the rest of the plunder. It contained a mechanism for electing a new emperor and another for dividing up the property of the Greek church. Still other passages governed the division of the lands of the empire outside the city and protected Venetian trading hegemony. Both contemporary sources and modern scholarship have used the pact as a template for talking about the division of spoils and have argued about the extent to which the crusaders followed their own plan.[1]

The March Pact does not mention relics or other moveable types of sacred items (altarpieces, works of religious art, icons, and so forth). In fact, no document written either before or after the pact reliably describes the process by which such objects were intended to be distributed or were in fact removed and dispersed. The only clear statement about plans for relics comes from the chronicler Robert of Clari, who writes that all the soldiers were required to swear an oath that they would not despoil churches or sacred objects.[2] Despite such oaths, of course, churches were looted or systematically stripped of value. Over the next few decades, unprecedented numbers of significant holy objects and uncountable numbers of fragments and forgeries from Constantinople appeared in the Latin West.

Due to the memorializing efforts of people such as Pope Innocent III and the Greek chronicler Niketas Choniates, the looting of Constantinople, especially the looting of its churches, has been fraught with controversy. In an angry letter that he widely distributed, Innocent wrote,

> How will the Greek Church . . . return to ecclesiastical unity and devotion to the Apostolic See, a church which has seen in the Latins nothing except an example of affliction and the works of Hell, so that now it rightly detests them more than dogs? . . . It was not enough for them [the Latins] to empty the imperial treasuries and to plunder the spoils of princes and lesser folk, but rather they extended their hands to church treasuries and, what was more serious, to their possessions, even ripping away silver tablets from altars and breaking them into pieces among themselves, violating sacristies and crosses, and carrying away relics.[3]

More verbosely, the Greek chronicler wrote,

> Their [the Latins'] disposition was not at all affected by what they saw. . . . Not only did they rob them [the Greeks] of their substance but also the articles consecrated to God. . . . What then should I recount first and what last of those things dared at that time by these murderous men? O, the shameful dashing to earth of the venerable icons and the flinging of the relics of the saints, who had suffered for Christ's sake, into defiled places! How horrible it was to see the Divine Body and Blood of Christ poured out and thrown to the ground! These forerunners of Antichrist, chief agents and harbingers of his anticipated ungodly deeds, seized as plunder the precious chalices and patens; some they smashed, taking possession of the ornaments embellishing them, and they set the remaining vessels on their tables to serve as bread dishes and wine goblets. Just as happened long ago, Christ was now disrobed and mocked, his garments were parted, and lots were cast for them by this race; and although his side was not pierced by the lance, yet once more streams of Divine Blood poured to the earth.[4]

The pope, the historian, and other medieval writers who agreed with their characterizations established the overarching narrative of sacrilegious pillaging that has remained the consensus ever since. Innocent and Niketas won the battle of memory.

There can be no doubt that horrific violence, rapine, and out-of-control looting filled the first three days after the conquest. Michael Angold has argued that the violence fell within medieval norms for a postconquest city, paling in comparison to the 1099 conquest of Jerusalem or the worst episodes of the Albigensian Crusade. Traditionally, commanders allowed their soldiers three days to pillage and then reasserted control, a process followed in 1204.[5] Angold thus writes against a long tradition of scholarship that adopts the positions of Niketas and Innocent. For example, Steven Runciman described the sack of Constantinople as "unparalleled in history," then declaimed, "There was never a greater crime against humanity than the Fourth Crusade."[6] In his text, the dispersal of sacred objects, linked to rapacious descriptions of looting and violence, serves as evidence for the atrocities of 1204. But even the myth-eroding work of Donald Queller and Thomas Madden implies a link between the taking of relics and the first three days of looting. After describing a prostitute dancing on the throne of the patriarch, they write, "Equally sought after in the churches and monasteries were Constantinople's numerous relics. For most, this 'pious thievery' was embarrassing enough that they later tried to conceal it."[7] Some must indeed have concealed their actions, especially after the looting of churches became the focus of Innocent's condemnation (the subject of chapter 2). Others, however, commissioned narrative accounts of their exploits, wrote letters and charters, or sponsored new liturgies. This evidence supports a more nuanced narrative than a tale of smash and grab, though plenty of smashing and grabbing occurred.

In this chapter, I argue against a loose conflation of the tumultuous initial looting of the city with the long-term extraction and dispersal of its sacred objects by the Latins in the aftermath of the Fourth Crusade. I offer an account of the various means, timing, and rationales employed by the victors of the Fourth Crusade to obtain and export relics. This account provides a context in which to examine the contested ways that crusaders and critics alike memorialized the treatment of Constantinople's relics.

Certain distinctions among the various cases of relic acquisition serve as organizing principles for the chapter. One can distinguish between *haphazard* and *targeted* looting of relics and between *authorized* and *unauthorized* acts. Sometimes, crusaders just grabbed whatever they could (haphazard). Other looters consciously sought out relics from saints who were already venerated in their home churches, that were especially valuable, or whose loss would not garner unwanted attention (targeted). At other times, commanding nobles and elite clerics took whatever they wanted from churches under their control and sent or carried the relics west without fear (authorized). However, some had to creep secretly through the treasuries or find a way to trick the guardians of the relic (unauthorized).

I also divide the movement of relics from east to west into three distinct phases in order to highlight chronological separation among various acts of relic acquisition. The first phase took place in the weeks immediately after the sack. This period is the most obscured by the chaotic nature of conquest and the concomitant lack of solid documentation, but the available source material does reveal enough fragments of data to draw some rough conclusions about those initial days. The second phase occurred over the next few years, as Constantinople's new occupants—people directly involved with the events of 1204—took possession of their city, took stock of their churches' possessions, and, sometimes, chose to send relics west. The great and powerful men of the crusade and new empire figure largely in this period. Doge Enrico Dandolo of Venice, cardinal and papal legate Peter Capuano, and Emperor Baldwin of Flanders stand out as the exemplars in this second phase. During the remaining years of the Latin Empire's short existence, which I mark as the third phase, relics continued to trickle west via theft, sale, and gift, particularly the latter. The great translation of the relics of the Passion to King Louis IX and many lesser-known translations fall into this category.

The Plan and the Looting: Context for the Relics

The looting of churches took place in a broader environment of postconquest plundering. Despite the reputation of the sack of Constantinople for indiscriminate slaughter, rape, and pillage, the internal sources on the crusade reveal many preemptive efforts to control the looting. The extent to which such plans failed is a separate issue.[8] The leadership, motivated by self-interest, sought to both monopolize distribution of the great city's riches and gather the needed coin to pay off their debts. The March Pact represents the culmination of their planning. It proposed a system for apportioning the throne, churches, land, fiefs, and coin of the Byzantine Empire. Sacred items, notably, do not appear in the document.

Why this absence? The Latins were well aware of the sacred richness of the city; indeed, crusaders and Western pilgrims had been marveling at Constantinople's relic collection throughout the history of the crusades. As early as 1106–7, a forged letter purporting to be from Alexius I invited Latin soldiers to come take possession of Constantinople in order to keep the relics safe from the Turks.[9] Robert of Clari, a knight of Picardy and author of one of the two main Western eyewitness accounts of the Fourth Crusade, revels in the majesty of the city's relics and grand churches.[10] Thus, the armies of the Fourth Crusade knew that the relics were present but made no plans regarding how to handle them. Ultimately, their decisions about secular wealth and offices shaped the fate of the relics and the later contest about the meaning of the fall of Constantinople in the Latin world.

The combination of the prohibitive costs of campaigning coupled with the potential bounty of a conquered Constantinople drove much of the crusade's action. By March 1204, the crusaders still owed another year's worth of fees to the Venetians. As the Latins drew up their pact, they hoped that the city of Constantinople would pay the now-deceased emperor's (Alexius IV Angelos's) debts to the crusaders and the crusaders' debts to the Venetians.[11] The realists among the army must have known that full conquest was highly unlikely, but they still needed a system for handling plunder, lest greed undermine a victory. Previous assaults on Constantinople indicated that they might be able to take, hold, loot, and retreat from a section of the city, even if a full conquest failed. The plan was to mandate, on pain of death, the collection of all valuable goods and coin in centrally guarded sites.[12] Anxious to avoid any conflict over the imperial throne, the crusade's leadership developed an electoral system that would go into effect as needed. The system would eventually work, but out of necessity the pact ensured that the leadership had not preselected an emperor at the moment that the crusaders entered Constantinople. Hence, as the crusaders began pillaging, no one could claim to be fully in charge.[13]

Toward the end of the March Pact, having dispensed with the apportioning of coin, food, and the throne, its authors turned to other forms of wealth. One paragraph of the pact ultimately not only shaped the division of the property and the offices of the Greek church but also set the stage for the next (postconquest) conflict between the Venetians and the papacy. Both subjects—church property and Venetian-papal dispute—pertain to the fate of the relics. The pact reads,

> Let it also be understood that the clergy who are from that party from which the emperor was not chosen will have authority to organize the church of Sancta Sophia and to elect the patriarch for the honor of God. . . . Certainly, the clerics of each party ought to organize those churches that have come into the possession of their party. To be sure, sufficient quantities of the possessions of the churches ought to be provided to the clerics and the churches so that they might live and be sustained in an honorable fashion. The remaining possessions of the churches, indeed, should be divided and distributed in accordance with the aforesaid agreement.[14]

The first part of this passage eventually gave control over Hagia Sophia to the Venetians. The subsequent text suggests that all sides would be claiming territory in the city as their own and that whoever took an area might also lay claim to the churches there. Any group of crusaders could seize an area and its churches, but it would not also receive all of the property and rents traditionally owned by a given church. Instead, such property (beyond "sufficient quantities") went into the general pool of plunder, was split according to the aforementioned guidelines, and was then apportioned by a given faction's leaders. The framers of the pact might have had relics in mind when they wrote about the "remaining possessions of the churches," but if so, their plans did not come to fruition. In the end, a central committee handled the issue of control over the churches and their properties, though arguments on this matter continued for decades.[15] Relics never received the same degree of citywide oversight as the churches themselves.

Evidence suggests that the leaders of the crusade made a strong attempt to keep to the terms of their pact, a finding that contrasts with the general tenor of external accounts of the days after the fall of the city. Some common soldiers, of course, had other ideas. Villehardouin, for example, laments that many soldiers did not deposit all of their plunder at one of the three central churches that the crusaders had set up as repositories, despite threats of execution for holding back loot.[16] Clari angrily accuses the treasure's guards of letting elite knights take whatever they wanted, leaving only the silver for the common soldiers.[17] The anonymous author of the *Devastatio Constantinopoli-*

tana scornfully characterizes the common shares of the spoil as "almost like certain down-payments."[18] Scholars argue about how to tally the total wealth collected. They also argue over why the shares were so low, whether the shares were actually as low as stated, how many people and what class of people were hanged for keeping back loot, the fate of jewels and other precious objects not easily divided, and other related issues.[19] If Clari and the author of the *Devastatio Constantinopolitana* were correct, then the collection system more or less worked (as evidenced by how unhappy they were with the official distribution). If Villehardouin is correct, then common soldiers concealed much of the loot for their personal benefit. Niketas and Innocent ranted about the wild looting, but neither was in as good a position to know the truth as the soldiers present in Constantinople. On the other hand, soldiers were unlikely to confess to sacrilegious outbursts of violence and destruction in internally produced sources. The totality of the evidence suggests that the initial days of the looting were indeed quite chaotic, as described to various degrees by eyewitness sources. Eventually, however, Villehardouin and his fellow elites took control of the city and its wealth and then made an honest effort to collect the treasure centrally. After all, the debt still loomed unpaid.

Thus, we understand the Latin army's approach to the secular wealth of Constantinople. The leadership tried to assert authority, the better to distribute loot and property in an organized and self-benefitting manner. The rank and file, risking serious punishment but aware of the great wealth available in the city and the difficulty that their leaders would have in enforcing their edict, helped themselves as they could. When able, the leaders punished those they caught, making an example out of the miscreants. Despite the many violent incidents that no doubt took place, no matter how much plunder the rank and file seized in bloody pillaging, the bulk of Constantinople's vast wealth passed into the hands of the great men of the crusade by the simpler process of occupation, appropriation, and negotiation with one another. The same holds true for the relics.

Phase One: Relics and Looting Immediately Following the Conquest

The crusaders took the walls, frightened off the Greek army, opened the gates, and stormed the city. Many citizens, expecting a more-or-less orderly triumph, lined the streets to welcome the new emperor; alas, for them, no emperor had yet been named and no single leader of the crusade could claim control over the whole city.[20] Instead, the various military commanders staked out their own territories. As was typical of the initial days following a conquest, chaos reigned, magnified more by scale than by ferocity. We will never know exactly what happened in the churches of Constantinople in these first hours and days, but out of the confusion and the scant textual evidence, a few faces and deeds emerge. We can begin to tease out a narrative based on scarce data points. An abbot sees soldiers looting the great monastic complex of the Pantocrator and uses that sacrilege to justify a more pious sacrilege of his own. He creeps into a remote part of the complex and bullies a Greek monk into revealing the location of relics, which he then takes into protective custody. A French bishop follows his friend, Boniface of Montferrat, into the Bucoleon Palace and takes command of one of the greatest collections of relics in the world. When the bishop leaves a month later, the collection is missing some pieces. Some Venetian crusaders take advantage of the confusion to scout out the crypt that holds the relics of their patron saint; a week later, while their comrades-in-arms are celebrating Palm Sunday, they steal them. A bishop from Troyes confiscates relics looted by soldiers and carefully apportions them to European and local churches. When he dies, the papal legate takes the bishop's collection and does the same.

None of the standard reports of the conquest reveal much reliable information about its chaotic first few hours. The incendiary rhetoric of Niketas quoted above represents just the barest fragment of his detailed and horrific description of the sack of Constantinople, for which he mourns. In lurid, tragic tones, the chronicler describes the breaking of the altar, the destruction of priceless works of art, and the stabling of mules in the sanctuary. In an ultimate act of impiety, a prostitute was placed on the throne of the patriarch. After describing the outrages committed against women and the old, Niketas concludes by attacking the crusaders for violating their crusading oath. They had promised not to deviate from their planned course until they found the Saracens, but deviate they had. They had promised not to have sexual intercourse, but now they were raping Greek women. "In truth," he wrote, "they were exposed as frauds. Seeking to avenge the Holy Sepulchre, they raged openly against Christ and sinned by overturning the Cross with the cross they bore on their backs, not even shuddering to trample on it for the sake of a little gold and silver. By grasping pearls, they rejected Christ."[21] Niketas attempts to present the incursion as an unholy war that played out in diametric opposition to the crusaders' holy mission. With such an agenda, he found the violation of relics rhetorically useful. Of all the crimes committed against the city by the conquering Latins, the chronicler chose to recount the sacrilegious looting first and the breaking of the sacred oath last, thus bookending his account with the worst offenses. Niketas sought to convey his horror at the atrocities committed in the name of Christ by these "Franks," who should have been trying to liberate the Holy Sepulcher in Jerusalem. He evoked the Antichrist and Judgment Day. He compared the Latins to the most despised people in the New Testament—those who participated in the shaming and execution of Christ. He did not eschew describing the other iniquities of the conquerors but began with the violation of the sacred.[22] That decision may reflect a quick sense on his part that the memory of the sack would be ruled by the postconquest behavior of the Latins. That said, his account must largely be rejected.

Niketas was working within the genre of lament, not history, and thus employed hyperbole as a rhetorical strategy. His goal was to blame and weep in prose, not to make a historical argument about causation. Even other elements of his own chronicle call his descriptions into question. Wisely, Niketas was in hiding during the initial chaos, so at best he knew only secondhand of the depredations. As Michael Angold has noted, when Niketas actually encountered crusaders, one Frank did try to rape a girl in his party, but several Italians intervened and threatened to hang the Frank if he did not give her back. She was returned unscathed. The *Chronicle of Novgorod*, naturally sympathetic to Orthodox clergy, complains about the robbing of clergy and nuns but not of their murder or rape.[23] Another Greek eyewitness, Nicholas Mesarites, tells the story of his brother John, who took refuge in a monastery and faced crusaders who broke into the sacred house without fear. Impressed by his faith, the crusaders treated him with respect and did him no harm.[24] If, as Angold has supposed, the leader of the Latins who met John Mesarites in the Monastery of St. George of the Mangana was Count Hugh of Saint-Pol, who took over St. George's after the conquest, this episode provides more evidence for the quick reassertion of control by the crusade leadership, especially over ecclesiastical properties.[25] The Latin leadership did what it could to roll back the fog of war.

The Latin accounts support the notion that the churches of Constantinople were spared significant damage from the looting soldiers, although the fires certainly scorched them. Robert of Clari, representing the viewpoint of the rank-and-file soldier in the army, reserves harsh criticism for the conduct of many of his fellows. He finds the vast riches of Constantinople amazing but also witnesses the tensions that they caused within the army. He writes that, according to the Greeks, Constantinople had been filled with "two-thirds of the wealth of the world."[26] Now that wealth belonged to the Latins. Yet, Clari laments, little of the profit made its way into the hands of the common soldiers. Instead, the victors fought over how much each one should take from the spoils, and many "who ought to have guarded this wealth took the jewels of gold and whatsoever else they desired, and robbed the spoil."[27] These moments of anger and disappointment with his lack of loot stand in stark contrast to his commentary on the relics of the city.

Relics, in Clari's narrative, receive nothing but words of wonder and praise. He exults in their capture, lists the major acquisitions, and recounts histories and provenance insofar as he knows them. He writes of the Holy Lance, the pieces of the Cross, the robe of Mary, the head of St. John the Baptist, and the shroud of Christ, and then adds that he saw even more relics than he could possibly describe. And these were just the relics that the crusaders found at the Bucoleon Palace. The chance for the Latins to view such holy objects as their "owners"—not as the somewhat unwelcome guests of the Greeks—delighted Clari.

The difference in tone between the descriptions of normal plundering and the capture of relics is striking. When a particular hoard of gold and gems or a piece of property fell into a crusader's hands, Clari names the crusader (or group) or at least labels the acquisition's point of origin.[28] These statements are usually accompanied by words of condemnation for not properly sharing the plunder. When a crusader found a relic, however, Clari rarely mentions the individual who uncovered it. He reserves his narration for descriptions of the relic and its resting place, expresses wonderment at the miracles associated with the object, and then moves on to the next one. The chronicler was not afraid to document internal divisions in the force or to criticize when his fellows erred or sinned. He presents the acquisition of the relics, however, as a victory for all of the crusaders.

Curiously, the most complete account of the Fourth Crusade, that of Geoffrey of Villehardouin, never refers to the acquisition or looting of relics. As is typical of accounts of crusades, God and providence play active roles in the narrative. Sermons and other religious affairs appear regularly, and relics are mentioned when oaths are sworn over them. Villehardouin even refers to the relics of Constantinople, specifically, in one key passage. After Alexius III had fled and Alexius IV had taken the throne with his father, the chronicler writes, "Now you may know that many people from the army went to look at Constantinople, its sumptuous palaces, its many impressive churches and its great riches, of which no other city ever had as many. It is impossible even to begin to describe all the saints' relics since there were as many in the city at that time as there were in the rest of the world put together."[29] Villehardouin notes the existence of the relics but omits any reference to the specific objects captured after the final conquest. He discusses plundering in general. He, like Clari, excoriates those who stole valuables for themselves and is quick to point out how the army's leaders—of which he was one—punished the offenders. Regarding the looting, he writes, "Individuals began to come forward with their booty and it was gathered together. Some were honest in presenting their spoils, others deceitful. Greed, which is the root of all evil, knew no restraint; from that time forward greedy people started to hoard things for themselves, and Our Lord started to love them less. Oh God—they had behaved so loyally up to that point!"[30] Villehardouin laments that even the threat of excommunication did not deter these men from keeping some portion of the booty for themselves instead of turning it over to their leaders to be divided "fairly." That they could ignore the sacred sanctions they were risking seems to have infuriated the chronicler more than their lack of fear of being hanged—the bodily punishment for theft. Had crusaders been breaking into vaults and claiming relics or stripping away golden reliquaries from their sacred bones with wild abandon throughout the city, Villehardouin could have described it as yet another outrage. His silence on the subject might speak to ignorance of such sacrilege or embarrassment about the conduct of his fellow crusaders. On the other hand, perhaps Villehardouin, the best-informed of the Fourth Crusade chroniclers, was silent precisely because whatever pillaging of Greek churches took place did not seem egregious. Rather, it fell within normal medieval conduct of war.

Villehardouin was not alone in omitting any discussion of relics from his account. The *Devastatio Constantinopolitana*, a harsh critique of the crusade, never mentions the sacred objects removed from Constantinople. This text is a curious and brief account—only five pages in the single extant manuscript—that expends most of its fury on the perfidy of the crusade's leaders. The author, who felt that the poor men of the crusade had been cheated, emphasized the misdeeds of the Frankish and Venetian leadership, especially when it came to the acquisition of wealth. Had the leadership immediately claimed the relics for themselves personally, rather than opening Constantinople's shrines and their sacred objects to crusader veneration, one might expect the *Devastatio Constantinopolitana* to discuss it.[31]

Taken as a whole, these arguments suggest the lack of direct evidence for the kind of widespread sacrilegious looting of churches cited by both Innocent and Niketas. Indeed, in their omission of descriptions of persistent sacrilege, the major Greek and Latin eyewitness accounts of the crusade do more to dispel mischaracterizations of the looting than to support any particular chronology of such events. Of course, absence proves nothing, but it ought to introduce some doubt into the conversation about the plundering of the city. For more concrete information about the treatment of relics following the conquest, we must look to hagiographical sources. It is from these that one can reconstruct the deeds of specific crusaders, track the fate of relics, and more clearly demarcate the knowable from the unknowable.

Four hagiographical texts in particular open small windows into the history of relics in the postconquest city—the "Gesta episcoporum Halberstadensium," "The Land of Jerusalem" (De terra Iherosolimitana), the *Historia Constantinopolitana*, and the "Translatio Symonensis." A fifth text, the "Translatio Mamantis," also contains a description of the initial relic looting, although secondhand at best, and it will be treated more carefully during the discussion of phase two. The four texts describe four acts of relic acquisition. Two depict the risk-free (authorized) acquisition of relics by Bishops Conrad von Krosigk of Halberstadt and Nivelon de Chérisy of Soissons; the other two record careful and surreptitious (unauthorized) raids by Abbot Martin of Pairis and a group of lower-status Venetian crusaders.

Bishop Conrad von Krosigk of Halberstadt

To piece together this relic-centered narrative, we must begin before the final capture of Constantinople. The crusaders spent months camping just outside the city walls while ostensibly working for the rightful emperor, Alexius IV, and they were free to enter in small groups. Among the crusaders was Bishop Conrad von Krosigk of Halberstadt, a supporter and client of Philip of Swabia, Alexius's brother-in-law and backer in the Latin West. During this time, Conrad ostensibly benefitted from a long-established practice of relic gifting. He later professed to have received several objects from Alexius, who in fact pillaged his own churches for gold and silver items to melt down in an attempt to pay off his debts. In the "Gesta episcoporum Halberstadensium," the anonymous author makes grandiose claims that Conrad returned to Halberstadt with "the blood of our Lord, Jesus Christ, [portions of] the Lord's wood, the Lord's Sepulchre, the Lord's crown of thorns, His shroud and *sudarium*, the purple garment, the sponge and reed," and other objects.[32] These were among the most venerated relics in all of Christendom, but Conrad did not acquire the main Byzantine relics of the Passion. Those ultimately ended up in the hands of the French king Louis IX. Instead, the author of the "Gesta" is following typical medieval practice by equating tiny fragments of a relic with the whole. For example, Conrad's "crown of thorns" was merely one thorn.[33] In truth, the fragmentary pieces that arrived in Halberstadt could easily have been products of looting. A contemporary Greek writer, Nicholas Hydruntinus, accused Conrad of being a relic thief, but Conrad's own 1208 proclamation of celebration for the sacred items (making August 16 a feast day) describes them as gifts from Alexius.[34] The claim is supportable. The extant reliquaries, small and ornate, are comparable to other types of reliquaries long used by Byzantine rulers in sacral diplomacy.[35]

If Alexius favored Conrad, the short-lived emperor perhaps favored other elite Latins similarly. While Conrad might have acquired additional pieces after the conquest, as there were plenty of relics to be gained and his hoard is impressive, the physical evidence supports the bishop's statement that at least some were gifts. The Halberstadt trove, overall, suggests that at least a fraction of the relics taken west after the conquest were not stolen, looted, bought, or otherwise acquired as a result of war; they were diplomatic mementos of contact with the last of the Angeloi emperors.[36] Such gifting served as one, largely unconsidered, vector by which relics of Christ proliferated in the West after 1204.[37]

One of the more precise descriptions of a relic muddies the water. Conrad acquired "a [portion of] the skull of St. Stephen the protomartyr, along with his elbow," in order to bring Halberstadt a relic belonging to its patron saint.[38] Venice had laid claim to the relics of St. Stephen, stealing them from Constantinople in 1107 or 1108. Nearly a century later, Conrad and others found more. We cannot say whether these relics were simply pieces the Venetians had missed, forgeries created by the Greeks after Venice's theft, or a postconquest invention by Greeks or Latins. Regardless, Conrad did not acquire a relic of his cathedral's patron by chance. Other crusaders made similar acquisitions.

Conrad's conduct, in conjunction with several examples discussed below, suggests that instead of just grabbing whatever sacred item was at hand, some crusaders sought out objects of special personal significance.

Bishop Nivelon de Chérisy of Soissons

The "Gesta episcoporum Halberstadensium" is suggestive about the postcrusade environment but not definitive. No sources attest to Conrad's whereabouts in the days after the sack, so one is left with some questions, especially given the mystery of St. Stephen's head and elbow. Thanks to Robert of Clari's description of the relics of the churches in the Bucoleon Palace complex, we know somewhat more about the activities of Nivelon de Chérisy, who served as the bishop of Soissons from 1176 to 1207 and was another notable translator of relics. The sacred items that Nivelon brought back to Soissons are recorded in "The Land of Jerusalem," an anonymously authored text that he presumably commissioned. The author framed the translatio within a discussion of the larger struggle to redeem the Holy Land, placing the recent conquest of Constantinople in the context of that struggle. The text begins with the loss of Jerusalem and the famed relic of the True Cross to Saladin in 1187 and ends with Nivelon's return to Soissons with four Constantinopolitan fragments of the True Cross, along with other relics.[39] Nivelon was one of the most important clerics on the crusade; he led the army's clergy, just as Boniface of Montferrat led the secular force. At the end, he served as one of the twelve electors of Baldwin of Flanders and crowned him emperor in Hagia Sophia.[40] While Peter Capuano, the papal legate, came and went (depending on the army's current relationship with Rome), Nivelon was the constant leading ecclesiastical presence on the crusade.[41]

Nivelon's relics, according to "The Land of Jerusalem," included another head of St. Stephen the Protomartyr, a finger and the head of the Apostle Thomas, the crown of the head of Mark the Evangelist, a thorn from the Crown of Thorns, a belt of Mary and a piece of her robe, a piece of the towel with which Christ girded himself at the Last Supper, a forearm and the head of St. John the Baptist, a rib and the head of the blessed Blaise, the pieces of the True Cross, the staff of Moses, and many other objects.[42] The text tells us that Nivelon divided them among churches in his diocese, where the newly translated saints began to work miracles.

"The Land of Jerusalem" does not record how Nivelon actually acquired his relics, but, as a source on the relic looting, it does permit some modest deductions. First, one can correlate its list with relics described by Clari. He lists the Crown of Thorns, the Virgin's robe, the head of St. John the Baptist, and two large pieces of the True Cross as residing in the church of the Blessed Virgin of the Pharos, which was located in the Bucoleon Palace.[43] Boniface of Montferrat, a friend of Nivelon's, took control of the Bucoleon in the initial weeks after the conquest.[44] A month later, Doge Enrico Dandolo of Venice suggested that everyone vacate their (fortified) palaces before the election of the emperor, presumably to stave off any thought of armed resistance from the loser. That month gave Nivelon ample time to organize the churches, go through the inventories, and take whatever he wanted. Indeed, the March Pact specifically stated that "the clerics of each party ought to organize those churches that have come into the possession of their party."[45] Nivelon followed the agreed-upon arrangement.

Thus, we can place Nivelon and the relics that he eventually took home in the same place at the same time and speculate about what might have happened. Regardless of what Nivelon did in the privacy of the Bucoleon's treasury—even if he personally went in with a tool or snapped finger bones off a dead saint's hands—his actions cannot be characterized as looting or relic theft. The bishop encountered no danger, which, as we will see, is a prerequisite for the narrative traditions relating to relic theft. Nivelon was organizing the churches that his faction controlled. As the leading clerical overseer of these churches, he was within his canonical rights to translate relics—hence, no sacrilege. Too often scholars have conflated the activities of marauding soldiers with those of confiscatory bishops or princes. In a brief summary, Donald Queller and Thomas Madden use the words "stole" and "seized" to describe the deeds of Bishops Nivelon and Conrad, linking them to the "hundreds of relics pilfered by the crusaders."[46] I suggest here that the looting of soldiers and the secretive thieves discussed below varies significantly from confiscations by commanding bishops, especially in terms of how such deeds are memorialized. The elites could authorize their own activity; the common crusaders could not. Surely Nivelon was not the only Latin cleric to extract a few sacred fragments from a newly possessed church's inventory.

Abbot Martin of Pairis

In the initial chaos, many crusaders no doubt plundered Constantinople's churches, but the record of their misdeeds emerges only in sources distancing themselves from such behavior. Bishop Garnier of Troyes seems to have tried to put a stop to the sacrilege; one source from a site that received a relic from Garnier labeled him *procurator sanctorum reliquarum* (manager of holy relics), but this is an uncertain attribution at best and is probably untrue, as will be argued below.[47] He certainly failed to contain the actions of Abbot Martin of Pairis, his ecclesiastical peer.

Abbot Martin's actions lie somewhere between the authorized, careful deeds of the bishops and the indiscriminate and largely untraceable looting that was not memorialized. Martin had left the main force of the crusade to protest the diversion to Constantinople, but he returned before the final conquest and entered the city after it was taken. According to the *Historia Constantinopolitana*, a text Martin commissioned from Gunther of Pairis once he returned home, he witnessed bands of soldiers ripping through the abbey church of the Pantocrator and decided to seek relics in a remote section of the monastic complex. These scenes may well accurately recount events that Martin actually witnessed, but as with all translatio narratives, one must be cautious. The neat positioning of Martin's pious looting against the impious looting of secular crusaders, for all its plausibility, may well function as a rhetorical device rather than correlate to fact.

By implication, Martin worried that he might lose his sacred plunder to the secular throng. Within the complex, he found a Greek priest hiding and threatened him with death if he did not yield the most powerful relics up to him. The priest, "thinking it more tolerable that a man of religion violate the holy relics in awe and reverence, rather than that worldly men should pollute them, possibly, with bloodstained hands,"[48] eventually submitted to Martin's demands. Martin took the best relics and hid them, then offered his protection to the priest and found him safe lodgings in the city.[49]

St. Simon and the Seven Thieves

The *Historia Constantinopolitana* suggests that Martin was concealing the relics from common pillagers, but he was likely also hiding his haul from other elites. As an abbot, perhaps he could have protected his plunder; other relic thieves were less fortunate. This conclusion may be drawn from the account of a successful theft carried out by seven crusading sailors from the parish of St. Simon the Prophet in Venice. Within days of the conquest, the sailors decided to steal the body of their parish's patron saint from the church of St. Mary Chalkoprateia.[50] According to the "Translatio Symonensis," which survives only in a fourteenth-century manuscript, they laid their plans, reconnoitered the site, and then stole the relic on Palm Sunday (April 18, 1204). They selected the holy day in order to avoid notice, as the citizens and other crusaders would be busy celebrating.[51]

The heist went off relatively smoothly, although some of the Venetians got lost on their way to the church. Having stolen the body, the remaining thieves found that they could not leave the city because Doge Enrico Dandolo would not let any ships depart. This had nothing to do with the theft of St. Simon; rather, it was an attempt by the leaders of the new empire to keep the army intact. According to the translatio, the doge then heard of the relic's theft and announced a reward for its recovery. After hiding St. Simon in an abandoned palace on the banks of the Bosphorus, the sailors waited for six months. Eventually, one of them received permission to leave Constantinople (by lottery) and took the body to his home parish.[52]

One can deduce many things about the looting of relics based on this rare narrative. First, these men clearly stole a relic as part of a heist. They did not simply authorize themselves to take possession of relics in their new church treasuries. Whereas Abbot Martin demanded to be taken to the most powerful relics and the looters he was avoiding grabbed whatever they came across, the Venetians were more discriminating. Theirs was a carefully planned and executed heist with a target chosen solely because of its particular value to the parishioners of St. Simon. Indeed, they even ignored the relics of St. Zachary, the patron of an important Venetian church, taking only the body of their own patron saint.[53] If Dandolo's attempt to obtain the stolen relic by offering a bounty is credible, as it may well be, another fact comes into focus. Had someone betrayed the fellowship of thieves and given the relic to the doge, the "Translatio Symonensis" would never have been written. We would not know about the band from the parish of St. Simon, although Dandolo might still have sent the relics to Venice in the end. Thus, we can conclude that there may have been other cases in which a member of the leadership, secular or clerical, confiscated a relic from a lower-status thief, condemning his story to oblivion, yet providing clues as to how bishops and counts acquired their relics.

The great majority of actions taken inside the churches of Constantinople remain invisible, and our few reliable examples cannot support a fully developed narrative. Yet our sources do suggest a range of possibilities. Bishop Nivelon and likely other leading clerics acquired relics by taking them out of churches under their control, confiscating them from errant pillagers, and receiving them as gifts. The deeds of the parishioners of St. Simon provide a counterexample, in which crusaders executed both a targeted and unauthorized theft. For Abbot Martin, the pursuit of saintly power, carried out surreptitiously, trumped other concerns about which specific relics he might acquire. The complaints from outsiders suggest that the stories of Martin and the Venetian parishioners may reflect a much larger, and now forgotten, pattern of theft and pillaging. If Dandolo and his cadre were ready to seize relics from lesser crusaders, no wonder most chose to remain silent.

The Second Phase: The Crusaders Go Home

Enrico Dandolo

Enrico Dandolo tried to recover the body of St. Simon at some point during the first six months after its initial theft. This attempted confiscation actually belongs to the second phase in the movement of the relics of the Fourth Crusade. In the weeks and months after the sack, the crusaders organized and disbursed their loot. They elected Baldwin of Flanders as emperor. The Venetians, as prescribed by the March Pact, took control of Hagia Sophia and the patriarchate. The crusade leadership divided up other properties and Greek territories, many still unconquered, in a process that led to great riches for some, conflicts among the Latin forces and other powers in the region, sales and exchanges, the settlement of Franks in Greece and Venetians in Crete, and many other changes. Boniface of Montferrat began his military operations in Thessalonica. The disastrous campaign against the Vlachs led to the death of the first Latin emperor of Constantinople and other leading nobles. Seeking to undermine the Venetian advantage, Genoa sent out privateers to plunder ships returning to the West. The pope attempted to reassert control. Peter Capuano lifted the crusade vows, and eventually the army dispersed.[54] As the crusaders returned home, relics returned with them; some were sent ahead as gifts to reward friends or to grease the wheels of diplomacy, as detailed below. In this phase, Dandolo, Baldwin, and Capuano all emerged as particularly important players in the authorized acquisition and translation of relics. Unauthorized actions continued as well, though as always they are harder to locate in the record.

In the most important Venetian chronicle from the fourteenth century, the *Chronica per extensum descripta* of Andrea Dandolo, who was the doge of Venice from 1343 to 1354 and a member of the same family as Enrico, one finds a description of Venice's share of the sacred plunder from Constantinople. Andrea lists an ampoule of Christ's blood, the arm of St. George, a piece of the head of St. John the Baptist, the body of St. Lucy, and the body of St. Agatha, which Enrico gave to an unspecified Sicilian pilgrim.[55] The chronicle depicts Enrico Dandolo as a grand distributor of relics. He probably brought back many more items, but any records of plunder housed in the treasury of the church of San Marco would have been largely destroyed in a great fire in 1231. However, relics from the conquest had also been distributed to other sites in Venice. And, in the 1260s, Doge Ranieri Zeno claimed that a small set of relics had miraculously survived the fire. These came to constitute the "official list" of crusade plunder that could be traced to Enrico Dandolo, and Andrea Dandolo's chronicle reflects that list.[56]

How Enrico Dandolo acquired most of his relics is unclear. According to a late fourteenth-century *translatio*, Baldwin of Flanders gave the relic of St. Lucy to Dandolo for Venice, raising the possibility that the doge received other relics as gifts.[57] Dandolo made some effort to acquire precious objects for the commune of Venice and San Marco, including, for example, the relics listed above, the relics of St. Simon the Prophet (although he failed), the quadriga that eventually adorned the church,[58] and large quantities of marble and other precious materials.[59] One cannot imagine the old, blind doge personally rummaging through a church treasury in Constantinople. Unlike the bishops of Soissons and Halberstadt, Dandolo was not a cleric who could inspect and seize relics in the course of taking charge of a formerly Greek church. Perhaps Dandolo sometimes succeeded in using bribery and threats against lesser crusaders, as detailed in the story of St. Simon and the Venetian thieves, even though he failed to seize those relics. His experience with negotiation and exchange could only have helped him in such an environment. Shortly after Dandolo's death, the Venetians demanded an icon of the Virgin in exchange for supporting Henry of Flanders's ascension to the imperial throne after his brother Baldwin died.[60] One suspects that the Latins traded with, offered gifts to, coerced, and bribed one another in order to acquire specific relics as the chaos of the capture subsided and they assessed their newfound lands and riches.

Baldwin of Flanders

Emperor Baldwin I figures in a number of letters and charters concerning relics. He used them in imperial diplomacy, thus continuing the practice of the emperors before him.[61] Like Dandolo, Baldwin of Flanders sent relics to his homeland, but not exclusively. He also included relics and other sacred items among the gifts that he sent to Pope Innocent III and the Templars in Lombardy. Genoese privateers captured the ship bearing Baldwin's emissary and pillaged it. According to the Genoese chronicles, the city's leaders sanctioned this expedition in order to profit from the fall of Constantinople in their own way; moreover, they hoped to limit the gains of the Venetians.[62] In November 1204, Innocent sent a letter to the archbishop of Genoa demanding restitution. By this time, the privateers had either released or received a ransom for the emissary, a Venetian named Brother Barozzi, who was the master of the Temple of Lombardy and about whom nothing else is known. Barozzi made his way to Rome, gave Innocent a letter from Baldwin (which survives), and told the pope about the piracy. As the relics and precious objects remained in Genoese hands, Innocent threatened to interdict Genoa if it did not immediately return them. Items intended as gifts for the pope, Innocent argued, became papal property immediately. He listed the objects owed to him and added those due to the Temple as well, insisting upon their return. These items included many gems and silver marks, in addition to two icons, a gilt reliquary, two golden crosses, a silver ampoule, and a relic of the True Cross that was bound for the Temple.[63] We do not know what, if any, response Innocent's letter inspired, but he did not place Genoa under interdict. One must assume an arrangement was worked out.[64]

Innocent listed only the one relic, a fragment of the True Cross. However, the Genoese chronicle of Orgerio Pane claims that many relics (*multas reliquias sanctorum*) were seized and eventually distributed among Genoese churches.[65] John Fotheringham argues that the medieval cross reliquary still in the Cathedral of San Lorenzo in Genoa is the True Cross relic mentioned in the letter.[66] It was given to Genoa by the men of Porto Venere, who owned one of the privateer vessels, in exchange for certain economic privileges. Fotheringham notes that the *Cronaca* of Jacopo da Voragine (who was Genoese) claims not only that the privateers captured many relics but that Jacopo himself obtained relics for the Dominican order in Genoa many decades later. The chronicler does not provide a specific list of these relics.[67] There are some likely explanations for the discrepancy. First, the Genoese texts could be confusing relics with altar cloths, icons, reliquaries (not the relics themselves), and other valuable items associated with the church. *Multas reliquias sanctorum*, however, seems to clearly describe relics.[68] Why, then, did Innocent not demand their return as well? Perhaps Brother Barozzi did not tell Innocent about the other relics, although why he would omit such a detail is unknown. Or perhaps the other relics were intended as gifts for other dignitaries and thus were considered to be outside papal purview. Regardless, the important detail is that Baldwin's envoy bore both a letter to the pope and sacred gifts for the Holy Father.

Baldwin had sent these gifts in hopes of easing the recommencement of papal-crusader negotiations after more than a year of discord. The letter to Rome, enregistered in October 1204, survives, as do three additional copies. These copies are addressed by Baldwin to the archbishop of Cologne, the abbot of Cîteaux and his Cistercian colleagues, and to "all the Christian people."[69] We do not know who received the last letter (and there may have been many other copies), but one can speculate that if Baldwin sent relics to Rome, he likely would have sent them to Cologne and particularly to Cîteaux. The Cistercians had been major players in the Fourth Crusade and would continue to be important to the Latin Empire.[70] Baldwin had plenty of relics to go around. Riant published a number of *instrumenta*, various types of documents mentioning relics, that describe cases in which an individual or institution received relics from the emperor. These are especially prevalent in Flanders and Hainault.[71] For example, Count Hugh of Beaumetz received a reliquary of the True Cross from Baldwin for his service as a crusader. The Picard count installed the relic in the Abbey of Mont Saint-Quentin.[72] Baldwin also sent relics to his titular liege lord, King Philip II Augustus of France. In a letter to the king from September 5, 1205, Baldwin records these gifts as a piece of the True Cross, Christ's suckling clothes and some of his hair, a thorn from the Crown of Thorns, some of the purple garment Christ wore before Pontius Pilate, and a rib of the Apostle Philip, which Baldwin perhaps included because the apostle was the king's namesake.[73] Notably, these relics overlap with those sent to France by Bishop Nivelon of Soissons, a detail supporting the argument that Nivelon acquired his relics from the same imperial treasury as Baldwin. The bishops of Beauvais, Noyon, and Senlis witnessed the arrival of the relics at Saint-Denis. The ritual reception of these gifts may have provided a template for the more famous translation of the relics of the Passion to Paris in 1239, after King Louis IX purchased them from Emperor Baldwin II through the agency of the emperor's Venetian creditors.[74]

The Papal Legates and Other Clerics

Baldwin sent relics to his homeland of Flanders, to the neighbors of Flanders, to the great ecclesiastical and political powers with whom he was already on good terms, and to those with whom he hoped to cultivate good relations as a result of the gifts, such as the papacy. Meanwhile, Rome's papal legates, Peter Capuano and cardinal-priest Benedict of Santa Susanna, played multiple roles in the history of the postcrusade translation of relics. Unlike Nivelon of Soissons, Conrad of Halberstadt, or Martin of Pairis, Capuano was not present when Constantinople fell in April 1204. Having left the crusade earlier because the crusaders were ignoring papal edicts, he did not want his presence to imply that the diversion to the city had papal sanction. He joined the "forgotten second front" of the crusade in Acre.[75] Once Constantinople fell, however, Capuano went there to take advantage of this sudden windfall on behalf of the pope. He lifted edicts of excommunication and absolved the crusaders of their sins. Reconciliation followed and the papacy's voice returned to the crusade.[76] Capuano's activity over the next few years exemplifies all of the roles played in the relic trade by the highest-status individuals connected to the crusade; he was an authority figure who granted permission, a relic translator himself, and an (accidental) enabler of crimes.

Having missed out on the first harvest of relics, Capuano seems to have become a voice of authority on the dispersal of relics in the second phase of their translation. For example, he took control of a trove of relics belonging to a deceased crusading bishop, Garnier of Troyes. Like Nivelon and Conrad, Garnier had provided an episcopal presence on the crusade. He, like his fellows, acquired relics immediately after the conquest, though not, I argue below, in any official capacity. He sent his chaplain to Troyes with the arm of St. James the Greater, the head of St. Philip, a cup that was allegedly the Holy Grail, and the body of St. Helen of Athyra.[77] Thanks to a letter from 1222, we know that Garnier sent additional relics with the chaplain, along with orders on how to distribute them. John of Poitiers (Iohannes Pictaviensis), canon of St. Victor of Paris, wrote to Peter, canon of St. Martin of Troyes and chaplain to Bishop Garnier, asking him to write an account of how Garnier had sent them the head of St. Victor. Both John's request and Peter's reply survive.[78]

Peter recounts that the bishop found the head of St. Victor in a church dedicated to the saint inside the walls near Constantinople's Golden Gate.[79] Garnier ordered Peter to take the head and "other relics of the saints" back to France.[80] There, Peter gave the head to Archbishop Peter de Corbolio of Sens, who later gave a portion of it to John the German (Iohannes Teutonis), the abbot of St. Victor's.[81] On the ides of April, Peter concludes, the relic was met with a procession and much rejoicing.[82] This short letter is particularly compelling because it describes not only the translation of the head from a church in Constantinople to Garnier's hands to the Abbey of St. Victor but also all of the intermediate chains of transmission. The process of exchange and division that took place in this case allows us to conjecture that this process of secondary gifting and sundering of larger relics may have happened often after they arrived in the West.

Garnier sent some of the relics that he had collected to France but died within a year of the conquest. As recorded in the "Historia translationum reliquiarum Sancti Mamantis" (history of the translation of the relics of Saint Mamas), or "Translatio Mamantis," Capuano took control of the rest upon his arrival in Constantinople.[83] In this text, an anonymous canon of Langres describes the actions of Walon of Dampierre, also a canon of Langres, who returned home from the crusade with the head of St. Mamas in 1209. This text is the third part of a larger translatio that describes the process by which various relics of the martyr came to Langres over the centuries, in order to authenticate each item.[84] The translatio contains a compelling description of the looting of relics, as well as the steps that Walon took to authenticate his relic. The relevant portion of the text reads,

> When Constantinople had been captured, the victorious Latins exulted over the booty which they had seized, for they had a vast amount of spoils. But blind greed, which persuades so easily, took the hands of the conquering conquerors, so that not only were the churches violated, but so were the vessels in which the relics of saints were resting, [their hands] shamelessly smashing the vessels [and] repulsively pulling off the gold, gems, and silver, and they thought nothing of the true relics. Having heard of this, senior officers of the army grieved greatly, and feared that this destruction might undo their victory. They therefore took counsel with the legates . . . and with the archbishops and bishops, who threatened to excommunicate anyone who unsealed the containers

of relics. . . . After this [threat of excommunication] the head of the glorious martyr [St. Mamas] was found.[85]

This paragraph is at best a secondhand account of the looting. Later, I argue that it responds to Innocent's successful employment of sacrilegious looting as a polarizing issue, the subject of the next chapter. This is the only Latin text that explicitly includes reliquaries among the sacred objects that the Latins despoiled for the sake of the external gold, silver, and gems; more important, it presents the responses of the crusade leadership to the sacrilege. According to the translatio, the leading crusader clerics gathered, threatened the defilers of relics with excommunication, and then took personal control over rounding up and redistributing the relics. If this account contains any truth at all, no wonder the bishops were able to send home such copious sacred largesse. Capuano would have had considerable clout in such proceedings, thanks to his lofty ecclesiastical status as papal legate and cardinal. He could not easily undo distribution decisions previously made by other high clerics on the crusade, but he could take charge of the deceased Garnier's relics.

According to the "Translatio Mamantis," the priest Walon visited Capuano and informed him that Garnier had planned to send the head of St. Mamas to Langres, long a center of the cult of St. Mamas, before he died. Agreeing that this seemed just, Capuano let Walon take the relic. The head thus passed to Walon through the legate's judgment that this was the best possible outcome, not through one of the acts of looting previously deplored by the text's anonymous author.[86]

By the time Walon spoke to Capuano, the time of chaos had long since passed. The acquisition of St. Mamas clearly belongs to the second phase of relic movement. The passage above indicates that later authors, concerned about the provenance of their new relics becoming tainted, took steps to make it clear that *their* relics had not been obtained through sacrilege. This concern has led to significant scholarly confusion about the looting of relics. Several medieval texts, including the "Translatio Mamantis," imply that Garnier had been put in charge of many relics in the city before he died.[87] Riant decided that this attribution was correct and argued that the crusader clergy had officially appointed him to that position.[88] Over the last century, other scholars have followed Riant's lead in arguing that Garnier was the official *procurator sanctorum reliquarum*.[89] This title implies a level of organization and oversight that simply did not exist until late in the second phase, probably after Garnier was dead. Most sources on relics never mention Garnier at all. The texts that do elevate him to such an official rank derive from sites that, like Langres, directly or indirectly benefited from relics that he collected in Constantinople. Such sources cannot be trusted because their authors wanted to de-emphasize the possibility of any sacrilege staining their new possessions. No neutral texts mention Garnier, in particular, as being more important than any other bishop; the situation was fluid until Capuano arrived. However, Capuano could not restore precrusade conditions and then reapportion relics. All he and his co-legate Benedict could do was try to control the situation as it developed after their arrival. The translation of St. Mamas offers one example of such attempts at control and regulation.

The papal legates' efforts to regulate the translation of relics, however, could backfire. Sometime after March 1206, according to the "Narratio exceptionis apud Cluniacum capitis beati Clementis,"[90] the legates accidentally enabled a brazen relic theft. We know very little about the two knights, Dalmacius of Serciaco and Poncius of Busseria, who stole the relic. The author refers to the former as "well learned,"[91] along with the more usual epithets for crusading knights ("noble," "faithful," and "good"). Once these two had served out their term in Constantinople, they tried to make a pilgrimage to Jerusalem. They failed, due to dangers on both land and sea, and found themselves back in Constantinople, disappointed. Dalmacius therefore went to the two legates to ask for permission to acquire a relic. The legates, speaking in "one voice," granted the request on one condition: the knight could not purchase a relic because of canonical prohibitions against the sale of such items. Undeterred, the knights went to the Monastery of St. Mary Peribleptos, where Dalmacius asked the monks, who appear to have been Greeks, about St. Clement.[92] Many Greek monks remained in their religious houses after the conquest until they were driven away by a new papal legate, Cardinal Pelagius, around 1213, so this encounter is plausible. While Dalmacius distracted the monks, his colleague, Poncius, simply walked off with St. Clement's head. The two returned home and gave it to the Abbey of Cluny.[93]

If this story reflects an actual conversation between the legates and the knights, it would give the impression that the legates were comfortable with the notion that crusaders might seek out relics to take home with them. Their concern was that such activity not be commercial in nature. On the other hand, the knights may have just bought the relic off of someone in Constantinople and the entertaining details are either their fabrications or the hagiographer's.

It is difficult to tell precisely when the theft or purchase occurred, but it could not have been in the initial days after the sack; this is a second-phase theft. Innocent sent Benedict of Santa Susanna to Constantinople sometime around May 1205, and he may not have arrived until the following spring.[94] Furthermore, the text indicates that the knights tried to go to Jerusalem only after they were released from their crusade vow, probably in March 1206,[95] and were subsequently turned back by harsh winds.[96] If this is true, then they would have returned to Constantinople just when both papal legates were definitely in the city. Hence, probably more than two years after the sack, the outright theft of relics was still occurring.

After many years of troubled service, Capuano finally returned to Italy, while Benedict remained, both continuing to dole out relics as opportunity arose.[97] Along his route through southern Italy, Capuano paused to distribute relics to various Latin religious houses. Amalfi, his hometown,[98] received the head of its patron saint, St. Andrew, in May 1208. Here, Capuano acted similarly to Conrad and Nivelon. He bore relics back to his home church, the locals greeted the relics with celebration, and the late saint worked local miracles.[99] Sometime between 1210 and the death of Capuano in 1214, an anonymous monk in Gaeta wrote a text celebrating Capuano's gift of the head of St. Theodore. Although brief, this account is exceedingly useful because it lists other examples of Capuano's generosity. The author begins with the gift of St. Andrew and then reports that Sorrento received the relics of the Apostle James. Naples received certain "true relics of other saints."[100] To the Abbey of Monte Cassino, Capuano gave an arm of St. Athanasius.[101] Gaeta's reception of St. Theodore finished the list.

This text serves as an excellent example of the most typical type of second-phase relic acquisition and translation. It was authorized, and the relics were physically carried by a high-ranking official and given to favored churches in his homeland. Capuano enriched the churches of southern Italy. Dandolo favored the churches of Venice. Baldwin sent relics to Flanders and the French king, just as Garnier did to Champagne. One notices a trend: relics of saints were often sent to places that already had a tradition of venerating those saints. St. Mamas went to the Cathedral of St. Mamas in Langres; a fragment of St. Stephen the Protomartyr went to the Cathedral of St. Stephen in Halberstadt; and St. Andrew went to Amalfi. In 1208, Henry of Ulmen brought the head of St. Pantaleon to Abbot Henry of the Monastery of St. Pantaleon in Cologne.[102] Henry of Ulmen also brought a spectacular cross reliquary to Limburg, although the precise provenance remains a subject of debate among scholars.[103] In 1222, the canon John the German of St. Victor's asked Garnier's former chaplain for letters of authentication concerning the relic of St. Victor that the abbey had received in 1205—yet another example of the trend. Many Western sites were dedicated to saints whose relics had long been housed in Constantinople; apparently, some of the leading figures on the crusade chose to use the conquest of 1204 as an occasion to fill these voids.

Dandolo, Baldwin, and Garnier sent relics west, but all of these men died in the East. For others, the voyage home marked the occasion when crusaders finally translated their gains, as well as the end of the second phase in the movement of the relics of 1204. Nivelon, Conrad, Capuano, and Martin are well known because they had the means to commission translatio narratives in their homelands. We know about the Venetian men who stole the body of St. Simon because a text that tells their story happens to have survived. A few fragmentary and non-narrative texts provide additional examples. According to one of these, Walon of Sarton, canon of Picquigny near Amiens, became a canon of a church in Constantinople. Having decided that he had experienced enough of the East after the disaster of Adrianople, he took a few silver reliquaries that he had found hidden in his new church and sold them to finance his journey home. He then gave the relics (a finger of St. George and yet another head of St. John the Baptist) to the cathedral at Amiens.[104] In another legend, an English priest who served as Baldwin's chaplain was sent back to the capital from the battle of Adrianople to fetch the Holy Rood, a relic of the True Cross traditionally borne into battle by the emperors of Constantinople, but which Baldwin had accidentally left behind. Unfortunately, Baldwin was killed before the chaplain made it back to the battlefield, so the chaplain hid the cross and took it with him back to Bromholm.[105] Henry of Ulmen's gifts also generated surviving documentation, including a new reliquary for the relic of St. Matthias that he had donated to Trier, with an inscription commemorating the donation.[106] Several seventeenth-century French church historians describe two cross-shaped reliquaries holding fragments of the True Cross that Robert of Clari had allegedly brought to the Monastery of Corbie from the imperial palace chapel. The reliquaries and inscriptions that attributed these items to Clari were lost, probably during the French Revolution, but an inventory from Corbie from 1283 mentions the relics that "Robert of Clari, soldier, brought from Constantinople."[107] The attribution is credible; as noted above, Clari catalogued some of the more important relics of the imperial chapel in his chronicle. It is interesting that he returned with objects from the chapel but never described his acquisitions. Does this represent an outright theft or evidence of sacrilegious looting in the first three days, or did Nivelon perhaps give Clari, his soldier, the tiniest of fragments of the relics that the bishop claimed from the palace churches? The sole complete copy of Clari's chronicle exists in a vellum book once belonging to Corbie's library, so one can at least note a connection between the knight and the monastic institution.[108] There must have been many more such relic translations as crusaders finished their terms of service or simply gave up. Clari made no note of his own translation, although Corbie's inventory did. Surely other soldiers offered similar gifts to their favored churches.

Not only have accounts of relic translation been lost to modern historians, but some relics themselves were lost during the transition from Greek to Latin rule. Three of the bishops on the crusade took or sent relics home. A fourth prelate, bishop-elect Peter of Bethlehem, could not have returned to Muslim-controlled Bethlehem, and he died at Adrianople before he might have selected an alternative site for his sacred plunder. A Greek text blames Conrad of Halberstadt and bishop-elect Peter for stealing the relic of consecrated bread from the Last Supper.[109] The "Gesta episcoporum Halberstadensium" never mentions this relic and most certainly would have noted its possession if Conrad had held on to it. Alfred Andrea speculates that Peter lost the relic at Adrianople. No post-Adrianople record of the relic's presence has been found.[110]

The second phase witnessed many translations of relics—some seized during the first weeks, some obtained later. Within about five years, although these dates are not firm, most of the people who participated in the crusade had died, gone home, or settled permanently in the Latin Empire. Many acquired relics—by theft, by gift, by purchase, or by authorized acquisition. As the participants' movements ceased, the great exodus of relics slowed, but it never stopped. Forgeries complicate the matter. As late as 1215, criticisms of relic-selling in Canon 62 of the Fourth Lateran Council indicate that relics, including forgeries, were being sold and distributed throughout Europe.[111] Invented items no doubt joined and perhaps even comprised the majority of the mass of looted relics in this black market of the sacred. When perusing the lists of Fourth Crusade relics, one sees many heads of St. John the Baptist, True Cross fragments, and other easily fabricated fragments of various objects. Authentication proved difficult, and the looting of Constantinople gave a reasonable provenance for the unscrupulous forger to employ.

The Third Phase: The Height of the Latin Empire

During the relatively short life span of the Latin Empire, Latins continued to send relics from Constantinople to the West. Again, one can divide the known cases of relic acquisition into two groups: authorized and unauthorized. The rulers of the Latin Empire and other newly conquered lands continued to use their relics as diplomatic gifts. The most important and best studied of these cases concerns the translation of the relics of the Passion to King Louis IX of France in 1239. But there were others. Emperor Henry (r. 1206–16) followed his brother's pattern of doling out minor, or small, relics, as did his successors.[112] Meanwhile, Latin clergy in Constantinople mined their treasuries for suitable objects for translation. In some cases, the clergy simply sent the relics west in their original reliquaries. At other times, they seem to have shaved off small parts in order to form new relics. The Venetians proved particularly interested in claiming relics from their churches in an expanded Venetian quarter of Constantinople, and our sources present some of these translations as unauthorized.[113]

Riant's collection of "Epistolae et Instrumenta" provides ample evidence of Henry of Flanders's emulation of his brother. The letters and grants are all relatively short and contain little information about where and how Henry obtained relics. As emperor he would have encountered no difficulty in doing so, and he sometimes provided bills of authentication for them. A *testimonium de reliquiis* found in Lyons, dated April 6, 1208, bears witness to the transfer of relics of the True Cross, St. Stephen the Protomartyr (yet again), St. Thomas, and St. Eustachius to Archbishop Raynaldo. Pontio de Caponay bore the relics, and Henry provided him with this short *authentica*.[114] Other texts give even less information. One simply records that Henry sent "infinite relics of the Savior, Mary, the apostles, the evangelists, the prophets, the martyrs, the confessors, and female saints, and pious benefactors" to two German monks, Thomas and Gerard.[115] What could this list mean? Did Thomas and Gerard somehow acquire dozens of tiny fragments one by one, or did Henry give them a sack filled with them? A 1215 document from Clairvaux is clearer. Hugo, formerly abbot of St. Ghislain in Hainaut (Henry's homeland), delivered a relic of the True Cross from Constantinople to Clairvaux as a gift from the emperor. The document provides a very brief history of the Fourth Crusade in order to show how the relic came to be in Henry's hands. Again, the purpose of this account was authentication.[116]

Documents that testify to the movement of relics out of newly Latinized churches by their new owners demonstrate that the phenomenon spread beyond Constantinople and lasted for decades. In 1215, Archbishop John of Neopatras, from Thessaly, sent a finger of St. Nicholas "and other relics" to the Monastery of Gembloux in Belgium.[117] In 1216, Archbishop Warinus of Thessalonica sent a finger of St. John the Baptist to a monastery in Phalempin, Flanders.[118] In 1218, the Cathedral of St. Albans in Namur, Flanders, catalogued its relics, which included a spine from the Crown of Thorns and some of Christ's blood, both from Constantinople.[119] We do not know their provenance, but Baldwin's and Henry's generosity to the religious houses of their region has already been noted. A 1224 testimonial on relics is attributed to William of Villehardouin but was almost certainly produced for Geoffrey I Villehardouin, "prince of Achaia" and nephew to the marshal of Champagne.[120] The prince sent a reliquary to the church of St. Remigius in Reims, Champagne, his family's home city, via an old monk named Arnuld de Lotti. Inside the reliquary were drops of blood that he "believed" to have been shed from the side of Christ on the cross.[121] We do not know where the prince acquired this relic. In 1230, Walter, reeve of Beata Maria of Cinctura in Constantinople, sent relics to Lambert, the reeve of Beata Maria in Bruges. These included an arm of the Apostle Bartholomew, an arm of St. Blasius, and relics of St. Laurence and Stephen the Protomartyr (again). In 1232, Anselm, the procurator of St. Mary Magdalene in Constantinople, brought together multiple relics of, yet again, St. Stephen the Protomartyr. Anselm, like Walter, sent these to Lambert of Bruges.[122]

The above are just a sampling of the relics sent from the Latin Empire and Frankish Greece to Western Europe. Relics had always flowed licitly from church to church in the Middle Ages at semiregular intervals. Guardians of relics rewarded friends and curried favor by offering small pieces of relics. Bishops redistributed relics within their sees.[123] But now there was a sudden influx of relics, some very important, coming from long-established religious institutions in the East, all of which were under new ownership.[124] Such institutions, backed by the Greek nobility and their churchmen, had gathered relics for centuries. Perhaps the Western clerics lacked a long-term commitment to their new properties and felt free to use them to enrich their old friends and allies back in the West. It is not clear that anyone tried to strip a newly acquired religious building of value entirely, but a certain amount of careful siphoning on behalf of the homeland definitely took place.

Venice figures prominently in the history of this siphoning. In 1222, the abbot of San Giorgio Maggiore, Venice's principle monastery, ordered the translation of a relic out of a daughter monastery, Christ Pantepoptes, which it had obtained in Constantinople after 1204. The prior of San Giorgio, who ruled the Pantepoptes, enlisted the help of the podestà, the chief official in Constantinople's Venetian quarter, in finding transport for the relics of St. Paul the New Martyr.[125] The translatio recording this story casts it as a sacred theft, as the abbot commands the prior to send the relic to him secretly (*abscondite sibi mitteret*). But it is not clear who the Venetians feared might catch them. The prior controlled the monastery. The podestà had absolute power within the Venetian quarter. Thus, we are left to question whether the translation of St. Paul's relics was authorized or unauthorized.[126] The timing is curious. Venice's leading monastery had acquired this property after 1204 but decided to send the relic to Venice fifteen years later. Other Venetian sources describe the acquisition of the relics of St. Helen, John the Martyr, and Paul the First Hermit (taken to Venice in 1211, 1214, and 1239, respectively), and the purchase of precious objects for the express purpose of decorating the churches of Venice. Venice also acquired the relics of St. Theodore the Martyr (1257) and St. Barbara (1258) just as the Latin Empire was weakening in the face of the Palaiologoi threat.

The translation of the relics of the Passion to King Louis IX, in 1239, is justifiably famous for its transformative effect on French royal iconography and Western devotional practice.[127] The art of Sainte-Chapelle, the eventual house for the relics, depicts the only two prior acts of translation in Christian history to rival it—the *inventio* of the True Cross by Constantine and his mother, Helen, and the recovery of the cross by Heraclius.[128] This chapter demonstrates that the translation of relics to Louis, although exceptional in scale, occurred within a larger ongoing pattern. Many relics were taken out of the Latin Empire. More specifically, Baldwin I gave relics of the Passion to Philip II Augustus, setting a precedent for the later translation. Baldwin II had used the Crown of Thorns as collateral on a loan from Venice. He saw the translation to Louis as a better deal for him than any other. Louis had to send two Dominicans to redeem the crown before the king would choreograph the great translation.[129] Using the great relics of Constantinople at the highest levels of statecraft was nothing new to the Latin emperors.

Unlicensed relic trafficking during the life of the Latin Empire completes the picture. We have almost no evidence of trafficking beyond the complaints of those who wanted to stop it.[130] These relic sales most likely happened on a retail level—not from a commoner to a church, but from one commoner to another. Such transactions would not have been recorded. Forgeries, as well as actual bits and pieces of relics stolen by common crusaders, probably flooded the West, but, again, details about these were not preserved by the sources. Capuano and Benedict's prohibition against purchasing a relic offers one piece of evidence for the phenomenon.[131] Canon 62 of the Fourth Lateran Council (1215) represents a later, and broadly applied, attempt by the Church to restrict the unauthorized translation of relics. By this point, a decade after the conquest, Rome would have had a solid understanding of the problem it was trying to solve. The canon forbids the sale or unauthorized exhibition of relics. It also establishes that only Rome may approve new relics, giving it control of the means of authentication.[132] While one cannot base claims about the quantity or frequency of the unauthorized sale of Constantinople's relics on the canon, the law does indicate the existence of the problem.

Conclusion

The details of the long process of stealing, looting, and redistributing Constantinople's relics after 1204 remain murky. The general patterns, however, are clear. The process began with a vow not to harm the Greek churches, but in the chaos of the conflict, that vow fell by the wayside. Undoubtedly, the translatio of St. Mamas, Niketas's lament, and Innocent's diatribe contain elements of truth in blaming the crusaders for destroying and desecrating relics, smashing altar plates, and breaking other sacred items in order to acquire gems and precious metals. During such acts of pillage, some crusaders, who had long venerated the relics of Constantinople, must have stolen tiny pieces and risked death in doing so. This type of theft led to trafficking, forgeries, and the widespread, uncontrolled, and largely undocumented dispersal of relics in Europe over the decades to come. Furthermore, various individuals took advantage of the chaos to pick and choose the relics they most desired. Abbot Martin and the Venetians of St. Simon's parish are the two best-documented examples. The abbot valued ease of access and safety, whereas the Venetians chose a specific relic that they wanted to steal regardless of the risk.

Once things had settled down, the leaders of the crusade began to claim the relics for themselves. The Latin bishops in Constantinople at the time of the conquest had prime access to the relics of their choice and also received important items as gifts. Garnier of Troyes died before he could disperse much of his collection, and papal legate Peter Capuano, who had missed the free-for-all of the initial conquest, took control of these relics. The secular leadership joined the bishops, perhaps using the power of confiscation to gain their plunder. By around 1210, the initial appropriation and apportioning of relics and territories in the East among Latins from and in the West had been accomplished. Many relics remained in the churches and monasteries of Constantinople, but they continued, in whole or in part, to be sent westward from time to time. The slow process of licensed relic translation joined with more illicit forms of relic trafficking to drain the sacred wealth of Constantinople; these translations included those that propagated the grand myths associated with the relics of the Passion, as well as the peripatetic wanderings of the Shroud on its way to Turin. In 1261, the "new Constantine," Michael VIII Palaiologos, had to begin Constantine's work of creating a "new Jerusalem" all over again.[133]

2

Pope Innocent III and Sacrilege, 1204–1215

When news reached Pope Innocent III that Constantinople had been conquered, he rejoiced at this clear sign of God's miraculous power. He publicly hailed the victory and predicted the speedy reunification of the Greek and Latin churches, which would then lead to the liberation of Jerusalem by the forces of a united Christendom and perhaps mark the beginning of the Apocalypse.

But the Greeks failed to convert in large numbers. Enemies of the new state pressed in from all sides, and the need to defend the empire sapped resources from other crusading activity. Jerusalem remained in Islamic hands. Worse, critical voices from the West questioned crusader conduct and papal complicity in that conduct. At the same time, the pontiff began negotiating with the secular leadership of the crusade over church property in Constantinople. The Orthodox churches of Constantinople had owned huge swaths of the most desirable property in the great city, and the secular powers in the new empire, Frank and Venetian alike, felt empowered to appropriate it. But for Innocent, all church property belonged to the "seamless garment of Christ," and he demanded its immediate return.

By then, however, Innocent had lost his leverage. The crusaders had defied him in their diversion to Constantinople and had been excommunicated for their trouble. They had also vowed, on pain of damnation, to fight for the Holy Land; until released from their vow, damnation threatened. These were cudgels that Innocent could have wielded to influence the postconquest environment. But, after the conquest, Innocent's papal legate, Cardinal Peter Capuano, released the crusaders from their vow and absolved them of their sins. In return, he demanded an additional year of service and little more. Innocent could not extract further promises in exchange for lifting the penalty of excommunication, nor could he demand further military action in lieu of a campaign against Muslim Jerusalem. Innocent needed a new approach.

This chapter argues that Innocent employed accusations of sacrilege and other sinful behavior during the postconquest looting as a source of new leverage and as a means of explaining the sudden loss of divine favor. Such accusations cited wide misconduct but named the violation of holy ground and the seizing of relics as the worst of the crusaders' many crimes. These complaints were made most explicitly in the summer of 1205, just as crusaders and their relics began arriving back in the West.

Within a year of the creation of the Latin Empire, papal writings consistently raised the issue of sinful misconduct after the conquest in order to push recalcitrant Christians to support papal positions or desires. Thus, the pope moved the contest over the meaning of 1204 to a religious battlefield. Even when not discussing the looting, he made moral or spiritual judgments on crusader conduct, thus keeping the conversation on the papal battleground of religious matters. Over time, other critics of the crusade echoed the papal approach in its moral condemnation of the crusaders and focus on illicit looting. The persistent criticism from Rome and other sites cemented the crusaders' conduct and moral decision-making during the pillaging of Constantinople as the locus of the conflict over memory and meaning of the Fourth Crusade.

Innocent and the Crusaders

The contest over the memory of the Fourth Crusade emerged out of a specific set of political, ecclesiastical, and economic postconquest issues with which the papacy and the leaders of the crusading army wrestled. As with so many other phases of the crusade, the terms of oaths sworn by the soldiers dictated the nature of the difficulties to follow.[1] Key terms of the March Pact at once incurred Innocent's wrath and mandated reconciliation between the crusaders and the papacy, a precarious situation indeed. The central passages—on election and division of secular spoils—caused no controversy with Rome. It was, rather, the lesser provisions that governed the disposal of the wealth of the church and the patriarchate of Constantinople that reignited tensions otherwise potentially eased by the victory. The lay leaders had disposed of church lands, other kinds of church property, and even the highest ecclesiastical office in Constantinople. Innocent could not let this stand. Meanwhile, in order to ensure that the co-signers of the pact would all meet the commitments to which they had agreed, the document mandated papal ratification. The crusade leadership, assuming that Innocent would eventually absolve them of their sins, actually wanted the coercive threat of papal excommunication in order to guarantee the crusaders' adherence to the document. Without papal ratification, the pact could have been annulled, thus potentially rendering Baldwin's ascension to the throne illegitimate and raising the chance for further internecine conflict.

Innocent's responses to the crusade are found chiefly in the register of his correspondence covering the most important years of the crusade's aftermath, 1204 to 1206.[2] The *Gesta Innocentii*, a second key source for papal engagement in the contested memory of 1204, offers the perspective of the larger papal organization. Its author, an anonymous member of the curia writing between 1204 and 1209, benefitted from his hindsight of the events of the Fourth Crusade, the sack of Constantinople, and the failures of the early Latin Empire. One of the chief purposes of the *Gesta* was to exculpate Innocent from any blame that might have accrued to him as the sponsor of the initial crusade.[3]

The interactions between the army and Rome during the close of the crusade shaped the papal response in the years that followed. Over the course of the campaign itself, before the sack, the tone of papal letters builds from mild reprimand to outright fury and condemnation. Questions of morality, ecclesiastical privilege, and divine approval—topics on which Innocent could claim ultimate authority—appear within these sources from the very beginning. As plans began to go awry, the pope deployed his limited tools of coercion and persuasion in order to get the crusade back on course to Egypt without antagonizing allies or potential allies, particularly the king of Hungary and Emperor Alexius III. He reminded the crusaders of their oath and threatened excommunication; in fact, each time the crusade diverted, an edict of excommunication against the army went into effect, though the crusade leadership suppressed this news. Innocent tried to divide the crusaders from their defiant leaders, or to split the French from the Venetians, with intermittent success. Many soldiers did abandon the enterprise (mostly because of internal dissent rather than papal machinations), but enough of them remained to provide a credible military force. Further undermining any sway Innocent might have had, clerics on the crusade preached to the rank and file that the diversion to Constantinople was part of the holy mission.[4]

Despite the crusaders' defiance of the papacy, this crusade was not particularly irreligious. The soldiers had taken sacred oaths on which they staked their very souls. Nor did the diversion to Constantinople mean that the soldiers intended to abandon their quest to free Jerusalem. To the contrary, Constantinople initially represented a means to the ends of financing and supplying for the campaign against the Muslims. Even in February and March 1204, the crusaders still planned to leave Constantinople and campaign in Egypt. But the successful conquest changed everything. The clause mandating papal approval of the March Pact demonstrates that the crusaders knew the papacy would have to be part of the new empire's future for it to survive. Moreover, the crusaders were operating under lingering burdens of excommunication. They now controlled a large region that would need to be assimilated into the Latin rite if the conquered people were to accept their Latin rulers. Most importantly, Jerusalem was nowhere in sight. The only military expedition the army would yet undertake was to pacify its new holdings and beat back both Greek and Bulgarian claimants to the throne. And only the pope or his representative could absolve the oath of a crusader.

Innocent knew that the crusaders cared about obedience to Rome, if not to the degree he might have wished. Throughout the Constantinople affair, Innocent and his legate remained optimistic that the force could be turned back toward Egypt and returned to the papal fold. To effect this desired turnabout, Innocent offered both spiritual inducements and threats. His main concern about the diversion to Constantinople had been that it might interfere with reconciliation talks or efforts to recover the Holy Land. Even after the death of Alexius IV, the idea that Constantinople could be conquered by the small Latin army, be ruled by a Latin emperor, and seemingly serve as a new beachhead for future crusades had not seemed likely to any of the parties involved.[5] However, presented with the reality of the new emperor Baldwin, in the first few months after the fall, Innocent stated his belief in the providential nature of the conquest and was ready to deal with the conquerors.[6]

In the initial aftermath of the conquest, therefore, it was a foregone conclusion among all parties that some form of agreement between the papacy and the crusaders could be reached. The shift away from diversion and toward looting, particularly sacrilegious looting, took place in an atmosphere of mutual distrust yet mandatory engagement. Each side had much to gain by dealing with the other, but Innocent had the moral upper hand. The crusaders knew that they had strayed and required papal forgiveness to lift the edict of excommunication. On the other hand, the crusaders were in Constantinople, held the city, and had already apportioned the wealth of the East among themselves. With the moral high ground balanced against fait accompli, negotiations concerning reconciliation and the ecclesiastical future of the Latin Empire began; so too began the contest over memory.

The First Postconquest Communications: Cautious Optimism

After news of the conquest reached Rome, the pope turned his efforts in the East to four new issues. First, he wanted to recover all of the church property that had been looted or secularized—this included both objects, such as relics, and the lands of the Greek church in the city. Second, he desired complete papal control over the patriarchate of Constantinople. Third, he wanted the newly conquered lands to serve as a base of operations for further crusading activity. Fourth, and perhaps most significantly, he wanted to convert the Greek people to a true Roman Catholicism. The Franks and Venetians, meanwhile, were dealing with two issues of their own. They needed, first, papal ratification of the March Pact to stabilize the new empire while, second, maintaining their respective new possessions in Constantinople—including the churches and church property they had claimed as their own. These matters directly pertained to questions of church and papal prerogative. Where agendas came into conflict, the debate often unfolded along moral or spiritual lines. The specifics of the contest over memory and interpretation emerged from that debate.

A short letter from Innocent to Baldwin from November 1204 reveals the pope's approach to the surprising conquest. Baldwin had sent his first letter to Innocent in May, but Genoese privateers captured the courier and delayed the letter's arrival.[7] Innocent began his letter by praising the miraculous nature of the conquest. This was not mere window dressing. The providential nature of the conquest was invoked by all involved across diverse genres (sermons, chronicles, diplomatic letters, poems, and so forth). But Innocent used his statement about God having miraculously effected the victory in order to assert his prerogatives over the new empire. He wrote, "[God] has deigned to work magnificent miracles with you for the praise and glory of His Name, for the honor and profit of the Apostolic See, and for the benefit and exaltation of the Christian people."[8] He placed Baldwin and his "land and people under the primary protection of St. Peter and under our special protection, resolutely ordering all archbishops, bishops, and all other church prelates, also kings, dukes, counts, and other princes, and all peoples that they support and defend your [Baldwin's] lands and people, and they neither personally molest them nor have them molested by others."[9] Innocent promised to order his prelates to excommunicate and place under interdict any who might "molest" the new lands, and he instructed all of his clerics to assist the new emperor. He also extended the papal crusade indulgence, offering a remission of sins to those "lay crusaders" who helped defend the new Latin Empire. Innocent pledged to send Baldwin additional assistance, because he recognized that by helping Latin-ruled Constantinople, "the Holy Land might be more easily liberated from pagan hands."[10]

Then Innocent issued a warning. In his view, the Byzantine Empire fell because God wished to punish the Greeks for defying Rome. He reasoned, "After the kingdom of the Greeks turned away from the obedience to the Apostolic See, it continuously descended from evil to worse evil until, by the just judgment of God, it was transferred from the proud to the humble, from the disobedient to the obedient, from the schismatics to followers of the Latin rite, so that it might rise through the virtue of obedience to goodness because through the sin of disobedience it fell into evil."[11] Therefore, Innocent continued, Baldwin had best remain "in obedience" to Rome lest the same fate befall his empire. Innocent informed Baldwin that to obey Rome he would have to "diligently and faithfully make sure that ecclesiastical goods, both fixed and moveable, are protected until they might be properly organized in accordance with our authoritative decision, so that those things that are Caesar's might be rendered to Caesar, and those things that are God's might be rendered to God without confusion."[12] Placed at the close of the first formal communication between pontiff and new emperor and closely approximating biblical phrasing, this reference has considerable rhetorical weight.[13] Innocent linked the survival of the empire to obedience to Rome and questioned the fate of church property. He probably suspected that some "confusion" had already taken place.

Innocent's letter epitomizes his approach to the postconquest situation. First, he affirmed the miraculous nature of the victory. Second, he demanded specific actions from crusaders who wanted to avoid divine retribution for their sins. He coupled his historical analysis and providential interpretations with specific warnings. Carrot and stick—Innocent offered his support while demanding obedience. The fate of the vast wealth of the Greek church particularly concerned him.

Although chaos had initially reigned in the days after the Latin soldiers took Constantinople, "confusion" was not the biggest obstacle to satisfying the pope—and the chaotic looting of church property might well be labeled "confusion." Rather, it was the more systematic appropriation of church wealth and position that demanded papal action. Two tenets of the March Pact addressed church matters. Following passages that detailed how six Venetians and six Franks would elect an emperor, the next section mandated that whichever party—the Franks or the Venetians—lost the election, that party would receive authority over Hagia Sophia and the patriarchate. Moreover, as noted above, the pact stated that "sufficient quantities of the possessions of the churches ought to be provided to the clerics and the churches so that they might live and be sustained in an honorable fashion. The remaining possessions of the churches, indeed, should be divided and distributed in accordance with the aforesaid agreement."[14] To secure this agreement, the parties asked that the pope "bind by the chain of excommunication" anyone who broke the pact.[15] Innocent had no quarrel with much of this treaty, including the method of choosing an emperor, the clauses that refused access to the empire to anyone at war with Venice, the creation of a council to determine who received which fiefs, and even the means of dividing the secular loot. No pontiff, however, could have accepted the provisions for church property and the patriarchate, let alone given them official papal sanction.

The patriarch of Constantinople was arguably the second most powerful prelate in Christendom, following only the pope himself. Thomas Madden argues that the Venetians had always planned on losing the imperial election and taking control of Hagia Sophia, since Doge Enrico Dandolo had neither the authority to claim the city for the Venetian republic nor the desire to start his own imperial dynasty. Moreover, along with the title of patriarch came the control of the cathedral itself and all of its vast properties, leadership of the local church, and, most important, the ability to keep the newly Latin patriarchate from eroding the privileges of the Venetian-dominated patriarchate of Grado, the patriarchal seat located on an island not far from Venice.[16] Under no circumstances would Innocent allow secular figures to determine the fate of the patriarchate, but his relationship with the Venetians and their leader had been especially fraught, and perhaps this contributed to the ensuing tensions over the issue.[17] These tensions would linger well into the second decade of the Latin patriarchate's existence.

The distribution of church property was an even more contentious problem.[18] The pope's urgent concern stemmed from the crusaders' decision to give themselves the right to redistribute the vast wealth of the Greek church.[19] The crusaders had agreed to reserve the churches—the actual buildings—for various clerics on the crusade, but such was the limit of their generosity. The churches of Constantinople controlled vast quantities of land and property throughout the medieval city. This city had served as the "new Jerusalem" for generations of Greek emperors and garnered wealth from the donations of pilgrims and the bequests of the devout.[20] The crusade leadership decided that it would give its priests only as much of the goods and property of the churches as the priests would need to sustain themselves appropriately. All other plunder taken from the churches was fair game for the secular crusaders. Furthermore, these secular leaders decided how much a given church needed to support itself.

Innocent was likely aware of at least the basic tenets of the March Pact by the time he wrote that first letter to Baldwin in November 1204. The pact itself was not enregistered in Rome until January 1205, and Alfred Andrea speculates that Baldwin delayed sending it to Innocent because he knew that it would "provoke papal ire."[21] A long letter from Baldwin to Rome from May 1204 (as opposed to the short missive that was delayed, as mentioned above) details the course of the conquest but does not mention the fate of the churches. Baldwin describes the battles, the multiple elections to determine the emperor in the last weeks before the sack, and his own election, and offers many hopeful words for the future, but he obfuscates the details of the pact, already enacted. He pretends, for example, that the appointment of electors occurred nearly of its own accord, rather than having been scrupulously planned out in detail weeks before the final assault.[22]

One might posit that Baldwin suspected that the provisions concerning the churches would cause problems. He may have wanted more time to assess and divide church property before receiving a specific papal edict forbidding any such action. Throughout the crusade, the army's leaders used fait accompli to counter papal objections, and they seem to have continued in this mode. This would explain Baldwin's delay in informing the pope of what, precisely, was going on in Constantinople. The word "confusion" in Innocent's first letter to the new emperor indicates that any attempts at suppression failed. The pope suspected that there would be problems, even if he did not yet know the details.

The March Pact, technically, was an agreement between the Venetians and the Franks. Thus, both Dandolo and Baldwin (as the leader of the Franks, once he took the throne) needed to send a copy to Rome and ask Innocent to ratify their agreement. The copy of the pact and their two letters requesting papal approbation arrived in January 1205.[23] With these in hand, Innocent could respond more directly. The two letters betray a certain discomfort. Baldwin asked for papal ratification of the "articles of agreement," then stressed the "good and faithful association" between himself and the Venetians, specifically Dandolo. He noted that, in order to show their devotion to Rome, the parties agreed to ask for papal approval even before they stormed the city. Innocent should ratify the agreement, Baldwin concluded, for the sake of the stability of the new empire, the "relief of the Holy Land, and . . . the preservation of church unity."[24] These three goals could not be achieved, he averred, without the Venetians' help. Baldwin feared that Innocent would still be so angry at the Venetians that he would reject the agreement and throw the entire mechanism for apportioning the new empire into chaos. A papal rejection might also erode Baldwin's legitimacy as emperor. In this letter, therefore, Baldwin emphasized the core goodness, faithfulness, and, above all, utility of the Venetians.[25]

Dandolo had an even tougher task in seeking papal approval. He had to retell the entire history of the crusade in such a way as to make his actions seem acceptable. His letter to Innocent constitutes the first known Venetian attempt at shaping the memory of the crusade—a text earlier than either the Venetian translatio texts discussed in part II or the Ravenna mosaics considered by Madden.[26] Whether Dandolo actually expected to change Innocent's mind is unknowable, but he did not necessarily have to persuade the pope of anything. The goal was to provide a willing pontiff a face-saving means out of the impasse between the two sides. He may have hoped that the pope would seek to make peace in order to play an active role in the new empire. Dandolo's case relies partially on claiming that he did no wrong and had never intentionally defied papal will. More importantly, Dandolo suggested that the clear evidence of divine approval and even direct intervention in the campaign meant that the pope must forgive him. God, after all, could outrank the pope in religious matters.

This letter from Dandolo provides us with the earliest evidence of an internal counternarrative of the crusade that would resist the condemnatory voices from Rome and elsewhere. Dandolo employs the types of arguments later made by the translatio texts of the Fourth Crusade. He stresses the presence of a divine hand guiding events, explaining how, "with (as we believe) divine inspiration rather than human planning overtaking events," Alexius Angelos met with the crusading army and asked for help. As a result of this "divine inspiration," the crusaders and the Greek prince signed the Treaty of Zara, agreeing to attempt to place Alexius on the Byzantine throne.[27] Dandolo was arguing that regardless of what had transpired in the past between the Venetians and the papacy, events had so clearly shown the signs of divine intervention that exoneration should be a foregone conclusion. Nevertheless, he did offer an exculpatory account of events. For example, he claimed that the Venetians had attacked Zara only because it was unjustly (iniuste) engaged in rebellion against Venice. He had heard that Hungary (to whom the citizens of Zara had pledged their city) was under the protection of Rome, but Dandolo did not believe this could be true.[28] He had "patiently endured" the edict of excommunication, but it had since been lifted by the papal legate Peter Capuano, so there was no need to ask for further official forgiveness on the matter of Zara anyway. Furthermore, the conquest of Constantinople was undertaken simply to correct a wrong (against Alexius and Isaac Angelos), and violence broke out after the Greeks proved to be treacherous liars (mendaces et fallaces).[29] In the diversions to Zara and Constantinople, claims Dandolo, the Venetians and crusaders only sought to fight injustice. And, of course, the city of Constantinople "had to be conquered for the honor of God and the Holy Roman Church and the relief of Christendom."[30] Dandolo concluded that Innocent should grant his petitions because all of the Venetians' actions had been only for the benefit of God and Rome.

Dandolo may have believed parts of his letter. He did not plan for the crusaders to become irrevocably indebted to Venice before they even departed from the city. He did not plan to divert the crusade to Constantinople. He probably did intend to use the newly constructed crusading fleet to pacify potential rivals in the Adriatic before sailing to Cairo, as this was in line with Venetian crusading tradition. Instead, he went so far as to use the crusading army to conquer the city of Zara.[31] He did support both diversions as a means for the crusaders to pay off their debts to Venice; one central thesis of Madden's work emphasizes the lack of his legal authority as doge to forgive those debts without such a solution.[32] The recasting of Alexius and Isaac Angelos as perjurers only occurred after the Angeloi had been overthrown, since they had started as allies. Venetian secular accounts of the Fourth Crusade would come to include an invented papal directive to assault Constantinople, but Dandolo's core argument did not rely on rewriting history or trying to alter papal perceptions.[33] Instead, the concept of God's will *superveniente*, which Andrea translates as "overtaking events," reveals Dandolo's hermeneutic.[34] Events happened. Dandolo could justify his decisions, but such justifications were unnecessary, he claimed. With God's will "overtaking" those events, the matter was moot. Dandolo did not admit to wrongdoing. He did not ask for forgiveness (Capuano had already absolved him, after all). He asked only for a favorable hearing of his petition. Later, the translatio texts of the Fourth Crusade would follow Dandolo's approach to addressing morally questionable deeds: deny, blame the Greeks, admit sin when necessary, and invoke divine will. If God had worked a miracle to give Constantinople to the crusaders, should not the pope now treat Dandolo, one of God's instruments in the affair, generously?

And the victory did seem to be a miracle. Before 1204, Constantinople had never fallen to an outside army. It is true that the Latins were greatly helped by internal dissension, but the city fell chiefly because French and Venetian soldiers made it over the walls. Only after this assault did the Greek army take flight.[35] For the crusaders, the success of the whole venture (and the promise it seemed to indicate for future crusades) proved that the deviation was part of God's providential plan. Medieval authors often argued that God's plan unfolds through otherwise disagreeable events, a theme to which authors of the hagiographies of 1204 frequently returned.[36] Dandolo turned Innocent's conceptual framework back on the pontiff. Innocent had never denied the presence of God in the conquest of Constantinople; instead, he set himself up as the arbiter of the meaning of God's presence. Dandolo offered an alternative interpretation.

In responding to the March Pact, the papacy tried to remain firm on certain points while otherwise staying positive and optimistic. The pope found much in which to rejoice when considering the new empire, despite any "confusion" about what should be "rendered" to the Church. Innocent's writings suggest that he believed, in an apocalyptic sense, that the shocking conquest of Constantinople signified salvation for the Holy Land.[37] His letter to the clergy of the crusade in November 1204, produced at the same time that he wrote his first official letter to Emperor Baldwin, contains a wondrous and complex invocation of both the Old and New Testament, including the book of Revelation. This letter argues that once the Greeks enter the Roman Church, "all Israel shall be saved."[38] The invocation of Revelation and the direct link between the conquest of Constantinople and the coming Judgment places the letter firmly in the category of apocalyptic writing. Innocent wrote that God, through the crusaders, had brought the reunification of Christendom to "divine completion." That reunification was a prerequisite for the salvation of the Holy Land, itself a prerequisite for the end of days. For all this to come to pass, however, Innocent concluded that the new kingdom must be stable and that the Greeks must truly be converted. Only the Apostolic See of Rome could make sure this happened.[39] Thus, Innocent's letter, like Dandolo's, contains an early attempt at control over the interpretation of the meaning of the conquest.

The possibilities of this great triumph for Roman Christianity persuaded Innocent to be forgiving and mollifying, though careful not to abrogate his prerogatives. Another letter to the crusader clergy in Constantinople demonstrates how Innocent sought to maintain his balancing act. Written in January 1205, the letter begins with a long excursus on the histories of the various patriarchates. Innocent cited the scriptural basis for each see and put Peter's church at the core. He lamented that he, as pope, had long since "cast out his nets," but only lately had been able to draw in pagans and schismatics so that they could be converted to the Roman rite.[40] He then turned to one of the specific issues presented by the March Pact. The Venetians had elected a subdeacon named Thomas Morosini to the position of patriarch. While Morosini would create considerable controversy during his career, this letter takes a curiously equivocal stance on the appointment. Innocent simultaneously rejected Morosini's uncanonical election and then appointed none other than Morosini as the new patriarch of Constantinople. The pope wrote that he had been assured (by the various secular lords of the Franks) that "the partnership of these same people [the Venetians] would be useful and necessary for the governance of the empire, for the relief of the Holy Land, and for preserving church unity."[41] On the other hand, despite these entreaties by the Franks in Constantinople, he had to reject this election on the grounds that no "secular prince" could select a patriarch, given that the laity had no right to manage ecclesiastical affairs. Innocent also made it clear that this principle was the only reason he was canceling the election of Morosini, not because of any challenges or appeals lodged against the Venetian subdeacon. Alfred Andrea speculates that it was the lower French clergy, not the Frankish elites, who sponsored such an appeal.[42] The voices of the lower clergy, largely unrecorded in extant records, offer another vector for oral memorialization in the aftermath of 1204. Overall, Innocent presented himself as a fair arbiter (not taking sides against Venice). He upheld canon law but was also flexible enough to keep the power-sharing agreement in Constantinople intact.

Innocent's decision to protect papal prerogative as much as possible while pragmatically seeking a reasonable solution was typical of his approach to tricky situations over his long pontificate.[43] In Innocent's solution, more importantly to this chapter, one can detect the principle of good emerging out of sin. By appointing Morosini, Innocent suggested that, if the situation were properly controlled, positive results might emerge for the church and the Latin Empire out of this secular transgression. No secular power could appoint the patriarch of Constantinople. But, the pope continued, leaving the Greek church without a head would do active harm to the church and, by extension, to the all-important process of converting the Greeks. He reasoned that "a transgression by people ought not to flood over to the injury of the churches." Furthermore, Morosini was blameless (after all, he had not elected himself uncanonically).[44] Innocent acknowledged the political reality that the new Latin Empire needed Venetian engagement and assistance to remain viable. The Franks had taken the throne, and Innocent understood that the Venetians needed something in exchange. The pontiff wrote that keeping the Venetians involved might be not only "advantageous but what is even truly necessary."[45] Therefore, Innocent yielded and allowed the subdeacon to become the new patriarch, without giving ground on principles of canon law or his prerogatives. As a result, Morosini had a very busy March in 1205. Innocent summoned him to Rome and ordained him as a deacon on March 5, a priest on March 26, and a bishop on March 27. He made Morosini patriarch on March 30.[46]

Morosini's appointment emerged as one issue among many in the aftermath of 1204. The official responses to Morosini exemplify the broader patterns of papal, Frankish (composed of many subgroups), and Venetian negotiations about roles and status in the new empire. As with so many other aspects of crusading, however, the rhetoric of the political debates, conflicts, and resolutions consistently employed ecclesiastical or theological concepts, and this came to shape memory and argument. Innocent introduced his bureaucratic decision to abnegate Morosini's appointment and to reappoint him by reciting church history in his letter. He depicted the creation of the new Latin patriarchate of Constantinople as a key step in the ending of the preapocalyptic chapter of human history. Judgment was nigh (a positive outcome), the pope wrote, if only the transition from the Greek to the Latin church could be truly effected. The letter contains a key concept: through transgression, properly controlled, great and transformative results could ensue. In the eyes of Rome, the Venetians overstepped their rights by appointing Morosini. On the other hand, Innocent seems to have decided that keeping Morosini as patriarch would help improve the future of both the new empire and the Greek church (via ensuring that the Venetians continued to support the enterprise). The key, for Innocent, was taking the transgression and recasting it as a blessing. This line of reasoning opened the door for the translatio texts of the Fourth Crusade. The hagiographers would defend the crusade by using the same line of logic—take sinful deeds and retell them as acts of devotion.

The Second Phase of Papal Reactions: Frustration and Accusations

From the middle of the spring of 1205 and into the following summer, Innocent dealt with two troubling issues. The conversion of the Greek people to the Roman rite did not progress apace and the property of the Greek church had been (in the eyes of Innocent) unjustly broken up among the victors. Several themes dominate the letters from the papacy during this period. First, the pope demanded the return of all looted church property and objects. To that end, he asserted the inability of secular powers to dispose of anything ecclesiastical—whether church offices, lands, or properties. He offered spiritual rewards to those who protected church property and threatened those who claimed it as their own with excommunication. Second, Innocent wrote more and more frequently about the conversion of the Greek people, a process with which he grew increasingly frustrated, and eventually furious, as the months slipped away. The letters from this stage contain many of the same general themes as those letters produced during the previous months. They continue to invoke ecclesiastical rights, powers, and purposes and to articulate the spiritual significance of events in the East. Their tone, however, shifts dramatically. Whereas the early letters express jubilation at the fall of Constantinople along with gentle rebukes for outstanding issues, as the months passed Innocent's hostility toward the crusaders grew.

For each of the two central issues, one can extract the core of the papal perspective from Innocent's letters to the East. First, on church property, Innocent flatly rejected the relevant provision of the March Pact. The definitive statements of rejection are located in a collection of letters enregistered on February 8, 1205. The papal chancery notes that Innocent composed a letter to Emperor Baldwin and made exact copies for the crusader clergy, Boniface of Montferrat, and the other Frankish counts. Innocent added a harsh additional paragraph to the copy destined for Doge Enrico Dandolo.[47] In the key passage contained in all versions of the letter, Innocent defended the church against the "carving up" that had taken place. He wrote,

> For expressly included in these agreements [the March Pact] was the provision that ecclesiastical possessions should be divided between the Franks and the Venetians, with a portion reserved for the clerics from which they can be honorably supported. Therefore, inasmuch as it is not possible for this to be ventured without injury to the Creator, the oath that was given on this matter appears to be totally illicit and might rather be called a false oath, except for the fact that "saving the honor of the Apostolic See" had been added to that very oath.[48]

Innocent observed, somewhat crisply, that the honor of the Apostolic See could not be kept very well if secular leaders picked apart the holdings of its "special member," the church of Constantinople. Yet he concluded all but one letter—the one to Dandolo—on a positive note. By protecting church property, the pope promised, one "might be worthy" (*merearis*) of not only a remission of sins and access to heaven, but also of God's aid in protecting one's secular holdings. If Baldwin and his fellows protected Christ's spouse (the church), then Christ would protect them. Because the papal scribe remarked that only the doge received a letter with a different ending, one can assume that Innocent made similar promises to all other recipients of this letter, with the exception of Dandolo.

The letter to Baldwin, and those like it, contained a clear, strong rejection of the practice of dividing up church property as described in the March Pact, but Innocent again displayed both the carrot and the stick. He reminded his reader of all the positive results that would come from cooperation with the papal agenda, even if, when hostile, he had become blunter than in his earlier letters. When amending the letter for Dandolo, however, Innocent first rejected the pact (as quoted above) and then made a direct threat. The pope ordered Dandolo to cease and desist; he must not partake in the division of church property. Furthermore, Dandolo must stop others from doing so (to the full extent of his ability). If the doge failed to comply in either regard, Innocent had given the clergy in Constantinople the power and obligation to excommunicate him immediately, without any opportunity for appeal. Dandolo's duty to Rome, according to Innocent, was to see that the Greek church was "restored to its pristine state."[49]

The pope had sought to bring the Greek church and its wealth under Rome's oversight "without confusion." But long before he wrote his first letter to the new rulers in the East, the alienation of church property had already taken place in a way that was new to the history of the crusades. The division of property within Constantinople, and indeed throughout the new empire, occurred through a combination of prearranged discussion, "first come, first served," and ex post facto negotiation among the victors.[50] Naturally, the conquerors of Constantinople were not willing to preserve the wealth of the local church, a wealth based on centuries of giving among the Byzantine elites in order to garner spiritual rewards for themselves and their families. The new Latin leaders wanted to begin new traditions while enriching themselves. It did not matter to them whether a given church had traditionally owned a particular plot of land or received specific rents—the new leaders would redraw the map of patronage and control as they saw fit. Because the papacy eventually relented from Innocent's uncompromising stance, one can regard his insistence on "pristine" restoration to be more of a negotiating point than a reflection of his actual expectations.[51] The entire wealth of the Greek church could never have been recovered, but the church sought to mitigate the losses. The letter's promises of reward and threats of excommunication created the circumstances in which the pope, his legates, and hopefully a pliant patriarch could negotiate for the return of lost property more effectively. Innocent also sought to keep the outcome of the Fourth Crusade from setting a precedent in which secular leaders would determine the reorganization of church land.

This was also a new kind of conquest for Latin Christendom. The lands conquered during the First Crusade had domestic Christian churches, but they existed within the power structures of Turkish and Arabic rule. Such churches, as landowners, were not as powerful as the churches in Constantinople, nor did they possess the same volume of precious artifacts.[52] Innocent was right to worry about the circumstances in Constantinople setting a precedent. Only a few years later, the Albigensian Crusade would present analogous issues when an entrenched, powerful local church was conquered by Christians looking to (among other things) increase their own wealth through conquest. Innocent did not, of course, know that the Albigensian Crusade was on the horizon. He did, however, express the hope that the rest of the Byzantine Empire would fall quickly into the hands of Latin conquerors. As new territories did succumb to the Latins, Innocent had to face the same issue of maintaining church rights and property. For example, Boniface of Montferrat sent a letter to Innocent pledging his obedience from his new kingdom of Thessalonica, a move presumably calculated to try to pull papal support from his rival Kalojan of Bulgaria. Negotiations over Thessalonica's churches ensued.[53] This is precisely the kind of circumstance that Innocent, with forethought, was attempting to ensure would develop in a way most beneficial to the Holy See.

No matter how fervently Innocent expressed his hopes that the Latin Empire would "Romanize" and enrich the papacy, the situation in Constantinople did not turn out to benefit him. After a little over a year, in a letter to Peter Capuano, his legate and erstwhile chief servant, Innocent's tone shifted again. He admitted that instead of bringing the papacy great "profit," the Latin Empire was causing "impoverishment."[54] By this time, several events had occurred that put an end to any remaining papal optimism about the future of the Greek lands. Emperor Baldwin had died. Enemies from all sides threatened both the crusader kingdom of Antioch and Latin Constantinople. Word of the extent of the postconquest pillaging seems to have reached Rome, or Innocent at least invoked the alleged atrocities of the sack for the first time. His letter consequently unleashed considerable venom at both the crusaders and the papal legate. Innocent blamed Capuano for badly mismanaging the situation.

The evidence for when, precisely, Innocent learned details about the conquest is circumstantial. Until this letter to Capuano, no papal texts specifically described the sack, although one would expect Innocent to have questioned the bearers of early missives quite closely. As members of the crusading parties or allies to them, perhaps those early messengers elided the details of the sack, taking care to match the rhetoric of the messages they carried (as any good envoy would). The letter from Boniface of Montferrat, mentioned above, contains a curious passage in which he discussed the transmission of information from the East to Rome. Boniface wrote,

I believe it has been announced many times over to Your paternal ears how many deeds the compassion of divine graciousness has mightily effected on us and around us. Indeed, lest the truth of our affection for and sincere good will towards the Apostolic See, which we have had thus far, will have, and do have, be utterly concealed from Your Majesty, and inasmuch as the chain of events is better conveyed by the spoken word rather than in a letter, we have sent over our most beloved and faithful knight, William Ariento, as a messenger to Your Apostolic Holiness regarding the present state of affairs, and we ask that Your Sincerity deign to have unwavering faith in this man sent by us.[55]

Boniface composed this passage as part of his effort to curry papal favor and win Innocent's blessing. The above lines may provide textual evidence for one of the first emissaries from the new empire who saw the conquest and had nothing to gain by concealing the details from the papacy. Boniface wrote as early as August 1204. The letter was enregistered in April 1205, still only a year after the sack.[56] Everyone else we know to have been present at the conquest who went to Rome before April 1205 appeared before Innocent with an agenda that necessitated keeping the pope in the dark about any wrongdoings. Baldwin and Dandolo, for example, wanted Innocent to ratify the March Pact, not probe acts of past sacrilege. Innocent could not have relied on the reports of the crusading clergy—they were the very ones who had helped suppress Innocent's edicts. Boniface, on the other hand, had left Constantinople to conquer his own kingdom. He lost nothing by allowing his emissary to describe other people's sins to the pope. In fact, we know that Boniface was trying to cast himself as the only truly loyal and competent servant of the papacy in the conquered Greek lands.[57] One cannot be sure, of course, what William Ariento said to Innocent when he had his audience, but the letter does suggest that the pope finally had both reliable and well-informed sources of information at his disposal.

In the letter to Capuano, Innocent vented his wrath. Capuano's biggest mistake, in the eyes of the pope, was releasing anyone who agreed to remain in Constantinople for another year after the conquest from the crusading vow. His second-biggest mistake was that he (or his agent, acting on the legate's orders) had absolved Dandolo after he had been excommunicated for the diversion to Zara. Both of these acts of absolution had, in Capuano's mind, followed papal guidelines on the subject. To Innocent, they were gross errors of judgment.[58] Innocent's first attempt at retaking the Holy Land, an effort begun almost immediately upon his ascension to the papacy in 1198, had ended without the bulk of the army campaigning against the Muslims. He well knew the work it took to organize such a campaign and must have wondered whether he would live to organize another; in fact, he died before the Fifth Crusade departed. Expressing both disappointment and rage, his letter condemns the crusaders for their sins and the legate for the absolution of said sins. In doing so, Innocent specifically addressed the looting of sacred objects for the first time and revealed the path by which future contests over memory would unfold.

The conduct of the crusaders in Constantinople, wrote Innocent, had made the task of converting the Greek people impossible. Conquering the Byzantine Empire was not enough, especially because, as noted above, fulfilling the conditions of the book of Revelation required the Greek people to reject their heresy and accept the ways of the Roman Church. The conversion of the Greeks, therefore, was not merely important for the prestige and power of the Holy See, but a key part of God's plan to see the Christians reconquer the Holy Land; this would lead toward the expected, and desired, apocalypse. Innocent lamented that the excesses of the crusaders destroyed the possibility for stability and true conversion. He cited the lack of mercy from the crusaders, who did not spare anyone for "reasons of religion, age, or sex, staining with the blood of Christians swords that they should have used on pagans."[59] The crusaders had defiled their holy purpose. They "exposed both matrons and virgins, even those dedicated to God, to the filth of the lowborn."[60]

Finally, Innocent turned to the spoiling of the churches, lamenting their "violation." Here, again, are the lines with which I began the first chapter: "It was not enough for them [the Latins] to empty the imperial treasuries and to plunder the spoils of princes and lesser folk, but rather they extended their hands to church treasuries and, what was more serious, to their possessions, even ripping away silver tablets from altars and breaking them into pieces among themselves, violating sacristies and crosses, and carrying away relics."[61] Whereas earlier letters mixed optimism and condemnation, the tone has become solely negative. Innocent blamed Capuano's shortsighted forgiveness of the sinful crusaders. Angry but articulate, he suggested that Capuano was responsible for losing control of the soldiers and then absolving them without forcing a campaign in the Holy Land.

Innocent embraced the power of this particular set of accusations and repeated the charges almost word for word in a letter to Boniface of Montferrat. He changed the order of the accusations, however, so that they ended with a powerful phrase comparing the Latins to dogs: "Ut iam merito illose abhorreat plus quam canes!"[62] Robert Wolff interprets the two letters from Innocent as a sign of the pope's "early spirit of understanding for the Greeks."[63] Regardless of whether the pope felt sympathy for the plight of the Greek people, the letter to Boniface (replete with insults and accusations) had another central purpose beyond expressing Christian brotherhood. Innocent was focused on setting the terms for the acquisition of new land.[64] After enumerating the sins of the crusaders (including Boniface), the pope ordered, "In fear of the Lord and with the hope of pardon from divine judgment, you are to hold and defend the land that has been acquired and acquire land to be held and defended, ruling in justice the people subject to you, preserving it in peace and conforming in matters of religion, so that you return ecclesiastical goods."[65] Thus, Innocent first set out the accusations of wrongdoing. He described the plundering of the churches as "more serious" than other crimes. Having set the moral tone and reminded Boniface that the road to salvation lay in defending Christ's bride, the pope then made it clear what he expected Boniface to do.

In the eyes of the papacy, the outrages enacted on the young and old, on women, and on the churches of Constantinople undermined the future of the Latin Empire and the Holy Land. By using the traditional medieval metaphor of the Church as Christ's bride, the Church became the most holy of the violated women. An empire fraught with anger at the violations, inhabited by rebellious people who could never accept their overlords or the church of their overlords, would not be able to drive back the Muslims. In Innocent's eyes, God's plan, made evident by the initial victory, had fallen into jeopardy. Both he and the crusaders had frequently stated during the first postconquest year that the fall of Constantinople was providential because it would aid the crusading effort. They kept the Holy Land at the forefront of their rhetoric. With the future of the empire at risk and the process of converting Greeks to the Roman rite stalled, this potent claim no longer stood up.

In fact, Innocent began referring to danger to the Holy Land directly. In his harsh letter to Capuano from February 1205, Innocent chided the legate for dereliction of duty at just the moment when the Holy Land needed him most. The patriarch-elect of Jerusalem had died in 1202.[66] The Count of Tripoli and the Armenians were at war. The king of Jerusalem, as well as his wife, Isabel (the power behind three husbands), and his son, died in April 1205.[67] Meanwhile, the pontiff wrote, enemies might be poised to attack the Holy Land. At that moment, Innocent lamented, "all of its friends" had followed the legate's lead and "abandoned it along with you."[68] Innocent reminded Capuano that he had dispatched him "not to capture the empire of Constantinople but for the defense of the remnants of the Holy Land and for the restoration of what had been lost (if the Lord should grant it), and . . . not to seize temporal riches but to earn eternal riches."[69] Here, again, looting becomes an issue. The pope then stepped beyond his criticism of Capuano to assault the whole diversion, including the men who went to Constantinople and were absolved of their oath by the foolish legate. According to the narrative from Rome, temporal riches lured the crusaders and Capuano away from the right path. No matter how providential the conquest of Constantinople had been, God's blessings were now being squandered.

Phase Three: The Contest over the Latin Patriarchate of Constantinople

The first two phases of papal response moved from cautious optimism to categorical denunciation. In the years that followed, papal relations with the various factions in the new empire varied as the issues changed. As the eyewitnesses to the conquest of 1204 wrote their chronicles and as the recipients of new relics began to write translatio narratives, the ecclesiastical disputes between Rome and the Latins in Constantinople took a new turn. One controversy embroiled the Venetians in particular and serves as an example of the type of situation in which the arguments about church property might have proved useful. Because of the circumstances of its creation, the Latin patriarchate of Constantinople spent its entire existence mired in various types of internecine conflict while tasked with the impossible job (at least given the conditions) of converting the Greeks.[70]

The most important aspect of these conflicts was that none of the players took absolute sides. Their motivations and alliances varied from case to case. In Constantinople, the Frankish clergy, the Frankish nobles, the Venetian clergy, the Venetian podestà, the patriarch and cathedral chapter, and Rome itself (represented largely by a succession of papal legates) all had complex agendas and were willing to argue against a given faction on one issue, yet ally with it on another. The same could be said for the representatives of all of these groups back in Venice, Rome, and France. The two central issues of debate both pertained to the looting of Constantinople. The first concerned the selection of canons for the cathedral chapter (the body that chose new patriarchs), and the second dealt with reparations to the Church for looted property. This latter subject could easily be connected to the pillaging of Constantinople, although the disassembly of religious houses may not have been as widespread as Innocent feared.[71] With regard to the former issue, while Morosini's appointment (and the appointment of canons) was not directly tied to the question of church property, Innocent tried to connect them. The pope specifically invoked the patriarch in his attempt to coerce Dandolo to help with the reparation efforts. Innocent wrote, "Since our beloved son Thomas, patriarch-elect of Constantinople, should soon arrive in Constantinople, none of the possessions of the church of Constantinople should be distributed by the laity or confirmed by us before his arrival because it could redound to the prejudice of his rights and a loss to his church."[72] Innocent wished to use Morosini to enlist the Venetians as partners in maintaining church property in Constantinople, though this attempt failed.

Having experienced a rapid promotion from subdeacon to patriarch, Morosini left Rome in March 1205. Innocent instructed him that his duty was to represent the church, not the Venetians.[73] Morosini then departed for Venice to choose new canons and find transport to Constantinople. Before the patriarch could leave Venice, however, the acting doge Ranieri Dandolo ordered him to swear that he would appoint only Venetians to the group that elected new patriarchs, the cathedral chapter of Hagia Sophia. Furthermore, Morosini had to disavow any authority over the patriarchate of Grado and its many privileges in the eastern Mediterranean. The Venetians wanted to be very careful to keep the revenues and rights of Grado, rights that extended into the Venetian quarter of Constantinople itself. Morosini, of course, recognized that these new oaths directly contradicted Innocent's orders to act as an independent and faithful patriarch, and he refused. A month passed. Morosini began to run out of money, and in May 1205 he took the oaths the Venetians demanded.[74]

Innocent promptly ruled that Morosini's forced oath was not binding and demanded that he renounce it. Having been released from this oath, Morosini nevertheless appointed only Venetians whenever possible. This infuriated the Frankish clergy, Innocent, and the papal legates alike.[75] To complicate matters

further, at precisely the same time that Morosini and the Venetians were arguing with the Frankish clergy and the papacy, Morosini, the Frankish clergy,
and the papacy sought reparations from the Venetian and French lords. Morosini became Innocent's lead negotiator (before Cardinal Benedict arrived) in
trying to undo the secularization of former Greek church property. The secular authorities were willing to offer some lands to the church and to promise
generous tithes, but would not relinquish the prime real estate they had
acquired in the sack. After extensive negotiations among all parties, Morosini
and other clerical delegates received the right to form a commission that
would determine a just settlement. Initially, the Venetians did not take part
in the hearings. Thus, any solution would be, at best, a half measure. Furthermore, although the Franks offered adequate reparations (according to the commission), Morosini and the Frankish clergy battled over how to divide the
reclaimed wealth among themselves. The pope attempted to adjudicate from
Rome, but with little success. The difficulty was that far too much of the church
land was unrecoverable. Constantinople had been conquered, divided up by
the conquerors, and settled. Retroactively undoing the effects of the conquest
proved nearly impossible; as unsatisfying as they were to the clergy, cash set-
tlements were really the only solution. Such payments paled in comparison to
the value of steady rents.[76] In new lands such as Thessalonica, where church
property had not been lost beyond recovery, matters were very different
(although the church there had not been as wealthy).[77] Within Constantinople, as late as 1223, this dispute continued unabated.[78]

Other issues similarly created a turbulent environment of shifting alliances. In 1213, for example, Innocent sent Cardinal Pelagius to work on the
land negotiations and to convert the Greeks. He tackled the latter mission
with verve and seems to have closed churches and even imprisoned priests
who insisted on maintaining the Greek rite.[79] By this point, however, the
Greek clergy and Greek nobility had become part of the status quo in Latin
Constantinople. The emperor protected them, and thus a new dispute between
Constantinople and Rome emerged.[80]

No extant sources detail the creation of the commission that tried to resolve
the questions of church property. Absent proceedings of the negotiations, we
can never know what pressures were brought to bear. The sources we do have
display Innocent's rhetorical approach. He mixed legal precedents that guar-
anteed the Church's rights with invocations of damnation and salvation. Vast
sums of wealth and vital aspects of ecclesiastical power were at stake. Innocent

insisted that Rome, and Rome alone, would determine the sacred significance of all questions relating to the conquest of Constantinople. Moral condemnation, warnings about the fate of sinners, and exhortations concerning the sacred purpose of the Latin kingdom of Constantinople served Innocent as tools in these debates.

Nonpapal Criticism

Innocent focused on moral condemnation of actions taken in the aftermath of the conquest in order to regain leverage. We cannot necessarily track his influence over the nonpapal voices that raised similar critiques. That the letters to Boniface and Capuano employ precisely the same language permits conjecture that Innocent may well have written similar letters to others. Many pieces of diplomatic correspondence have been lost. For example, although we have additional communications between Boniface and Innocent, the letter from Boniface to which Innocent responded with accusations and exhortations no longer exists. If the pope spread his interpretation of the sack of Constantinople throughout Europe, then the dissemination of the letter comparing the Latins to dogs may have set the tone for others to emulate. One can find, however, other explanations for the emergence of anti–Fourth Crusade rhetoric. The crusade had operated in an air of controversy from the moment of departure, and those who felt wronged could easily find many grounds on which to criticize the crusaders. In both the Latin and Greek traditions of criticism, looting took a central role.

The eyewitness accounts of Niketas Choniates, Geoffrey of Villehardouin, Robert of Clari, and the anonymous author of the *Devastatio Constantinopolitana* all accuse the crusaders of egregious rapacity. Each characterizes the crusade differently, as befits the distinctions among the authors. Niketas levels the harshest critiques, but there is no evidence that his work was disseminated to the West during the thirteenth century.[81] His impact was limited.

Villehardouin wrote from inside the crusade and generally tried to defend his actions and the actions of his comrades. He singled out the looting, however, as the key moment when God's favor was lost. He argued that God had been generous to the army in enabling the conquest of Constantinople, but because too many soldiers hoarded loot and did not share according to the March Pact, God became angry. After describing the plan to collect all the booty in three churches that were guarded by an equal number of Franks and Venetians and lamenting the lost loyalty of those who chose to loot for themselves, the marshal of Champagne opines on God's favor. He writes, "Oh God—they had behaved so loyally up to that point! And Lord God had demonstrated that in all their affairs he had honored and exalted them over all other people. But on many occasions good people suffer because of the wicked."[82] This final line is critical because it offers Villehardouin's interpretation of events. According to the marshal, who hoped to be numbered among the righteous, good people pay for the sins of the wicked.

The lay knight Robert of Clari also pointed to the looting as the cause of God's disfavor but offered a different interpretation. Clari describes Mourtzouphlos's flight from Constantinople and the announcement to the soldiers that the city had been taken. He explains,

> Then they had it cried through the host that no one should take possession of a house until it had been decided how they should be divided. Then the high men, the rich men, came together and agreed among themselves to take the best houses of the city, without the common people or the poor knights of the host knowing anything about it. And from that time on they began to betray the common people and to keep bad faith and bad comradeship with them, for which they paid very dearly later, as we shall tell you.[83]

Clari admits that although the best properties went to the richest conquerors, the city was large and everyone found a house. The key here is not the secret meeting among the wealthy that, Clari alleged, took place after the victory, but the reference to later events during which God punished the rich for their sins against the common soldiers. Thus, when describing the disaster at Adrianople later in the chronicle, Clari laments that three hundred knights were lost there and lists the refugees who fled back to Constantinople after the rout. He concludes, "And thus did God take vengeance on them for their pride and for the bad faith which they had kept with the poor people of the host, and for the terrible sins which they had committed in the city after they had taken it."[84] Like Villehardouin, Clari pinpointed the looting as the moment when the leadership incurred the wrath of God, for which they would suffer at Adrianople. Although the two French chroniclers each blamed the other's social stratum for illicit looting, they picked the same moment as pivotal, identified the same sin, and blamed a terrible defeat on that sin. Clari's account was not disseminated until the nineteenth century, but the correlation between the two texts is striking. Could it reflect a broader Frankish tradition?

The author of the *Devastatio Constantinopolitana*, probably a poor cleric on the crusade, echoed Clari's assessment with even more vituperation, offering it credence.[85] He argued that the wealthy participants in the crusade wronged the poor soldiers of Christ and stripped them of their rightful plunder. The common booty was distributed "almost like certain down-payments," with but a few silver coins going to each man.[86] The foot soldiers who participated in the sack of the richest Christian city walked away with a mere five marks, according to the author. Thus, Alexius IV, the doge of Venice, and the Frankish leaders betrayed the mission to save the Holy Land, won a great victory, and broke their vows to the common soldiers, robbing them of their rightful share of the spoils. A negative text, the *Devastatio Constantinopolitana* bases its criticisms on the divide between the wealthy and the poor; greed and ill-gotten gains figure prominently.

Not only do these eyewitness accounts fixate on the looting, but various critical texts produced back in Latin Christendom do likewise. The *Historia Constantinopolitana*, the story of Abbot Martin of Pairis, provided a source for the contemporary chronicler Burchard of Ursperg. Burchard relates that "a certain abbot . . . from the place called Pairis . . . carried many relics back to his monastery, which are still kept there. Whether they were stolen, let him who reads decide. Or can the lord pope clearly justify such thievery made on a Christian people, just as the thievery of the people of Israel in Egypt was justified by divine authority?"[87] Writing at some point in the early thirteenth century, Burchard invoked the looting of relics and put the burden of judgment squarely on the pope's shoulders. His comparison of the plundering of Constantinople in 1204 to the meritorious plundering of Egypt draws on a standard trope in medieval Christian discourse, one invoked as far back as St. Augustine in *De doctrina Christiana*, but it could also be read as a subtle dig at the failure of the crusade to reach its original destination, Cairo.[88] Such criticisms reflect the voices of the crusaders who protested the diversion to Constantinople. Clari reports that when presented with the decision to go to Greece with Alexius Angelos, "there were some who did not approve of going to Constantinople. Instead they said, 'Bah! What shall we be doing in Constantinople? We have our pilgrimage to make, and also our plan of going to Babylon or Alexandria.'"[89]

It is difficult to assess whether these criticisms troubled the victorious Latin crusaders, or whether Innocent felt defensive about the result of "his" crusade. One detects an atmosphere of general criticism toward the crusades emerging in the early thirteenth century. Most people still fervently supported both the crusade ideal and individual crusades in particular, but dissenting voices have left some records. Those such as Burchard voiced criticism of the pope for allowing his crusades to go awry. Writers who were critical of the Albigensian Crusade often lumped the diversion to Constantinople together with the assault on the Cathars. For example, a Cluniac monk named Guiot de Provins (ca. 1145–ca. 1208) lambasted the papacy in his Old French satire on the church entitled "La Bible." He named avarice as a papal sin in general and then credited avarice as the force behind Innocent's decisions to direct crusades against the Greeks, as opposed to Muslims.[90] Other Provençal poets picked up this line of reasoning, and it only grew more intense as the Albigensian Crusade developed.[91]

The *Gesta Innocentii*, written with the benefit of hindsight, unlike the letters, reflects a curial attempt to structure a narrative of the Fourth Crusade that would burnish Innocent's image in the eyes of history.[92] The *Gesta* contained an edition of Innocent's critical letter to Capuano that invoked, as the worst of sins, the violation of sacristies and the "carrying off of crosses and relics."[93] The author adds that Baldwin of Flanders, rather than the cardinal, was chiefly to blame for having "summoned [Peter Capuano] to his presence by ambassadors and by his imperial rescript."[94] This assigns further fault to the crusaders, rather than to a member of the clergy. Condemnatory phrases appear in both papal writings and external sources. For example, in Innocent's February 1205 letter to Capuano, the pope referred to the Holy Land as "bereft of men and of strength."[95] He repeated this phrase in a letter to King Philip II Augustus of France, dated July 10–15, 1205, in which he reported on the abandonment of the Holy Land and asked for help in Outremer.[96] The same phrase reappears in the copy of the letter in the *Gesta*.[97] Innocent was not one to waste a good rhetorical device, and one can be sure that this sort of phrasing appeared in other papal communiqués, public statements, and discussions behind closed doors.

Three early thirteenth-century chronicles repeat Innocent's argument that the conquest of Constantinople and greed for temporal plunder led to the departure of pilgrims and locals from the Holy Land. For example, the *Historia Albigensis* by Peter of Vaux-de-Cernay, a soldier on the Fourth Crusade, lambastes the crusaders who cast aside the "schilling of God" in order to embrace the "schilling of the Devil."[98] Peter's uncle, Abbot Guy of Vaux-de-Cernay, joined Simon de Montfort in refusing to divert to Constantinople; both left Zara for the Holy Land rather than make a deal with Alexius Angelos. Naturally, the chronicler Peter could serve his own agenda by emphasizing the diabolical nature of those departing from the Holy Land out of greed.[99] But the *Eracles*, a text written in the crusader states (initially),[100] also notes the departure of manpower, though it lacks the polemical touches of Innocent's writing and the *Historia Albigensis*.[101] Finally, Robert of Auxerre's general *Chronicon* (a history of the world to 1211, when he died) mirrors Innocent's response to the crusade. The text first expresses joy at the providential victory over the Greeks and then turns sour, just as Innocent's letters do. Robert states that the Holy Land, as a result of the Fourth Crusade, was becoming "destitute of men and resources,"[102] the same phrase used twice by Innocent and found in the *Gesta*. There is no way of tracking whether, or how, Robert might have read one of Innocent's communiqués, but the point is clear. After Capuano left the Holy Land to go to Constantinople, others followed.

Sin, greed, disregard for vows, and disobedience to the pope are all, at their core, issues of morality. From both inside and outside the army of the Fourth Crusade, medieval writers argued that the crusaders' sins, especially looting, led to the perversion of a sacred quest, the weakening of the new empire, and dire threats to the Holy Land.

Conclusion

In the aftermath of the Fourth Crusade, critics of its outcome connected condemnations of the looting to larger spiritual issues of sin and absolution. Innocent used the moral superiority implicit in the papal office to gain an advantage in disputations about ecclesiastical oversight, office, property, and wealth. From the very pragmatic issues of rents and the makeup of a cathedral chapter to the grandest of visions about the fate of the Latin East, the Holy Land, and even the Apocalypse, hostile memorialization relied on a moral critique of postcrusade conduct. A counternarrative would have to contend with the papacy on the matter of interpreting divine will, a tricky task at best.

Enter the medieval concept of pious thievery. The next chapter examines the narrative sources produced by those who received relics after the Fourth

Crusade. The texts offer arguments calculated to undermine the portrayal of sinful crusaders and moral failures and to valorize the very behavior that the pope criticized. They contain a counternarrative that, according to the logic of the genre, revealed divine providence at work in the conquest of Constantinople. Although the thieves (and by extension all the crusaders) had sinned, God had already mandated forgiveness. God trumped Rome.

PART II

TEXTS

3

The Translatio Narratives of the Fourth Crusade

Within a few years of the rise of the Latin Empire in Constantinople, an anonymous cleric at the Cathedral of Soissons produced a narrative account of the deeds of his bishop, Nivelon de Chérisy. The text, a combination of theodicy and translatio, begins with catastrophe. The forces of the Kingdom of Jerusalem are scattered so that their sins might be purged.[1] The relic of the True Cross is lost.[2] Jerusalem falls. And yet, even out of this disaster, the author claims, great good can emerge. At the end of the text, the bishop sends a great collection of relics to Soissons. Curiously, the author describes the relics as having come from the "mountain of Maquerel," a site in the Holy Land. When the bishop returns home after his long absence, he carries four of them—"two great crosses of the wood of our Lord" and two smaller crucifixes.[3] Thus, a text that begins with the loss of the True Cross in the Holy Land ends with the arrival of similar relics in France, and all is well. But, in truth, Nivelon never made it to the Holy Land, and neither did the army he accompanied. His relics came from the sack of Constantinople.

This text joins eight other extant translatio narratives. They were written in France, Germany, and Italy (see map 2) and collectively offer an interpretation of the Fourth Crusade that celebrates the very behavior condemned by the papacy and other critics. The texts function as a hagiographic corpus in which ideas about relics and the necessity of memorializing acts of transfer and installation intersect with the desire to respond to hostile narratives about both great and iniquitous deeds in Constantinople. In some cases, such as the Soissons text, the positioning of the campaign in the broader context of the

crusade to the Holy Land diminishes the narrative significance of Constantinople. Other accounts avoided mentioning the Fourth Crusade as much as
possible. Venetian hagiographers, in contrast, invoked it whenever possible,
sometimes even needlessly. Each author, perhaps guided by his patrons, faced
similar pressure to render the possession of a new relic or relics licit in the face
of opposition, but they took distinct paths, and these choices led to revealing
idiosyncrasies.

When Conrad von Krosigk, bishop of Halberstadt, retired, he commissioned a *gesta* that included an account of the relics he had brought home from
the Fourth Crusade. The author writes about Conrad's journey to the Holy
Land and his return home to Germany. He packs the text with many interesting and detailed anecdotes. But when describing the Fourth Crusade, the
author compresses the entire narrative into a few phrases. He simply writes,
"Qualiterque ultimo, civitate capta, Alexius Alexio suppositus fugatus fuerit,
et ab Alexio Alexii patruo exoculatus."[4] After this proliferation of emperors
named Alexius, which when read in Latin seems calculated to confuse, the
author mentions that many miraculous things happened, but they would
require a special tract (*specialiem . . . tractatum*). He skips past the miracles,
even though they enabled Bishop Conrad to acquire his relics. Why omit these
deeds that display God's favor?

The translatio relating the delivery of the head of St. Mamas to Langres also
skips miracles, instead focusing on the authentication. The author authenticates the relic by citing Peter Capuano, in addition to Bishop Garnier of
Troyes, the translator himself (Walon of Dampierre, bishop of Domoko), the
monks of St. Mamas, and finally St. Mamas himself (through a miracle). The
hagiographer accepts the papal premise of widespread iniquity in the postcrusade moment but then characterizes all involved in St. Mamas's translation
as nonlooters. His account thus localizes the exculpatory effect of the translatio narrative without engaging in a broader contest over the meaning of the
Fourth Crusade.

Some texts are direct about the means by which a relic fell into Latin hands.
In Gaeta, the recipients of the head of St. Theodore Tyro depicted their benefactor, the papal legate Peter Capuano, as a defender against the unlicensed
spoliation of relics. This narrative contains elaborate details about the nature
of the cult of saints and Byzantine history leading up to the Fourth Crusade.
The author lingers on Emperor Manuel Comnenus and the betrayals among
the Angeloi. But he skips over the crusade itself, especially in the face of events

that must have caused some embarrassment and irritation for Capuano. On the other hand, despite the legate's threats and pleas, the crusaders ignored him, so an apologist could conveniently excuse Capuano.

To celebrate the translation of the relic of its titular saint, Amalfi's Cathedral of St. Andrew also produced a narrative involving Capuano. This text connects multiple themes. It skirts the boundaries between authorized and unauthorized relic acquisition by depicting Capuano escorting two priests from Amalfi, who stole the relic, back to their (and his) native city with their precious cargo. Miracles enable their movement along the way, but we are provided with no description of the profane or the sublime during the crusade. The author weakly skips over the subject by noting that the crusaders diverted to Constantinople because of "human or divine leadership."[5] In a genre predicated on interpreting the will of God through his actions on earth, this hesitancy stands out as unusual.

In contrast, a narrative produced in Venice after 1222 is not at all hesitant to cite the will of God. The story of St. Paul the New Martyr employs imagined danger to universalize the meaning of a relic translation. The text sets the stage for a story packed with danger and intrigue by opening with an account of the Fourth Crusade. But the actual theft took place nearly two decades after the conquest, and the participants in the translation—both monks and merchants—were in no danger. Rather, they were canonically within their rights to transfer the relics of St. Paul and were protected by all the relevant secular powers of the Venetian quarter of Constantinople. The danger was all fabricated to turn an authorized translation with no risk into a more powerful story of relic theft.

However, in 1204, eighteen years before the smooth transport of St. Paul, would-be relic thieves had faced real threats. Seven Venetian crusaders had decided to steal the relics of St. Simon the Prophet, their parish's patron saint. Venetians from the parish had worshipped at the shrine in Constantinople for generations; now here was their chance to take the relics home. The narrative recording their deeds emphasizes threats from the Greek populace—a patently impossible situation given that the theft took place on April 18, 1204, just a week after the conquest. Rather, the real thieves had to protect themselves from their own leaders, who might have wanted the relics for themselves. The narrative ostensibly memorializes the theft as anti-Greek so as to link it to the crusade and to imply that the power of St. Simon's miracles manifested divine absolution for the crusaders' sins.

Rostang of Cluny, like the cleric from Soissons, makes the case that his institution's acquisition of the important relic of St. Clement signified the restoration of God's favor to the West. God had taken Jerusalem from the Latins because he was angry about the city's intercultural mixing and insufficient purity, but perhaps the tide of history was changing. As befits a monk of Cluny, Rostang emphasizes the necessity of avoiding the lure of secular wealth; according to his account, the two crusader knights who acquired St. Clement did just that. They wanted to buy a relic before heading home from Constantinople, but the papal legates forbade them to do it. So instead they stole one.

Finally, Gunther of Pairis's masterpiece, the *Historia Constantinopolitana*, the best-studied and longest of these texts, extends its reach far beyond contemporary traditions of translatio or the earlier Carolingian tradition that Patrick Geary called *furta sacra*. The prosimetrum links its protagonist, Abbot Martin of Pairis, to St. Martin of Tours. It binds the fall of Constantinople to the fall of Troy. The battle scenes are stirring. The poetry following the prose passages serves the didactic purpose of guiding the interpretive process of the reader. Gunther uses humor to point out the flawed nature of human action in contrast to divine perfection. And yet, at what should be the climax of the translatio, the moment in which a miracle authorizes relic theft, he addresses the reader directly, admitting that everything he is writing might be false. But, even if so, the reader ought to believe that everything contained within the *Historia Constantinopolitana* reveals the providential will of God.

This chapter presents the above texts in a series of short summaries that highlight the structural elements of each. The next chapter will then apply various categories of analysis to this corpus in order to explore narrative techniques and the diverse approaches to commemorative hagiography.

Soissons

Nivelon de Chérisy, the bishop of Soissons from 1176 to 1207, played a significant role at many critical moments throughout the Fourth Crusade. He led the Latin clergy.[6] He helped recruit for the crusade in its early stages and ultimately placed the cross on the shoulders of Boniface of Montferrat.[7] He served as an emissary from the crusade to Innocent III and then as a messenger, albeit a poor one, from the pope back to the army.[8] He led the preaching that took place outside the walls of Constantinople in April 1204, delivering (along with other clerics) a sermon that cast the conflict with the Greeks in terms of a just and holy war.[9] He announced the choice of emperor to the gathered crusaders.[10] Before abandoning the Bucoleon Palace, Nivelon also acquired a considerable hoard of relics from its churches.[11] He sent some of the relics home at once and, in 1205, became the archbishop of Thessalonica.[12] After the disaster at Adrianople, the barons sent Nivelon to seek help from the papacy, the French, and the Flemish.[13] He subsequently returned from Rome to Soissons with the remainder of his haul of relics. He died in Soissons in 1206 or 1207.[14]

The text that records Nivelon's deeds, "Concerning the Land of Jerusalem and the Means by Which Relics Were Carried to This Church from the City of Constantinople,"[15] places his acquisition of relics in the larger context of the struggle for the Holy Land.[16] The anonymous author repeatedly connects the recovery of relics of Christ's life to the eventual recovery of the land where Christ lived. He begins with the fall of Jerusalem to Saladin in 1187. Bishop Nivelon appears in the middle of the text and takes a leading role in the latter third. However, even as the author attempts to link the conquest of Constantinople to the larger crusade endeavor, the text does more to reveal dissent and concern over the nature of the Fourth Crusade than to defend Nivelon and his fellows.

As with most translatio narratives, "The Land of Jerusalem" authenticates the newly arrived relics and promotes their veneration in their new locale. The decision to focus on the Holy Land, rather than Constantinople, represents the author's response to obstacles to authentication and promotion. The work has four distinct parts: the opening passages on the loss of Jerusalem and the Third Crusade, a section on the Fourth Crusade, an accounting of the relics brought back to Soissons, and a final section defending the liturgical veneration of the relics of the Apostle Thomas. The first and second sections follow a narrative format. The third and fourth provide a traditional hagiographical list of relics, liturgical notes, and several accounts of authenticating miracles.

As noted by Alfred Andrea, the first section shifts from negative to positive and back to negative on a nearly sentence-by-sentence basis, a method that allows the author to show the complexity of God's judgment.[17] The text states that the Latins captured Jerusalem and Antioch (during the First Crusade), only to lose the former in 1187 "for the purgation of their sins."[18] The Third Crusade brings hope, dissension leads to defeat, and the Fourth Crusade restores hope. God's will moves in cycles, punishing and blessing the people of the Holy Land and beyond. Impurity of spirit results in the loss of providential blessing over the Latin enterprise in Jerusalem, and the Fourth Crusade becomes the new blessed venture of redemption; it too proceeds cyclically through success and disaster. In this manner, the author creates a rubric by which a reader may interpret the ongoing struggles of the Latin Empire. Adrianople was not a sign of total disaster but rather another cyclical event that would, he hoped, soon be followed by a providential blessing. And if that blessing had not yet come by the time the author was writing in 1206–7, surely it was nigh and Jerusalem would soon be redeemed.[19] This is a clever structure, given that the author must conclude with Jerusalem in Islamic hands and the Latin Empire in danger.

As the author shifts his focus to the relics, he splits them into two groups—those sent west after the conquest and those brought west by Nivelon after Adrianople.[20] The first group contains relics of the Passion, the Virgin's belt, relics of St. John the Baptist, the finger of Thomas (with which, doubting, he probed the wounds of Christ), and other objects.[21] The author neither explains how Nivelon acquired these relics nor includes any specifics about their transportation. This lacuna is important, especially when compared to the other texts that follow. Miracles at the moment of acquisition and during transit serve an important role in authentication and signify saintly approval of a translation. Devoid of such details, the text instead describes local miracles. For example, after the relics were deposited with proper veneration, "many out of the scores of weak, infirm, and sick were cured on that very day and weekly in the mother church of Soissons."[22]

This type of miraculous healing is standard fare. However, the author describes the relics not as plunder from 1204 but as "having come down from the mountain of Maquerel."[23] "Maquerel" seems to be Mount Machaerus near the Dead Sea, the site where Herod executed John the Baptist. His relics were taken from there to Alexandria and then to Constantinople, and now, according to the author, they have arrived in Soissons.[24] But only the forearm of the Baptist could possibly have come from Machaerus, and that was not the most important relic in the group. Nivelon did not even keep the forearm relic for his own cathedral, but sent it to the Abbey of St. Jean des Vignes.[25] The attempt to place all of Nivelon's diverse relics within a tradition that properly belonged only to the relics of the Baptist reminds the informed reader of the first part of the text on the liberation of the Holy Land. The author thus begins to link the relics to his grand theme, albeit subtly. The second list of relics similarly recalls the earlier passages. The author reassures the reader that although the "wood of the holy cross had been lost" at Hattin, Nivelon recovered new "crucifixes from the wood of the Lord."[26]

The author's argument is that we must suffer in order to be purged of sin and all that is good will be lost. Once that purging is complete, God's providential judgment will restore the good. The author binds Nivelon's translation of relics to the history of the Holy Land and the Christian quest to "redeem" it. The Fourth Crusade was thus part of the process by which God would give Jerusalem to the Christians, much as he gave the relics of the life of Christ and the apostles to Nivelon.

The problem with this argument is one of scale. Does the translation of a few splinters of the True Cross equal the loss of one of Christendom's most important relics, not to mention Jerusalem? Perhaps not, but the text issues a warning to any who might dispute the affirmed will of God. After the bishop brought the head of the Apostle Thomas to join the finger, sent earlier, the text states that

> In the same year, although it was not usual for the translation of the blessed Thomas to be celebrated so solemnly, it was so decreed by the bishop and was solemnly performed and celebrated by the clergy throughout the whole diocese. In consequence, many persons, inspired by the spirit of the devil, objected. Among these was a certain woman, driven insane with the loss of her sight and hearing. When she was led to the cathedral church . . . her neighbors and relatives prayed and made offerings for her, and she was healed on the very same day.[27]

That woman was lucky. A "certain carpenter" in the region decided to work on St. Thomas's feast day but was "fatally struck as soon as he picked up his tool, since he began to do his work, neglecting the precept of the church." The reader should not be too horrified with this rough justice, the text reassures, because "his death was preceded by confession and amends for the evil of his labor." Furthermore, many others in the area "experienced such losses from their work, either corporally or in their affairs, that thereafter they dared nothing of the kind; rather, equally flocking together with the multitude of the people at the church and giving thanks for things seen and heard, they established and made the day solemn by their throngs."[28] The author weighs positives against negatives even in this final coda. The carpenter sinned and was punished (the negative), but died in a state of grace (the positive).

This final section deviates from the structure of the first three in order to address local issues of veneration pertaining to the introduction of the cult of the Apostle Thomas. The author invokes three great powers to support Nivelon's decree—God, the bishop himself, and the community, of which the third was arguably the most important. "Neighbors and relatives" brought the first dissenter to church, and there she was cured. Many people suffered because they chose to work on the feast day of St. Thomas, but they were forgiven when they returned to the multitude. It was their "throngs" that made the day "solemn." The authority of the bishop mattered, but the power of communal action supported the hierarchy.[29]

The particular features of "The Land of Jerusalem" reveal the challenges of writing a translatio in the wake of the Fourth Crusade. The focus on the Holy Land is unusual in the corpus precisely because it draws attention to the failure of the crusaders to save Jerusalem. It may present a path to apologetic memorialization, but it also diminishes the power of translatio to use relic movement to reorder the local sacred landscape. The absence of a narrative of acquisition removes the opportunity for a miracle to stave off disaster and to demonstrate the divine sanction for the translation and its enablers (the crusaders). Thus, "The Land of Jerusalem" was written about Jerusalem, the crusades in general and the Fourth Crusade in particular, and the reception of relics back in France—everything but the deeds of Soissons's bishop. Only in its expression of the concept that great good can emerge out of disaster and wrongdoing does the text hint at a path for a more potent narrative. With Jerusalem still in Muslim hands in 1206–7, the author and his readers were left waiting for the tables to turn from negative to positive once again.

Halberstadt

Although the final passages of the text from Soissons imply the presence of otherwise unknown local conflicts, Bishop Conrad von Krosigk of Halberstadt's history and the "Gesta episcoporum Halberstadensium" are more transparent. As a result of the complicated politics of the Holy Roman Empire, both Conrad and his anonymous apologist operated in difficult circumstances.[30] Conrad became caught up in the great power struggles among imperial claimants and their supporters. In the "Gesta," the genre of translatio serves as one way, among others, to defend Conrad from his local and papal critics. Thus, the author hoped, the Fourth Crusade could become the path to exoneration instead of condemnation.

Conrad went on crusade in order to escape from the consequences of having supported Philip of Swabia against Otto of Brunswick in the ongoing Welf-Hohenstaufen conflict.[31] Pope Innocent III worked diligently to ensure ecclesiastical solidarity behind the papal candidate, Otto. But Conrad, who became bishop in 1202, had already sworn an oath to Philip and refused to renege. He was thus excommunicated and hoped that going on crusade would restore papal favor.[32] Alas, for Conrad, the crusade resolved little. When he returned from the East, he was still identified with Philip's cause and regarded with suspicion. He may even have been forced into retirement at the Monastery of Sittichenbach in 1208.[33] The "Gesta" was probably composed in 1209, perhaps in the monastery and perhaps with Conrad's oversight.[34] He died that same year.[35]

Except for the dramatic events of the conquest of Constantinople, which are omitted, the text offers a clear and detailed narrative of the crusade through Conrad's eyes. The author pauses frequently to describe political, religious, and personal anecdotes. For example, we get the details of a lunch between the crusader prelates and the orthodox archbishop of Corfu, during which the clerics debated the issue of papal primacy.[36] The text also includes Conrad's postcrusade pilgrimage to the Holy Land, his voyage to Rome in order to seek absolution from Innocent, and the installation of new relics in Halberstadt.

In this text, translatio functions within the larger history of Conrad's career (this text is a full *gesta*) and reinforces the central message that divine grace demonstrated Conrad's righteousness, even when matters looked grim.[37] Throughout, miraculous episodes speak to his piety and the favor he found in God's eyes. For example, a hermit in Ragusa predicts the fall of Constantinople to Conrad.[38] In Syria, "divine aid" cures Conrad of the "quartan fever" (malaria) while he prays at the church of the Blessed Mary, a famed pilgrimage site.[39] "Divine Clemency" carries Conrad back from the Holy Land to Venice, after briefly pushing him toward North Africa.[40] Moreover, many holy people acclaim and praise Conrad in the text: the king of Jerusalem, the knights of the Temple and the Hospital, the citizens of Tyre and Acre, the citizens and clerics of Venice, and, after some disputation, even the pope.[41] God and good Christian people all favored Conrad, according to the "Gesta," in spite of his many travails and denigrators.

These miracles, signs, and acclamations attest to Conrad's personal sanctity. One's attention is drawn, however, to an unusual lacuna: the author dispenses with the entire first and second sieges of Constantinople (and all the complex dealings between those sieges) in the single Alexius-packed sentence quoted at the beginning of this chapter. The author seems to crave the confusion engendered by this statement. He goes on to extol "the wondrous manner in which the Lord effected miracles through an army as insignificant as it was underrated," but then skips past the miracles.[42] It strains credulity to think that the author had time enough to describe a meal in Corfu but could not squeeze in more than one sentence on one of the greatest military events in history. Could this omission be a response to broader criticism? The author was surely aware of the papal discourse, at least through Conrad, his source. Conrad had, after all, directly received absolution from Innocent in 1205. The author might also have been aware of the insinuations of Burchard of Ursperg against Abbot Martin of Pairis.[43]

By leaving the sack of the city out of the text, the author could hint about divine favor in Constantinople while avoiding controversy. Miracles directly favoring Conrad appear early in the text, whereas miracles ratifying communal acceptance of his relics proliferate in the later sections. The entire region benefits from Conrad's piety. After the arrival of the relics in Germany, the community, from high clerics to high nobles to "an innumerable body of commoners,"[44] receives, glorifies, and blesses the bishop because "this man carried with him tokens of the saints in connection with which undoubtedly peace and salvation were introduced to the Fatherland."[45] Whereas the text from Soissons argues that the translation of relics (to France) would transform the fate of the land of Jerusalem in an unspecified future, for Halberstadt the relics had already changed the fate of Germany. The author explains the mysterious workings of these saints in an extraordinary paragraph. Their "propitious arrival"[46] ended the schism between Philip of Swabia and Innocent III "through the strange death of King Philip." Philip had defeated his imperial rival, Otto of Brunswick, and gained papal approval, only to be murdered by one of his neighbors in an act of private vengeance. Otto thus emerged as the undisputed emperor. It must have seemed a strange result both to Conrad and to the author of the "Gesta," but the text accepts that Philip's death occurred through the "wondrous judgment of God" and that all should rejoice in the end of the civil war.[47] Besides, the concept that God's will could be expressed through negative and unusual events (or *mirabilis*) was useful with regard to the author's quest to exonerate Conrad. The effects of Philip's death included the quieting of rebellions and the achievement of concord. Plenty overcame scarcity. And thus, by the "arrival of such patrons" (that is, the saints), the scourges of "famine, pestilence, death, rebellions and wars took their rest in every quarter."[48] The saints from Constantinople defeated the four horsemen of the Apocalypse. The people should, the author insists, give thanks both to God and to their bishop for these blessings.

And so they did. The author redescribes the people welcoming Conrad to the Cathedral of Halberstadt. "The Lord has led forth the just man," they sang,[49] and Conrad preached a sermon about the relics. The day he arrived (August 16, 1205) became a perpetual feast day.[50] Translatio, then, functions as the clearest indication of divine and communal approval for Conrad's decisions over the three years between the regional troubles that forced him to depart on crusade and his return home. He left a war-torn region in disgrace. According to the text, he returned in triumph, accompanied by saints who then brought peace to Germany on his behalf.

The author of the "Gesta" had a clear task—to defend his bishop. As with the text from Soissons, he adopts the concepts of translatio in arguing that negative actions could reveal the will of God and that the translation of relics, regardless of the circumstances, had an exculpatory and providential force. Still, the author never employs the key elements of the genre in his narrative. He implies that miracles occurred during the crusade but does not credit those miracles to a specific saint acting on the behalf of the translator in order to enable the translation. Peace came to Germany, but the hand of God showed itself through the murder of Conrad's secular lord. Conrad was cured at a shrine, but not by a saint whose relics he then brought home. The effectiveness of the idea of pious theft depends on the literary creation of a link between the miracle, the saint in question, and the person bearing the relics. "The Land of Jerusalem" describes no miracles in the act of translation but at least recounts those that occurred after the relics had been installed. The "Gesta" lacks direct miraculous connections between Conrad and the relics that he brought home to Halberstadt. This could be a response to the condemnation of relic looting from Rome and elsewhere, but the precise reasons behind this odd omission remain unclear.

Langres

Bishop Garnier of Troyes's untimely death in Constantinople in April 1205 has rendered the textual tradition concerning the relics he sent west necessarily murkier than the directly commissioned accounts of Nivelon and Conrad.[51] He indirectly figures as an authorizing figure who distinguishes the acquisition of his relics from blasphemous looting. Garnier took the cross after his overlord, Count Thibaut of Champagne, led the way on November 28, 1199.[52] Like Nivelon, Garnier commanded one of the great Venetian ships, the *Peregrina* (Lady Pilgrim).[53] He had advocated accepting Alexius's offer while in Zara and thus bore significant responsibility for the diversion to Constantinople.[54] Both Nivelon and Garnier were among the preachers who rallied the troops against the Greeks the day before the conquest,[55] and they were two of the six Frankish electors who helped select Baldwin of Flanders as emperor.[56] Garnier, like Conrad and Nivelon, was present at the sack, presumably organized some of the Frankish churches in the aftermath, and perhaps found his relics in that context. Although he sent many relics back to various churches in Champagne, his untimely death in Constantinople prevented him from commissioning narrative works analogous to those sponsored by his episcopal colleagues. And while those benefiting from his gifts did produce various texts that commemorate the arrival of the new relics, only one fully invokes the themes of the genre of translatio.[57] Within this narrative, the "Translatio Mamantis," the papal legate Peter Capuano acts as the arbiter of the late Garnier's wishes on behalf of the cathedral in Langres and that most unusual priest Walon of Dampierre.

After the crusade, Walon became bishop of Domoko in Thessaly, but found it too poor and so decided to return home to France. After abandoning his see, Walon asked Capuano for the head of St. Mamas and carried it from Constantinople back to the Cathedral of St. Mamas in Langres, as Garnier had intended.[58] Langres had been a center of the cult of St. Mamas for many centuries,[59] and Walon invoked this history when presenting his request to Capuano. The anonymous canon of Langres who penned the translatio could ignore some of the problems faced by the anonymous writers from Soissons and Halberstadt. He did not have to justify the creation of a new cult or quash local dissent, though rival churches might have envied the Cathedral of St. Mamas's access to donations and prestige.[60] Just as Conrad found when he gave St. Stephen's head to the Cathedral of St. Stephen, offering the relics of a cathedral's patron saint to that cathedral required little reordering of local sacred landscapes. Because St. Mamas's cult was so well established in Langres, the new relic enhanced existing prestige and practice. On the other hand, authenticity was critical. A forged relic would besmirch the value of Langres's already great collection of St. Mamas's relics. Because the head arrived in the hands of a man who had no particular local status, rather than in the possession of a local or neighboring prelate (as had been the case in Soissons and Halberstadt), the author focused on proving authenticity above all other concerns.

Although forgeries must have been prevalent, most Fourth Crusade translatio texts avoid the subject or at least rely on miraculous, rather than human, agency to prove authenticity. But not so in this case. The author inserts an *inventio*, or story of the discovery of a relic, into a larger, local text—a *vita* of St. Mamas and the *acta translatorum* of his relics to Langres.[61] In order to deal with the question of authenticity, the author ironically begins the *inventio* by describing the sacrilege of the crusaders—the very actions that enabled forgeries and desecration. However, having acknowledged the potential for deceit, he distinguishes the moral and sacred deeds of Garnier, Capuano, and (most of all) Walon from the sacrilegious pillaging of the crusaders, assuring the reader that the head is authentic.

Garnier, the narrative begins, did not participate in the looting or acquire the relic of St. Mamas as a result of any personal misconduct. Instead, he and other clerics took charge of the Greek relics in order to prevent any mishandling of sacred items, an assertion addressed above in chapter 1. The author—a canon of a cathedral that received relics more or less directly from Garnier—had every reason to exaggerate the propriety of the translation. Thus, instead of being an accurate attribution of status, the statements made in this source and other pro-Garnier texts[62] are part of the process of ex post facto authorization and authentication that constitutes the genre of translatio.

After discussing the steps Garnier took to counter the violation of churches, the narrative turns to a particular reliquary, containing the head, that had the words "Saint Mamas"[63] inscribed upon it in Greek. Although the author never says where the object was found, Garnier reclaimed it, by implication preserving it from sacrilegious damage or sale, and took it to his chambers. According to the "Translatio Mamantis," he intended to send the relic to Langres because that was its natural destination. Thus, the chain of events that concluded with the head of St. Mamas in Langres did not begin with impious plundering or a violent sack, but through clerics acting to protect sanctities from fellow Latin crusaders. The author describes the reliquary in the text, and presumably the item delivered to his church five years later was a match. Even poorly understood Greek, such as the inscription on the reliquary, could serve as an authenticating device in the Latin West.[64]

Enter the cleric Walon, "an honest man of good character,"[65] and the papal legate Peter Capuano. According to the narrative, Walon sought to prove by every mortal means possible that he had a true relic and to make sure that the translation was fully canonical. First, he gained an audience with Capuano and convinced him that Langres had the best possible claim to St. Mamas's relics. This gave the author the chance to rehearse the history of St. Mamas's relics in Langres and to invoke the wishes of the late Garnier. Capuano accordingly gave Walon the reliquary from the bishop's chambers. Thus, whereas the opening passage of the text describes Garnier's confiscation of the relic and thereby establishes that the translation happened in defiance of desecration, the second passage serves three purposes: to establish a chain of possession from Garnier to Walon, to state the cathedral's historical claims to St. Mamas, and to demonstrate that both a bishop and the papal legate approved the transfer.

But this impressive level of authentication was not enough for Walon or the text's presumed audience. According to the author, Walon then took the relic to the Monastery of St. Mamas in Constantinople, from whence it had been pillaged. If this story reflects a historical event, one can only imagine the actual encounter between the ambitious Walon and the now-bereft Greek monks. One wonders whether he was accompanied by guards or took other precautions to make sure that he did not lose the relic at that moment. The narrative certainly does not hide the feeling of loss among the former guardians of the relic. Yet their exchange with Walon ultimately clears the translatio of any element of sacrilege or theft.

Walon's stated purpose for the visit to the monastery was to receive verification, not permission. Ultimately, he received both. When asked about the head, the abbot and monks wept. They begged Walon to return their relic to them, in the process verifying its authenticity (otherwise, why weep?). They would, they vowed, rather have lost all their wealth and possessions than the head of St. Mamas. But Walon responded with his own tears and entreaties, begging the monks to change their minds. He cited the history of Langres, focusing on the exquisite and constant veneration already given to St. Mamas within the cathedral and the community. According to the translatio, his vow to glorify St. Mamas even more fervently in Langres moved the Greek monks. They gave Walon their blessing, and he departed to unite the head with its body.[66] Thus, according to the source, not only did Walon have Garnier, Capuano, and history on his side, but even the Greek monks who suffered the violation of their sanctuary by rapacious crusaders were willing to see the relic translated to its new home.

The author largely elides the four years between Walon's departure from Constantinople and his arrival in France.[67] We know that he accepted the bishopric of Domoko in Thessaly but left after three days because of its poverty.[68] We do not know whether this was before or after he acquired the head. The translatio makes no mention of Walon's episcopal status, and he might well have wanted to keep his abandonment of the see quiet. The text does refer to Walon's history in Champagne, his devotion to the church of Langres (the dominant church of the region), and his service in the "Latin army." The author refers to Walon with such basic honorifics as *venerabilis*. The translatio sheds no light on his decisions, conduct, or motivations, other than to cite his piety and good reputation. After marking the passage of time between the conversation in the monastery and his departure to the West, the author introduces one of the enduring tropes of this type of narrative—the hazard-laden miraculous voyage. While Walon was returning to France by ship, the weather turned dangerous. All aboard feared for their lives. Walon (tearful once again) prayed to St. Mamas for deliverance, not in order to save his life or the lives of the men on the ship, but to protect the priceless relic. The saint calmed the waters, the ship survived, and "through many labors, many dangers, and with many tribulations," Walon eventually arrived in Langres. The author concludes by folding this translatio into the larger narrative of the history of Langres and local veneration of St. Mamas.[69]

Taken as a whole, the "Translatio Mamantis" provides a mixed example of hagiographic memorialization of the Fourth Crusade. Walon was a crusading priest, not so different from Nivelon or Conrad, except in rank—and he even became a bishop as a result of the crusade, albeit briefly. However, the text expresses none of the concern about the holiness of this crusade that appears in the other narratives. The positioning of Garnier as a nonlooter provides an answer to papal critique, as does the unlikely episode in which the Greek monks gave permission for the translation of the relic. This is a fantasy of ecumenical rapprochement, not an account of division. It follows the form of a classic translatio narrative, replete with a miracle that lends divine authorization to the translation. Of paramount concern was the need to authenticate Langres's new prize; therefore, the hagiographer cited Garnier, Capuano, Walon, the monks of St. Mamas, and finally St. Mamas himself (through the miracle). Garnier was no official *procurator sanctorum reliquarum*, but he did oversee postconquest confiscation and control of relics. In fact, the attribution of this title to Garnier demonstrates that the clerics of Champagne found their new relic's dubious past concerning enough to be worth the exaggeration. Carnage and a failure to free Jerusalem shrouded that past. To assuage any doubts about propriety, the canon of Langres cast the cathedral's benefactor as the one who stopped the sacrilege in the East and wiped away any sin.

Gaeta and Amalfi

By dying, Garnier escaped blame for what happened after the fall of Constantinople. Peter Capuano was not so lucky. Despite trying to make the best of a tricky situation, the legate's failure to reassert control (probably an impossible goal) drove the papacy toward its harsh assessment of postcrusade conduct and sparked the formation of the pope's negative narrative. The unfortunate legate bore the brunt of Innocent's harshest rhetoric, though the author of the *Gesta Innocentii* tried to ameliorate that critique in later years, as discussed in the previous chapter. The texts that document Capuano's efforts to take control of the relic situation reveal the pressures on recipients of Byzantine relics to exempt themselves from criticism.

On Capuano's way home from Constantinople, he endowed various sites with relics. Two translatio narratives regarding these gifts survive. The earlier of the two avoids discussing the Fourth Crusade, while the later text, from Amalfi, produces a smooth retelling of the Fourth Crusade without concern for sacrilege. However, even this latter translatio does not contain an account of where and how the priests who eventually brought their relic to Capuano found their prize.

The "Translatio caput Beati Theodori" is a contemporary account of Capuano's doings. Penned by an anonymous canon of Gaeta's cathedral between 1210 and 1219, the translatio condenses a great deal of information into a short text. The author begins with a general discussion of the cult of relics and then turns to Byzantine dynastic history following the death of Manuel Comnenus (1180), eventually connecting the Fourth Crusade to that history. Only then does the author arrive at the raison d'être of the narrative—Capuano's return to Italy with relics.

By the time Capuano arrived in Gaeta, it was a major city with a long history of trading within the Mediterranean world—a history discussed in the text.[70] The author also demonstrates a high degree of familiarity with the tumult in late twelfth-century Byzantium, but he heavily abridges the events of the Fourth Crusade. Riant dismissed the abridgement as "mal racontée,"[71] concluding that the poor account simply reflects limited awareness. Riant's analysis, however, does not explain the lacunae adequately. The text's author, a resident of a Mediterranean city, displays a detailed and accurate level of awareness about Byzantine affairs. He eloquently explains why Christians venerate saints and their relics and provides a credible account of the aftermath of the crusade. But out of 149 lines of text, the critical years of 1202–4 are covered in a mere 13. By comparison, over half the text is given to the years 1180–1202, despite the fact that these are outside the ostensible scope of the narrative. The text thus comes across as uneven, though thoughtful.

All the other Fourth Crusade translatio narratives take the importance and veneration of relics and saints for granted. The canon who penned this text, however, begins by discussing the propriety of saintly devotion. He writes, "As the stars shine in the sky, so do the saints shine in the church of God, and their radiance . . . is of Christ."[72] The relics of saints, furthermore, create the locus where mortals celebrate the saints' glory both in life and death and ask for their intercession in heaven. For this reason, the author continues, he will try his best to relate how the head of the martyr St. Theodore Tyro was translated to Gaeta.[73] These opening paragraphs set the stakes for the rest of the text. The saint's glory in heaven reflects on the place that housed his relics and on the local people who venerated him. Thus, all of Gaeta (not just the church) would benefit from St. Theodore's grace.

The author then turns to Byzantine politics in a manner not seen elsewhere in the translatio tradition. Many texts briefly mention the betrayal of Isaac Angelos, but this author takes the reader back to Manuel Comnenus and the challenges that he and his successors faced. He then proceeds through the preconditions for the crusade: a new dynasty, brotherly betrayal, and an escaped heir in the court of Philip of Swabia.[74]

These two opening sections reveal much about the author. He thought conceptually about sanctity and the practice of relic worship. He demonstrated his broad knowledge of the political events of the past forty years. Although he recounted the betrayal and blinding of Isaac with considerable emotion, he never dipped into anti-Greek polemic. One can imagine him thinking systematically about the significance of the translation of relics from east to west. In that light, his reluctance to discuss the events of the crusade could not have been due to ignorance or laziness. The author made a choice, and that choice perhaps betrays some discomfort with his task.

The author knew that Capuano, his monastery's benefactor, had a clear mandate: to bring aid to the Holy Land.[75] But whereas the anonymous author from Soissons used similar language to assert that the Fourth Crusade would ultimately lead to the liberation of Jerusalem, the Gaetan author made no such claim. Instead, the "Translatio caput Beati Theodori" offers a weak narrative of the crusade in just a few lines and skips from the conquest to the flinging of Mourtzouphlos off a column.[76] The author then shifts abruptly into the aftermath of the conquest, using the spoliation of Constantinople to reinvoke Capuano's divine mandate. In this key piece of the text, Capuano claims to have come to Constantinople only at the request of Emperor Baldwin—the same story that was circulated in the Gesta Innocentii.[77] There, "as was fitting," Capuano "reverently" began to investigate the pillaging of the city and specifically the "violation of churches."[78] In the process, he gathered together relics and "things of the saints"[79] in order to honor them and then personally took some of the relics to his ship. Two key lines follow. First, the narrative invokes "the will of God," who governs all mortal affairs. Second, the author states that Capuano, "out of caution and circumspection, concealed the relics and secretly hurried to the city of his birth, Amalfi."[80]

From whom could the legate have been hiding—pirates, other clerics, the crusaders who violated churches, or the pope? Was Capuano or the canon of Gaeta seeking to add elements of a furtum sacrum to the legate's story and thus provide canonical justification for a secret act of translation? One is left hungry for more details. Instead, the narrative lists the various relics Capuano distributed among Amalfi, Sorrento, Naples, the Monastery of Monte Cassino (not far from Gaeta), and finally the church of the Blessed Virgin in Gaeta itself. As with most translatio narratives, communal acceptance and veneration of the translated relic play an important role in finishing the narrative. Bishop Egidus of Gaeta led the clerics, and the populo universo followed with hymns and laud. The whole throng proceeded to the cathedral in order to deposit and install the relic. The narrative concludes with a peculiar exhortation to the author's brethren. He commands them to ask the martyr to extend his protection over the city of Gaeta and then returns to the theme of his first paragraph—the redemptive power of relics and saints. Just as St. Theodore triumphed over the flames of his oppressors (by "living" on as a saint), so he could help the citizens and clerics of Gaeta to "extinguish the flames of their own defects."[81]

Riant suggested that this text offers a view from Gaeta.[82] It is not surprising that a canon from its cathedral church had acquired considerable knowledge of Byzantine political history. But few Latin sources on the Fourth Crusade link the crusade to the Byzantine decline after Manuel Comnenus's death. Even Greek texts, such as Niketas Choniates's chronicle, attribute the conquest of Constantinople to Alexius III's failures as a military commander and his treason against Isaac, the event that sparked the deal between Alexius Angelos and the crusaders.[83] Clari tells the story of Manuel's death but uses it as a way to introduce Alexius Angelos—a small excursus in a much longer text.[84] The Byzantine material in the Gaetan account does not indicate an attempt to blame the crusade's failure to liberate Jerusalem on the Greeks (as other authors would do). Instead, it demonstrates a systematic approach to the author's subject. The abrupt ending of the careful history just before the crusade began thus stands out all the more starkly against the first two-thirds of the text.

The Amalfi text, written in the late thirteenth or early fourteenth century, is not so truncated. On his way back to Rome from Constantinople, Capuano stopped in his hometown of Amalfi, on which he would subsequently bestow considerable largesse. He offered its cathedral, a church long dedicated to St. Andrew, the head of its titular saint.[85] As recorded in the "Translatio corporis S. Andree de Constantinopoli in Amalphiam," Capuano acquired this relic just after arriving in Constantinople in 1205, but he did not steal it (despite Werner Maleczek's depiction of the act as a "pious theft").[86] Instead, two unnamed priests from Amalfi who were already in the city stole the relic and brought it to Capuano, who escorted both priests and relic home. The author, Matthew of Amalfi, brackets this theft with a panegyric for Amalfi and the usual trope of the dangerous sea voyage and saintly intervention. He rehearses the history of the crusade and mentions its task to help the Holy Land, but dwells neither on the failure to accomplish that task nor on the abandonment of the sacred region. As for the diversion to Constantinople, the author simply states that the crusaders were led there by "human or divine leadership."[87]

The exquisitely written translatio of St. Andrew's head mirrors the accounts of other episcopal translations in many ways. Capuano bore a relic back to his home church, the locals greeted it with celebration, and the late saint worked local miracles.[88] The author, it must be remembered, operated in a different era. The issues of the immediate postconquest years were no longer pressing, the story of the crusades had moved on from the rise and quick stagnation of the Latin Empire, and contemporary crusaders were more concerned with Egypt, the failures of the Fifth Crusade, and the actions of Frederick II. The author could thus easily develop the story of a native son returning to his home city with a valuable relic of a saint that the city already venerated.

The Amalfi text serves as a transition from the erratic and uneven exculpatory narratives about the clerical elite—narratives steeped in authority and discomfort—to those that embrace the power of pious thievery, unauthorized actions, and direct miraculous approval. The previous sources are all purely local narratives that focus on exonerating those responsible for specific acts of relic translation while avoiding the complications of the Fourth Crusade. The subsequent sources, in contrast, universalize their claims and construct a narrative of the crusade in which relic translation is but one piece of a holy endeavor.

Venice: St. Simon the Prophet

On Palm Sunday of 1204, a group of Venetian crusaders ventured from their ship into the chaotic city of Constantinople in order to steal a special relic from the crypt of St. Mary Chalkoprateia.[89] Their humorous story, preserved in the "Translatio corporis Beati Symonensis Prophete de Constantinopoli Venetias anno 1203," or "Translatio Symonensis," combines theological anecdote with heist.[90] Boilerplate elements, such as a miraculous scent exuding from the saint's corpse, mix with context-specific idiosyncrasies, such as when the thieves compare themselves to the Three Magi or stash the relic in an abandoned chapel on the Bosphorus. The text contains four distinct parts—preamble, the hatching of plans, theft, and aftermath—dotted with various religious digressions.

The first few sections of the text set the scene and offer various kinds of background material. They begin by introducing Venice and the parish of St. Simon the Prophet. The Venetians were "eager to serve the army of Christianity," for "they were born of a noble race, but indeed had a faith even more noble."[91] According to the text, Doge Enrico Dandolo of Venice, Count Baldwin of Flanders, and other counts took up the cross and went to Constantinople to wage a just war on behalf of Alexius Angelos, the deposed Greek prince. Greek iniquity and impiety serve as *casus belli*. The author claims that God "incited" Dandolo and Baldwin to attack the Greeks in order to "put down their [the Greeks'] arrogance and lift up their humility, [and] in order to destroy the malignant and bring peace to the benign."[92] Thus, the author can argue that this holy war, intended to put a stop to the iniquity of the Greeks, was a success.

The text indicates that twelve Venetians originally planned the heist, but it only names seven, because only seven made it to the crypt and carried out the actual theft. The narrator positions the seven relic thieves in contrast to crusaders motivated by secular loot. Most of the victors sought out mere gold and silver, but these "better" men, who were "citizens of the Rialto," had deeper motivations.[93] The Holy Spirit drove them to desire "justice," not common plunder, and from here the author pivots to a gospel-laden homily on the seven gifts of the Holy Spirit—wisdom, understanding, counsel, fortitude, knowledge, piety, and a spirit that fears God.[94] He provides the names of the thieves, who, although they were seven, had one spirit and all of the aforementioned qualities.[95]

After these three preambles—on Venice, on the Fourth Crusade, and on the Holy Spirit—the author begins the real story. Just after Constantinople falls, two men, Andrea Balduino and Pietro Steno, discuss the body of their parish's patron saint, Simon the Prophet. Steno reveals that he saw the relic years ago when visiting the city with his uncle, and Balduino opines that God may have "predestined" the two of them and their comrades to find the relic.[96] They gather ten coconspirators, locate the right church and tomb, and then return to their ship to plan the heist for Palm Sunday.

The central section of the narrative details the journey to the tomb, the theft of the relic, and the return to the ship—each phase fraught with peril. Five of the thieves get lost; four of the remaining seven guard the church door, and three actually enter the tomb. These three are stricken with fear, return to the door, are chastised, and then return to the crypt. Here we reach the pinnacle of any good relic-stealing text, the moment when the thieves finally see the relics. Just before opening the final container, Steno announces that the previous night he had dreamed about being home in Venice, attending mass in his own church. In the dream, Steno was the only person present and thus the only one able to help the parish priest with his duties. The other two thieves solemnly agree that this dream was a sign that he should take up the relics. Steno prays, asks the saint for mercy, and reaches into the ark. A miracle follows: a sweet aroma fills the entire church. "With a mixture of joy and fear," the men gather up not only the bones of St. Simon but also other sacred items.[97]

However, the thieves' trials are not done. Returning to their ship, they find the relics glowing with holy light, making concealment difficult even as their risk increases. When Greek citizens discover the loss of St. Simon and raise a great "murmur," the doge of Venice orders all the *uxeria* (ships used to transport horses) to be beached so that no one can depart.[98] In addition, the doge and "other princes of war" offer the relics' weight in gold for their safe return. The Venetian thieves thus take the relics off their ship, so that no other sailor finds them, and hide them in a little local chapel connected to an abandoned palace on the Bosphorus. They pay an old, pious Greek woman to care for the chapel, though they keep her ignorant of what is inside. "God be praised," none of the conspirators becomes tempted to turn in his comrades or to return the relics in exchange for the bounty.[99] Finally, after six months (the text skips ahead abruptly), one of the thieves receives permission by lottery to head back to Venice. Andrea Drusiaco (presumably one of the guards at the church door) takes the relics and a letter describing the events of its acquisition, journeys home without incident, and gives everything to Leonardo, rector of the thieves' parish church. Shortly thereafter, with great pomp and ceremony, Leonardo installs the relics in the church with the help of Venice's two highest-ranking clerics, the bishop of Castello and the patriarch of Grado. Here, the narrative concludes.

What should we make of this text? It stresses the unauthorized nature of the acquisition, and the verifiable details in the text support this characterization. Yet the author found ways to heighten tension, to emphasize honesty, sin, and redemption, and to elaborate on dangers that probably did not exist. For example, the text implies that the thieves had to act surreptitiously lest the Greek citizens of the city catch them, and that Dandolo was merely acting on behalf of those citizens and their "murmur" of distress at the loss of the relic when he placed the bounty. In reality, the thieves would have been in trouble only if they had been caught by the crusade leadership, whether Venetian or otherwise. The Venetian crusaders had no authority over the relic, over the church of St. Mary Chalkoprateia, or within the crusading army. The miracle of the scent specifically authorized the theft of their chosen relic, but the miracle of the sacred light created danger. Hagiographical and religious interpolations function similarly to the miracles, providing a didactic space in which the author can instruct his reader. Through prayer, digressions, miracles, and a constructed Greek threat, the "Translatio Symonensis" uses the power of translatio and local traditions of memorializing relic theft to support its narrative of the Fourth Crusade as divinely ordained and appropriately beneficial to Venice.

Venice: St. Paul the New Martyr

The "Translatio Symonensis" is the only Venetian translatio narrative from the first few years after the Fourth Crusade to survive intact, but it is joined by a single narrative from the second decade of the Latin Empire, the "Translatio corporis Beatissimi Pauli Martyris," or "Translatio Pauli." Although written in a context much changed from just two decades earlier, the story is presented as a Fourth Crusade narrative and thus reflects the continued utility of translatio in shaping the local memory of the Fourth Crusade. By 1222, when the theft of the relic of St. Paul the New Martyr took place, Venice had solidified its economic position, lost control over the patriarchate of Constantinople but preserved the patriarchate of Grado's rights, and, along with so many others, suffered through the disaster of the Fifth Crusade.[100] Venice contributed significant naval support to the Fifth Crusade, lost many men, and responded to the disaster by erasing the records of its participation in the crusade from local memory. It was, as Louise Robbert writes, "a bad dream to be forgotten by the men on the Rialto."[101] In this context, a Venetian monk produced the translatio as if nothing had changed since 1205. After beginning with a short account of the Fourth Crusade, the text continues with the discovery of the relic, the loading of the relic onto a ship, a storm, and the ship's ultimate arrival at Venice. Throughout the account, the author frequently digresses into homily and parable.

The account of the Fourth Crusade blurs the objectives of the campaign—the assault on Egypt and liberation of the Holy Land—in order to link crusade and translatio. The author contrasts the Greek people (*gens*) with the Venetians. The Greeks, filled with pride, were disrespectful to God, and thus all good people "in the whole world" hated them.[102] God turned to the Venetians, a people who, in contrast, were wholly devoted to him. This devotion was evidenced by their decision to join with "other counts from over the mountains" to aid the Holy Land against the Saracens and "other barbarians." Although God did want the Saracens conquered, he decided that the "renowned nobles" of Venice should first punish the Greeks and avenge the victims of their injustice.[103]

After a short account of the conquest of Constantinople, the monk pauses to draw a lesson from the events. Throughout, he explores his central themes by abandoning the narrative flow in order to instruct his readers. He first states that the awesome power of God handed the Greeks over to their conquerors on account of their contempt for him. Then the author suddenly changes his mode of expression from third-person narrative ("God handed over the Greeks") to address his monastic brethren directly: "We have said these things, o my most beloved brothers, so that nobody will be prideful, even if someone is disrespectful to you: because God hinders the proud, whereas to the humble, God bestows grace."[104] He concludes, in a critical passage, "The empire formerly of the Greeks was thus made into the empire of the Latins."[105] He returns to his third-person narrative with a description of the appointment of a Venetian, Thomas Morosini, to the patriarchate of Constantinople.[106]

After a brief discussion of the correct interpretation of the causes of the Fourth Crusade (Greek sin), the text jumps to the acquisition of the Monastery of Christ Pantepoptes[107] by Venice's Monastery of San Giorgio Maggiore, the discovery of the relics of St. Paul the New Martyr by a Venetian monk named Paulus, who was serving as prior, and Paulus's subsequent return to Venice to assume the position of abbot of San Giorgio.[108] The author forgives Paulus's joy at the discovery of the relic because the sacred treasure was worth more than all of the secular treasures in the world, a theme to which he returns.[109] As we have seen, the contrast between the greater treasure of relics and the lesser treasure of secular wealth is not atypical. The author draws a further contrast between the saint's body, which is dead, and his soul, which is alive in the celestial kingdom with Christ.

From Venice, Paulus, "not unmindful of the so very great treasure that had been relinquished"[110]—in other words, left alone in the monastery in Constantinople—quickly ordered the new prior in Constantinople to retrieve St. Paul's body and send it to Venice by stealth, lest the treasure be violated. The prior, named Marcus, obeyed, although the author curiously points out that he had no choice but to obey his abbot, as the abbot's word "was held [*tenebatur*] as law."[111] Here is the first of several key passages in which the author adds elements of sin, danger, and stealth to an otherwise straightforward "authorized" relic translation. Marcus is aided by Marino Storlato, podestà of the Venetian quarter—the supreme relevant secular authority there.[112] Storlato was a good friend to the religious house of San Giorgio, where he had buried his parents and would eventually be buried himself.[113] Marcus recruited his friend Iacobus Grimaldus to bear the "precious gem" to the abbot, so that it might adorn "not only the monastery, but also all of Venice, with its presence."[114] The involvement of these secular men extends the significance of the event from a simple instance of monastic relic thievery to an act that engaged the political and economic elite of the city. As if to reinforce this point, the author invokes St. Mark the Evangelist's presence in Venice. He writes, "For just as innumerable men and women come from all parts to visit the blessed Mark, so too it will become the glorious custom to see the blessed Paul."[115] Increased pilgrimage would be the reward for Venice's possession of St. Paul the New Martyr.

The voyage, as is so often the case in Venetian narratives, provides the central drama of the tale. Iacobus conceals the nature of his cargo from the captain and crew of the ship, and the author launches into a lengthy digression to excuse Iacobus's decision to lie. He plays with dichotomies of light and dark, wisdom and gold (sacred versus spiritual wisdom), sight and blindness, purity and impurity. He notes that glass remains pure even if hidden in darkness. The ship then encounters darkness in the form of a terrible storm sent by God, because, the author writes cryptically, "light is not able to be hidden by darkness." In other words, without an episode of darkness, there would be no opportunity for the saint's light to shine. The ship loses its oars, beam, mast, and sails, and all begin to despair as if "not their bodies, but their eternal souls might be dragged down as punishment for their sins."[116] They bring up the casket, discover that it contains a relic, and consider throwing it overboard, referencing the story of Jonah. Instead, all eventually decide to pray to the saint. The author avows that just as the "[martyr's] brother in name, the apostle Paul, said to Caesar . . . that faith in Christ would profit Rome greatly,"[117] so too would the veneration of St. Paul offer a similar blessing for Venice. The sea and winds grow calm ("within that hour"), and the sailors marvel at the power of the relic, which they refer to as "the limbs of the body," again invoking the themes of corporeal versus spiritual existence.[118] The rest of the text

relates a straightforward narrative of the ship's arrival at Venice and the ensuing celebration.

The "Translatio Pauli" presents itself as yet another tale of Fourth Crusade
relic theft. The actual translation, however, took place eighteen years after the
fall of Constantinople and was supported by elite secular and spiritual Venetian leaders. Other than the alleged storm, the translators encountered no
genuine threats. The author of this translatio embellishes the story to suit his
own purposes, linking medieval ideas about relic theft to his narrative of the
Fourth Crusade and his overarching themes of purity and grace concealed by
dark sin.

Cluny

Like the Venetian texts, the final two narratives surveyed in this chapter each
embrace the unauthorized nature of acts of acquisition and translation of relics. Rostang, a monk of Cluny, wrote the "Narratio exceptionis apud Cluniacum capitis beati Clementis, ex ore Dalmacii de Serciaco, militis, excepta" at
some point after 1206, the year that Dalmacius of Serciaco arrived at his monastery with the head of St. Clement.[119] The theft took place during the second
phase of relic looting. The thieves were both Burgundian knights who tried to
go to the Holy Land after their year of service in Constantinople was up, but
were thwarted by storms. Upon returning to Constantinople, they sought permission to acquire a relic from Peter Capuano and Benedict of Santa Susanna.
The cardinals granted their request but ordered them not to corrupt the process of acquisition by buying a relic. Presumably, they imagined that the
knights would seek some small fragment of a relic as a gift. Instead, the two
men stole St. Clement's head. In chapter 1, I suggested that the story demonstrates the following: First, by 1206, the papal legates had more or less assumed
a position of general authority with regard to the fate of Constantinople's relics, or so thought the knights. Second, relic stealing occurred anyway. Third,
relic trafficking also continued unabated, because otherwise the legates would
not have bothered warning the knights against the practice.

The narrative structure of the text exhibits an unusual conglomeration of
the features found in the cognate narratives discussed above. Rostang presents
an odd double text consisting of two parts: one is a narrative by Rostang
himself, while the other is, allegedly, Dalmacius's unabridged report of the

relic theft. Rostang delves into crusade history and tries to link the relic to the redemption of Jerusalem, while simultaneously relating a tale of brazen theft.

The text begins with a long, if erratic, account of the history of Jerusalem, moving rapidly from Nebuchadnezzar through various prophecies and finally to the era of Pope Urban II, whose Cluniac connections are trumpeted.[120] After a brief account of the early crusades, Rostang informs the reader that he will leave off this "Historiam Hierosolymitanam" and that "we will truly turn our stylus to modern times and modern things, and shortly tell . . . how the head of St. Clement was translated from Constantinople to Cluny."[121] Rostang blames "modern things"—Saladin and failed attempts to free Jerusalem— on luxurious living and diversity in the holy city. "True pilgrims," the monk writes, go on foot and suffer. This focus on the polyglot and multicultural nature of crusader Jerusalem as a negative aspect is intriguing and unusual, although a cloistered monk's scorn for the pleasantries of the city cannot be considered surprising.[122] He blames the devil for stirring up the pride of the kings and claims that the ensuing discord led to the neglect of the *iter Hiero-solymitanum*.[123]

The passage on the Fourth Crusade begins with the Western lords and bishops "from France, England, Germany, and from all the provinces of the world" instigating a new campaign for the *iter Hierosolymitanum* in order to save their souls.[124] Among this host, Rostang finally introduces the two relic thieves: Dalmacius of Serciaco, a "noble and well-learned man, who himself enlisted a certain soldier by the name of Poncius of Busseria, a faithful man and good comrade."[125] Rostang then rehearses the familiar story of trouble in Venice, as the crusaders failed to generate enough money to pay the Venetians for constructing the crusade's fleet of ships.[126]

Rostang compresses the remainder of the campaign into a few brief points. The arrival of the "emperor of Constantinople" (clearly meant to indicate Alexius IV) "freed them [the crusaders] from the labyrinth."[127] The crusaders signed the treaty of Zara, went to Constantinople, fought the Greeks, suffered great losses, took the city, and named Baldwin of Flanders emperor. Rostang makes no attempt to handle the intricacies of the situation. Nothing here is inaccurate, however, and perhaps he felt that it was a familiar enough tale to elide the details. Even the usual denigration of the Greeks as schismatics is relatively mild. Rostang describes them only as having "turned their backs to the divine truth;" thus, the smaller Latin army was able to defeat the great city.[128]

Abruptly, the text turns to the relic theft. Rostang writes that "the afore-mentioned Dalmacius, when he was not able to go to Jerusalem, deliberated with his comrade over how he might be able to piously steal the head of St. Clement. He had heard that the head had been translated over the sea to Constantinople by some emperor. . . . And how, with God willing, Dalmacius was able to obtain the head of St. Clement, you will hear how he, himself, narrated it."[129] These transitional lines are the key to understanding the entire translatio. Rostang acknowledges that the act was a pious theft, for the knights had debated the best way "to steal piously" (*pie furari posset*). He reinvokes Jerusalem, the subject of most of the text to this point, though he has trouble clearly connecting the relic theft and conquest of Constantinople to the holy city. The knights tried to go to Jerusalem and failed. The Fourth Crusade tried to go to Jerusalem and failed. Both failures, however, produced positive results for the West.

Dalmacius's account begins, "I, Dalmacius of Serciaco, and my comrade Poncius of Busseria . . . decided to visit the land of Jerusalem."[130] Except for its final few lines, the story is told in the first person, perhaps reflecting the knight's status as *valde litteratus*.[131] Dalmacius laments that after suffering through the campaign in Constantinople, he just wanted to get to Jerusalem, but the land and sea routes were much too dangerous. Tearfully, he begged God for an opportunity to serve him in some other way. God, Dalmacius claims, must have heard "the voice of my weeping"[132] and put the idea of acquiring a relic into his mind. In Constantinople, relics were cheap (*vilius*) and plentiful (*copia*), and to take one across the sea would bring both glory and praise to the bearers. Hence, Dalmacius and Poncius sought out the papal legates to request permission. The legates agreed that they could acquire a relic, but not through mercantile sale, as it was against the law to "parcel off" martyrs.[133] Interestingly enough, like the thieves from the parish of St. Simon the Prophet, Dalmacius and his comrade decided to steal their relic on Palm Sunday—March 26, 1206. Perhaps the knights knew that transport would be easily available two years after the conquest because crusader vows were expiring.

First, Dalmacius had to find a relic. He learned the location of the head of St. Clement from a Latin priest who had seen a gold-leafed reliquary on which was inscribed "*o ayos Clementios* [sic], quod latine dicitur sanctus Clemens."[134] Dalmacius scouted out the monastery and then returned to steal the relic.[135] He distracted its guardians while his comrade, Poncius, entered and snatched the head. The two then fled the monastery ahead of the hue and cry raised by the monks. The knights disguised themselves, evaded capture, and returned to their lodgings. There, they venerated the relic secretly until late May, when they were able to return home.[136]

As we have seen in previous texts, however, a terrible storm threatened their homeward progress. Some on the ship were so afraid that they abandoned the vessel on little boats (*barcellis*); others were frozen in fear by the winds and high seas. Yet others, guided by the knights, came together to pray. By implication, the knights informed everyone on the ship (or had told them previously) that they were carrying the head of St. Clement and that they should ask him for "clemency."[137] All prayed, lachrymosely, and when they finished the waters instantly became tranquil. They rejoiced, promised to venerate St. Clement mightily and in perpetuity, and (the text summarizes) evaded all other dangers on their way to Cluny. There, the relic was deposited with other relics of saints and all due honor was paid to them. Dalmacius's alleged narrative ends at this point. Rostang finishes the text by dating the arrival of the relic to the year 1206, while Innocent was pope and Philip II Augustus was king of France.[138]

Pairis

When Abbot Martin of Pairis returned from the Fourth Crusade with his sacred plunder, he commissioned a translatio, the *Historia Constantinopolitana*, from a skilled author within his community.[139] Gunther of Pairis reworked his story in an unprecedented way, creating a text that deviates rhetorically and structurally from the others in the corpus yet participates in many of the same processes of memorialization.[140] Alfred Andrea, the foremost expert on the text, writes that Gunther "crafted a tightly constructed masterpiece of interspersed prose and poetry in which every element is subordinated to the work's overarching theme: all the deeds mentioned in this history, even those that are apparently impious, were done under the direction of God in order to effect a historically significant change in the course of human events and to offer his servants an opportunity to cooperate in the salvation of their souls."[141] The text is a prosimetrum, a literary form that features alternating sections of prose and poetry, with the latter usually serving as a commentary on the former.[142] The genre thus combines straight narrative with didactic interludes.

Gunther's work is much longer than the other sources discussed in this chapter, but it reflects the same purpose of linking relic translation to an overarching interpretation of the Fourth Crusade. Like the texts from Venice, the relics and related miracles support an apologia, doing more than just authorizing the translation in question. One must wade through the overabundance of detail, pious verses, and base inaccuracies to assess the text as a relic-theft narrative. The very title of the work, preserved in two of the three best extant manuscripts, reads *Historia Constantinopolitana: The Capture of the City of Constantinople from Which, Among Other Relics, a Large Part of the Holy Cross Was Translated to Alsace.*[143] With this title, Gunther immediately instructs the reader that the fall of Constantinople should be seen as the vehicle by which relics were translated, not as a diversion from the holy war for Jerusalem. He establishes his central theme through a general discussion of divine will, stating that it is more marvelous when God works through "simple persons" than the great, because "the less God's works are joined to human ability, the more the majesty of divine power shines forth with them."[144] These first lines present the critical interpretive rubric through which Gunther hopes his readers will approach the ensuing story. Later in the narrative, he uses humor to mock even his patron, Martin, making the abbot seem somewhat foolish in his relic thievery. Gunther depicts him as one of the "simple persons" through whom God can work.[145] The text also extends this concept to the Greeks. Because the Greeks were schismatic, duplicitous, and heretical, they were the strangest tool of all that God used in redeeming the Holy Land and bringing relics to Alsace. Gunther concludes the first chapter with a warning to the reader: "We want the reader to be forewarned that even if things done by our own people appear impious, he must not doubt that they were, nevertheless, effected by the Divine Will, which is always and everywhere just."[146] Accounts of impieties, mistakes, sins, and confusion, in fact, should enhance the reader's wonder. Each chapter ends with a verse instructing the reader in the meaning of the preceding prose.[147] The first poem therefore reminds the reader one more time that "[God] made possible what was done."[148]

The bulk of the text is divided into three distinct sections: first, Martin's travels to the Holy Land and Constantinople; second, the conquest of Constantinople; third, the looting and transportation of the relics. In the first section, chapters 2–10, Gunther recounts the preaching of the crusade (in which Martin took part), the familiar stories of hardship in Venice, and the assault on Zara. Gunther heightens the protagonist's importance by comparing him to St. Martin of Tours. Both Martins reluctantly left their monasteries, says Gunther, in order to do the will of God.[149] The author exaggerates Martin's role in the crusade, making him central rather than adjacent to key diplomatic and religious moments.[150] Throughout the text, people ask Martin to speak for them, represent them, advise them, or serve as a diplomat or messenger, though none of these roles can be independently verified in the other source material.[151] Martin, in fact, skipped much of the crusade's early misbehavior by avoiding Zara and heading right to Acre, where more troubles ensued in the form of plague. Gunther concludes the first section by bidding the reader to "take a breath" and think about the sins of the Greeks and their rulers.[152]

Gunther's imagination, fueled by Martin's vague sense of the complex battlefields, leads him to stray wildly from the actual events on the field. The few contributions of the *Historia Constantinopolitana* to the military history of the crusade have been dealt with elsewhere.[153] Chapter 11 addresses the reasons that the Greeks needed to be conquered, including the overthrow of Isaac, the widely held Latin perception that the Greeks had hindered previous crusades, and, of course, their refusal to accept Roman Christianity. Moreover, Gunther includes this key passage on relics:

> There was also, we believe, another far older and more powerful reason than all of these, namely the decision of Divine Goodness which so arranged, through this pattern of events, that this people, proud because of its wealth, should be humbled by their very pride and recalled to the peace and concord of the holy Catholic Church. It certainly seemed proper that this people, which otherwise could not be corrected, should be punished by the death of a few and the loss of those temporal goods with which it had puffed itself up; that a pilgrim people should grow rich on the spoils from the rich and the entire land pass into our power; and that the Western Church, illuminated by the inviolable relics of which these people had shown themselves unworthy, should rejoice forever.[154]

These lines contain a clear articulation of the ex post facto justifications not only for relic theft but for all the looting and conflict in the course of the crusade. Notice, in particular, how the relics conclude the passage and provide the strongest excuse for looting. Gunther argues that secular and religious looting is part of God's just punishment, while it also provides for the just enrichment of a "pilgrim people" and the "Western Church." Through the taking of sacrosanct relics, the war becomes sanctified.

The next seven chapters contain Gunther's description of the siege and conquest. Both his prose and poetry are powerful; he fills them with images of heroism, fire, and death. Gunther sought to emulate both Vergil's *Aeneid* and a Latin version of *The Iliad* that was well known in the Middle Ages.[155] In one poem, Gunther asserts that the victory of 1204 should replace the Trojan War in the annals of history, poetry, and memory. Constantinople should take the place of Troy; the Greek warriors should give way to the Latin crusaders.[156] The entire section makes for stirring reading, as it describes the campaign far more evocatively than the chronicles of Clari or Villehardouin and matches Niketas in its epic flights of rhetoric. However, as engaging as they might be, the passages on the conquest add nothing to the titular task of the *Historia Constantinopolitana*—telling the story of the relics. Only in the nineteenth chapter (out of twenty-five) does Gunther turn to the purported climax of his piece.

Seeing his fellow Latins plundering the city, Martin decided that he must participate in the looting "lest he remain empty-handed while everyone else got rich." Therefore, "he resolved to use his own consecrated hands for pillage." The abbot deemed it "improper to touch secular spoils with those same hands, [so] he began to plan how he might scrape together for himself some portion of those relics of the saints." Martin tried the abbey church of the Pantocrator but found it filled with Latin soldiers. Thus, he headed for a remote spot in the religious establishment where he could avoid those "greedily occupied with other matters, such as stealing gold, silver, and every sort of common article."[157] He found a Greek priest there and, pretending to be filled with rage, threatened him with death if he did not reveal the location of powerful relics. The priest, "thinking it more tolerable that a man of religion violate [*contrectaret*] the holy relics in awe and reverence, rather than that worldly men should pollute them, possibly, with bloodstained hands," eventually submitted to Martin's demands and showed him the iron chest in which was kept the "desired treasure."[158] As Andrea notes, *contrectare* has illicit sexual overtones, and Gunther's invocation of rape, which accompanied the plundering of the city, seems deliberate.[159] Here the message of the first chapter comes into concrete effect. God acts through simple, even seemingly incompetent or wicked, means in order to display his will more clearly. Martin was but a crude vehicle for divine will.

Martin concealed the relics from his fellows, although, in another comical image, Gunther describes the abbot "unceasingly cherishing" the relics in private, trying "by his respectful devotion" to make up "for what was lacking externally."[160] On the voyage home, Martin skirted so many "mischances and dangers" that "it is not easy to recount" them. The last few chapters include a long list of the translated relics and descriptions of a few episodes (detailed below) that Gunther hopes will further prove the righteousness of Martin's actions. Much as he ended the first chapter, Gunther concludes the work with an exhortation to the reader:

> No one ought, therefore, to imagine that this, like many other phenomena, happened by chance. That would be nothing more than falsely denying God's great deeds their deserved honor. For if we carefully consider the utterly unbelievable and sudden capture of this very great city, from which all of these relics were translated, and the pattern of events as they happened, and Abbot Martin's journey on land and sea—filled with peril and yet, through God's protection, undisturbed at every point—it will appear clearer than day that all of these were surely not matters of chance, but divine gifts.[161]

Gunther then recounts the circumstances of the production of the manuscript (naming himself and asking for God's forgiveness for his own sins) and details the further translation of relics from Pairis to Philip of Swabia.

As a work of medieval literature, the *Historia Constantinopolitana* is an extraordinary piece of writing. As a translatio narrative, the long digressions distract from the story of Martin, the pious relic thief. The abbot vanishes from much of the text, including the most stirring passages. These passages, describing the conquest and battle, outshine the less ornate account of relic thievery and veneration back in Germany. While warfare is naturally dramatic, other authors de-emphasized the military events in order to heighten the miraculous. Examples of stirring miracles in transit abound in the genre, as we have seen in this chapter, so the emphasis on warfare seems a matter of choice. In the *Historia Constantinopolitana*, "mischances and dangers" are simply elided. The focus on war and the de-emphasis on journey limits the ability of the text to operate as a narrative of relic theft. In fact, the act of translation from east to west plays such a relatively minor role that a clear discontinuity emerges between Gunther's stated (and many times restated) purpose and the execution of that purpose.

Conclusion

This chapter has presented the nine extant full narrative sources as a unified body of texts accompanied by an array of fragments, later redactions, and *perdita*. Collectively, they reflect a pattern of memorialization that offered affirmative and valorizing narratives in the service of authentication and legitimization of translated relics. These stories were intended to accompany the relics into perpetuity, shaping meaning, guiding liturgical and artistic innovation as appropriate, and perhaps even helping to raise funds. By necessity, these narratives conflicted with the views on looting, theft, and translation offered by Rome.

By appealing to the redemptive and transformative power of translatio, authors were able to claim the benefits of the crusade without necessarily contradicting critical counternarratives. But not all invocations of the principles of translated relics and pious thievery operated in the same way. Claims of authority tended to lead toward local meanings. Those admitting to theft, or even fabricating theft where none took place, found themselves empowered to proclaim universal significance for even the most trivial act of relic theft. In the next chapter, I explore these distinctions of method and scale as we start to see the Venetian examples distinguished from the larger corpus.

4

Interpretations

This chapter explores the various methods by which the authors of Fourth Crusade translatio narratives shaped their arguments. These texts converge around efforts to locate providential blessings in even the most difficult of circumstances. The authors, mostly monks or canons of a religious house recently endowed with at least one relic from Constantinople, deploy evidence of divine sanction to cleanse their relic or relics of any stain of iniquity or misconduct.

The sources fall along a spectrum between two distinct categories. The first, which I label "translatio only," suppresses both the details of the Fourth Crusade and the deeds of the relic translator in a way that diminishes the direct connection between redemptive miracles and translation of the relics. These texts present the translations as authorized acts fully in compliance with contemporary norms and canon law, based on the approval of a relevant bishop or cardinal. The texts from Soissons, Halberstadt, Amalfi, Gaeta, and Langres all fall into this category. Translatio-only texts accept the critical narrative of the corrupted crusade and sacrilegious pillaging of Constantinople as valid, but then exempt *their* relics or site from this corruption and sacrilege. In turn, they often suppress key details in order to maintain an authorized facade and localize the exculpatory power of the genre.

Ironically, the second category, "pious-theft" narratives, finds power in the self-proclaimed unauthorized nature of acts of relic translation. The sources from Venice, Pairis, and Cluny fall into this category. By de-emphasizing human authority, in contrast to the localizing translatio-only texts, these stories of pious theft universalize their message, extending it beyond the walls of the home institution. Instead of claiming an exemption from sacrilege for a single relic or group of relics, such texts support an alternative interpretation of the Fourth Crusade that glorifies the very deeds so criticized by Rome. They attempt to memorialize the crusade writ large, not just for all the crusaders, but in terms of its universal meaning.

The narrative space occupied by the relics themselves governs the distinctions between the two categories. A medieval relic possessed agency in a way not generally granted to material possessions. The body parts of saints acted as metonyms for the saints themselves. By moving such an object, one repositioned the saint in the sacred geography of the medieval imagination, a move that had potentially destabilizing repercussions for both human and neighboring divine inhabitants of that geography. Buildings possessing the relics of saints could function as super reliquaries themselves, concentrating both the miraculous activity of the saint and the devotional activity of the mortal community. The enormous power of a relic to reorder and redefine space, power, and community created very high stakes for the translatio narrative's author.

Traditionally, the climax of any medieval narrative of relic acquisition, whether licit or illicit, occurs at the moment when the human agents of translation encounter the relic, via sight, touch, and smell.[1] These sensory interactions form a conduit between saint and mortal through which the blessed may communicate. Translatio-only texts elide the moment of revelation, discovery, or theft. Lacking this denouement, the texts lose the opportunity to follow the claiming of the relic with a ratifying miracle. Such miracles signify divine approval for the translation as it occurs, rendering mere mortal objections (or permission) irrelevant before the will of heaven. Indeed, in narratives of unauthorized relic theft, the path to exoneration lies in the manifest absolution of a miracle that binds the thief to the relic, the saint, and God, excusing any misdeeds that occurred during the theft. Without these two moments—acquisition and miracle—an account relating the translation of a relic from Constantinople to the West might describe the theft of a sacred object, or at least the process of translocation and installation in a new locale, but find it more difficult to connect the events of the Fourth Crusade to a broader exculpatory message. However, the need to answer papal criticism with exculpatory rhetoric remained, so the authors of translatio-only texts sought other means of constructing their defense.

In both categories, authors carve out didactic spaces within otherwise often formulaic narratives. These are moments in which the authors reveal their shaping choices and efforts at influencing memorialization. In this chapter, I have identified four techniques used by all nine of the sources, as well as three additional techniques used most commonly by the pious-theft narratives. All of the translatio narratives contain moments of digression, depictions of communal ratification, miraculous interventions, and invocations of providential history. Each of these four techniques, or concepts, allows the author to link the specifics and the complications of the Fourth Crusade to broader, less contested ideas or events. The authors of the four pious-theft sources further deploy retrospective prophecy, miraculous interventions, and direct exhortations in order to universalize the significance of their relic translations. Whereas in the previous chapter I proceeded text by text, looking at the structure, form, and content of each source on an individual basis, here I draw comparisons by moving through these concepts, tropes, and authorial strategies that span the corpus. In the end, I suggest that translatio-only narratives, by blurring the significance of the Fourth Crusade, focused their narrative force on the local memorialization of relics and their accompanying stories, whereas the concept of pious theft enabled the articulation of much more grandiose claims.

Providential History

Gunther of Pairis opens the first chapter of the *Historia Constantinopolitana* with the following passage:

> All manifestations of divine power excite such intensive wonder that unextraordinary phenomena should not be judged divine. Still, we are particularly in the habit of marveling at those great and difficult deeds which that divine power deigns to display through simple persons— persons who humbly in their own sight are the least of humanity and are deemed unequal to such tasks by others. . . . Certainly, the less God's words are joined to human ability, the more the majesty of divine power shines forth within them.[2]

Statements like this operate solidly within the norms of the medieval construction of providential history—the practice of attempting to locate and explicate divine will within human events. Gunther refers to Abbot Martin as filled with *humiles*, thus invoking the standard humility topos of hagiographical discourse. He subsequently extends his analysis to the complexity of the events that brought holy relics from Constantinople to Pairis. He speaks of the judgment of others as untrustworthy and instead bids the reader to seek the will of God in the extraordinary and unlikely. This is the context in which he introduces the reader to Martin and the Fourth Crusade. He implies that had the crusade gone as planned and retaken Jerusalem (via Egypt), it would have been too easy to see God's hand at work. But through the complications of the Fourth Crusade, divine power shone forth even more brilliantly. This interpretive theme reemerges throughout the *Historia Constantinopolitana*. For example, in chapter 11, Gunther carefully links the diversion and the treaty with Alexius Angelos to divine approval. He opens the chapter with a summary of all the human factors that drove the crusaders to divert and then shifts tone: "Yet there was also, we believe, another far older and powerful reason than all of these, namely, the decision of Divine Goodness which so arranged, through this pattern of events, that this people, proud because of its wealth, should be humbled by their very pride and recalled to the peace and concord of the holy Catholic Church."[3] Gunther finds it appropriate that the Greeks lost their temporal goods and that their "sacrosanct" relics would pass into the hands of the Western church. The poem that concludes the chapter makes the same point. In the next chapter, Gunther credits the "incontrovertible Providence of God" as the driving force behind the decisions made after Zara.[4]

Like Gunther, the anonymous monk of the Monastery of San Giorgio Maggiore, in the "Translatio Pauli," repeatedly considers the relationship between divine light and the occluding darkness of sin and doubt. At two critical moments in the story, the author veers from the narrative to pursue explanatory digressions (covered more fully below) on the nature of light and darkness. He works abstractly in his consideration of the nature of divine grace, but also metaphorically. He uses the storm at sea and the fear that the ship's passengers felt as a metaphor for those who, seeing dark clouds on the horizon, doubt God's presence. When the bearer of the relics of St. Paul, a merchant named Iacobus Grimaldus, lies to the captain and crew, here too is an opportunity for explanation. The author asks the reader whether it is believable that a sin, a mere lie, could conceal the grace brought by the relics. As it happens, Iacobus claims that the box containing the relics holds only glass painted with gold. Even painted glass retains its purity, the author notes. Light passes through it. There is no shame in rendering ornate something so pure.

The author's focus on secrecy and lies, which he then excuses, emerges as an odd feature of the text. From whom were the Venetian monks hiding their theft? San Giorgio legally controlled the Monastery of Christ Pantepoptes, and the 1220s were not a particularly dangerous decade for Venetians in Constantinople.[5] The monks and Iacobus had the podestà, Marino Storlato, the quarter's absolute ruler, on their side. Perhaps they feared the privateers and pirates that frequented the Aegean and Ionian Seas, but only a fleet of warships or the blessings of a saint could have defended against these. A Venetian ship was fair game, and concealing the relic would not have helped. Moreover, no hint of that type of external danger appears in the narrative. The author wrote this as a tale of relic theft, but the monks were really only stealing the relics from themselves, and even that skirted around violations of canon law.

Even stranger than the monks' secrecy is the insistence on presenting this tale as a Fourth Crusade story. While it is true that the Pantepoptes came under Venetian control as a result of the crusade, the author ignores the passing of time between the conquest of Constantinople and the discovery of St. Paul's relics and links these legally gotten relics to the plundered sacred and secular *spolia* of 1204. In this text, the conquest does not justify the relic theft, but rather the relic theft justifies the conquest. Here, the author's theme of God's light emerging from the darkness of sin becomes central. He claims that pride and arrogance sparked God's wrath and led directly to the holy war against the Greeks. As Giorgio Cracco notes, the author stresses that the Venetians obeyed God by assaulting Greece but would have preferred to fight the "Saracens and barbarians,"[6] a point that also emerges in the Venetian text "Translatio Symonensis." The anonymous author of the "Translatio Pauli" weighs intentions against results and finds that the results reveal God's hand. Enrico Dandolo wanted to save the Holy Land but, according to the source, was driven to Constantinople. Iacobus wanted to bring St. Paul's relics home to Venice and thus lied to the sailors. The monk chastises those whose faith is weak and those who fear death, asking them to look beyond the superficial trappings of earthly life and to embrace the deeper meanings of events. He stresses that one must not be fooled by rough trappings or crude exteriors because true internal light cannot be hidden. One can read this as a commentary on the practice of relic theft. Such acts seem illicit and sinful on the surface, but the careful observer can detect an underlying sanctity and piety. One can also apply this approach to the Fourth Crusade, especially as presented in this narrative. By the 1220s, the crusade seemed to be, at best, a distraction from the Holy Land and ultimately something of a failure. Looking deeper, the author could argue, one must see the result as a manifestation of God's will.

The known disjunction between the actual events surrounding the translation of St. Paul's relics and the narrative presentation of these events renders the "Translatio Pauli" particularly revealing, but similar themes appear in most of the other texts in the corpus. "The Land of Jerusalem," commissioned by Nivelon of Soissons, nimbly shifts from success to failure to success, as discussed in the previous chapter, in an effort to reveal God's providential judgment in the seemingly disastrous events in Jerusalem in 1187 and Adrianople in 1205, when the new Latin Empire suffered a grave defeat at the hands of the Bulgarians. In making these shifts, the anonymous canon of Soissons faced a considerable rhetorical challenge. The Fourth Crusade never reached Jerusalem. The emperor and many other important crusaders, including some in Nivelon's own party, died in battle. By the time Nivelon returned to France, the new Latin Empire was already imperiled and critics were already setting the patterns of historical memory. The text's references to Jerusalem, itself a sort of relic of Christ,[7] reflect an attempt to reshape the meaning of the crusade, at least in the context of memorializing the acquisition of relics for Soissons and its ecclesiastical allies. Whereas other authors, particularly the Venetians, would use an act of relic theft in an attempt to cleanse the Fourth Crusade, the canon of Soissons tried to use the greater mission of the crusades, the liberation of Jerusalem, to remove any perceived stain on an ill-gotten relic resulting from a misguided campaign. Thus, the exculpatory power is localized for the benefit of Soissons, rather than extended to all who had been involved in the Fourth Crusade.

Conrad of Halberstadt's biographer simply left the Fourth Crusade out of the "Gesta episcoporum Halberstadensium" and thus, like the canon of Soissons, localized the effect of the narrative. When Conrad commissioned the text, he was concerned about his local legacy after a long career fraught with difficulty. His biographer located providential guidance amid these difficulties, culminating in the astounding interpretation of the death of Philip of Swabia, Conrad's patron. The author credits the arrival of Conrad's relics (and the saints themselves) in Germany with the death of Philip and the sudden restoration of peace to the empire. Once again, an author of a Fourth Crusade translatio bids the reader to look beyond seemingly baleful circumstances.

The pattern continues. Rostang of Cluny binds apocalyptic teleology to the events of Constantinople and Jerusalem, searching for divine guidance at work in both victory and defeat, but breaks away from such inquiries when addressing the relic of St. Clement.[8] Rostang permits the knight Dalmacius to narrate his own story, creating a disjunction in the narrative. The text from Amalfi is even weaker, as it simply wonders whether God moved the crusaders to divert to Constantinople, leaving open the possibility of human weakness as the central cause. By contrast, the "Translatio Symonensis" and the "Translatio Pauli" similarly seek to locate the will of God in both relic theft and the Fourth Crusade. Whatever the case, the complex and controversial circumstances of the crusade drove the hagiographers who memorialized relic acquisition not just to seek providential blessings, great and small, in the darkest of circumstances, but to argue that God's light shines best when emerging from the darkness of human failing.

Digression

Digression offered medieval writers a space to explore themes not readily relevant to the primary action of a narrative. The Fourth Crusade translatio authors used this in two different ways. Translatio-only writers employed digression as a means to draw attention away from the actual acquisition of relics or the complications of the Fourth Crusade. Pious-theft authors, in contrast, segued neatly off the main thrust of their narrative to extend their message beyond the confines of discrete action. For example, the author of the "Translatio Symonensis" twice uses digression to explore the nature and significance of the relic of St. Simon, and then links that significance to both the relic thieves and the parish in Venice from whence they came. A long exegesis of the seven gifts of the Holy Spirit[9] appears between the storming of the walls and the relic thieves' first foray into the city. In this section, the author alternates between lines of scripture and explanatory sentences, a structure not used to this extent elsewhere in the translatio. He ends the discussion by stating that, because of their seven holy virtues, the seven thieves were as one, and "because they shared one spirit and one faith they discovered the body of the blessed Simon, prophet of the Lord."[10] This line guides the author and the reader back toward the story itself. The thieves are named and the section concludes, "Now let us turn our stylus to their deeds and actions from which came the translation of the body of St. Simon the Prophet."[11] The phrase "let us turn" (*vertamur*) links the author to the reader via the text's unusual use of the first-person plural.

Thus, the first digression links scriptural numerology, the seven virtues, to the seven actors. The second roots the story in the hagiographical traditions of the parish of St. Simon the Prophet. It reads,

> Exploring, they went through the whole temple, and came upon a confessional where the precious body rested in a marble ark. In the right part of the confessional there was another ark, in which lay the most blessed body of St. Jacob the Just. In the left part a similar ark contained the body of Zachary, prophet of God. In the wall above the ark in which Simon lay, there was an image that displayed his miraculous work. It showed a likeness of the boy Jesus being put into Simon's arms by Jesus's most sainted mother during the presentation at the temple. Before the altar there was a deep well, not of stagnant but of living water. By virtue of the holy relics, the well had such grace that a glowing sphere (as if made of burning wax) appeared in it by day, and those who were perjured were not able to see it. Oh wondrous things which show the greatness of sanctity! Those who were not perjured could see it, and those who were perjured were not able to see it. In this way, most dear ones, we are able to consider how heavy a fault is perjury. Therefore, we must, most beloved ones, be wary of perjury and all sins, so that we might be worthy to see his glowing sphere.[12]

Although the initial lines of this passage provide a setting for the denouement that is to come, the second part plays no further role in the translatio. Perjury is not an issue in the text. The thieves do not converse about the well, the miracle of the glowing orb, or any other details of the tomb during the theft itself, perhaps because these elements were well known to the parishioners of St. Simon in Venice. According to internal evidence in the text, Pietro Steno had visited the shrine before; as a pilgrim, he would have heard sermons and stories about St. Simon's life—including his biblical role at the circumcision of Jesus, as portrayed in the painting—and the miracles that followed his death. Furthermore, although no other descriptions of this well and its miracles have been located, medieval travelers' accounts do attest to the presence of a mar-tyrium in St. Mary Chalkoprateia. Such accounts cite the relics of St. Zacha-rias and other objects related to Christ's infancy, including the circumcision. One might reasonably speculate that parishioners of St. Simon, when visit-ing the martyrium, would have focused their attention most heavily on their patron saint's relics and his stories. Other pilgrims and visitors, including those whose accounts survive, surely paid more attention to St. Zacharias, the nominal focal point of the crypt.[13] The Venetian parishioners who had been to the crypt would have promulgated the story of the tomb, well, and miracle upon returning home. The description in the "Translatio Symonen-sis" would then reflect local Venetian hagiographical traditions about the tomb of St. Simon. The digression thus binds relic, relic theft, and relic thieves to the parish that ultimately received the relic and memorialized both cru-sade and heist.

The later Venetian text on the relic of St. Paul the New Martyr uses digres-sions not only to link the theft to the crusade and Venice but also to enhance the potency of the invented components of the narrative. At two points, the anonymous monk uses a specific sin as the launching pad for digression. After Iacobus lies about the contents of the casket he carries, the author engages in a lengthy and complicated excursus on St. Paul the New Martyr, his namesake St. Paul the Apostle, and the nature of glass, gold, knowledge, and wisdom. The monk begins by stating that glass remains pure even when hidden and when we are ignorant of it; so, too, the glory of the martyr St. Paul remains present even when we are unaware. St. Paul, he claims, was never duplicitous or fraudulent. The martyr's virtues can be contrasted against "those who have not known humility of self, and inside they are full of pain and fallacy."[14] The monk says that the virtues of prudence, temperance, fortitude, and justice can be depicted as gold—as if virtue were something ornate. For scripture instructs, "Acquire wisdom as if it were gold."[15] Therefore, the author asserts that "knowledge is ornate."[16] He qualifies this statement at once by stating that he is not speaking of terrestrial, animal, or diabolic knowledge, nor the "worldly knowledge of princes, which destroys." Instead, he means that the knowledge "hidden in the mystery of God" is ornate. This digression on wis-dom concludes with a passage from James: "[As regards] the wisdom that is from above, first indeed is chastity, then peacemaking, modesty, not being stubborn [suadibilis], good unanimity, being full of mercy and good works, without judging, and being without dissimulation."[17]

When the sailors on board the ship fear for their lives during the storm—
some even thinking to cast the reliquary into the sea—the author chastises the
fearful in a second digression. He asks, rhetorically, why a child should be
born blind. He answers that it is neither because of the parents' sin nor the
child's, but a manifestation of the work of God. Thus, "if blindness comes to
be, then let us be blind. Oh marvel! Oh wonder!"[18] He admonishes his readers
to glorify the mind and not the body, and to see in the storm the hand of God
and the glorification of St. Paul. By turning his scorn upon the sailors who
feared death, the monk returns to the theme of light and darkness. In a lovely
turn of phrase (in Latin, at any rate), he writes, "O sailor, why do you fear to
perish? You were carrying that which you were carrying, and you did not know
it; you had your salvation, but you were ignorant."[19] He informs the sailor that
the light of the saint cannot be extinguished, just as the name of any man "written in the book of life" cannot be blotted out. So one should not fear the death
of the body. Indeed, if he accepts the punishment of death, he will reign with
Christ and "shine" with all things in faith.[20] Thus, the monk's two digressions
speak both to sin's inability to occlude the grace of God and to the ways that
others ignorantly misinterpret the hand of God. He extends the analysis from
the relic to the crusade to the glorification of Venice by using unimpeachable
arguments about the movement of a relic, ratified by a miracle at sea.

The digressions in the Venetian texts employ biblical quotation in a homi-
letic manner in order to claim authority for an expansive narrative. The text
from Gaeta, on the other hand, uses its long discussion on the nature of relics
and saints to bolster the significance of the relic of St. Theodore and extend its
beneficence over the community. Although perhaps paltry in scale compared
to the grander Venetian texts, this is still an example of universalizing rather
than limiting impact. Biblical quotations naturally punctuate the other hagiographical narratives, but they do not generally provide a foundation of authority for making claims about the meaning of the Fourth Crusade or relic
translation. Instead, such digressions support specific claims about the piety
of the translator and the holiness of the relic. The Halberstadt text repeatedly
veers from the important deeds of Conrad in order to explore his piety, concluding with the liturgical chant for the wrongly accused: "Iustum deduxit
Dominus."[21] Digression exalts the bishop and does nothing for the endeavor to
which he committed himself.

Digression does not serve the translatio-only narratives in the same way
as the pious-theft texts. Instead, the authors of two translatio-only texts

sought exculpatory power in the broader crusade endeavor. The most striking example, as discussed above, appears in "The Land of Jerusalem." The author of that text binds Nivelon's recovery of a fragment of the True Cross to the loss of that cross at Hattin, while similarly linking the conquest of Constantinople to the loss of Jerusalem. Conrad of Halberstadt, according his *gesta*, spent considerable time in the Holy Land, thus establishing the importance of his crusade to Jerusalem.[22] In a similar manner, Rostang of Cluny generates an apocalyptic reading of the fall of Constantinople, situating the broader crusade endeavor within an eschatological framework.[23] The Venetian texts both set up the crusade to Jerusalem as the initial goal, then credit the divine hand with shifting the focus to Constantinople.[24] These topics were covered more closely in the previous chapter but deserve mention here, as they demonstrate tactics for shaping memorialization and sharpen the comparison between translatio-only and pious-theft texts. In the latter, digressions run far afield from the main narrative thread. In the former, the narrative thread is pulled to Jerusalem and the broader crusade endeavor in order to bind the events of Constantinople to the central mission of the liberation of the Holy Land.

Direct Address

In three of the texts, authors break from third-person narrative in order to directly address the reader—monastic, ecclesiastical, or lay communities, depending on the text. Verbs shift to second person or to first-person plurals, and the authors use the vocative to instruct readers in proper interpretation. At times their tone is contentious, reflecting the bitter contestation over the meaning of the Fourth Crusade; at other times, authors write more as guides or teachers to willing followers. These passages of direct address not only reveal authorial direction but also stress points around which the authors felt a reader might go astray.

In the *Historia Constantinopolitana*, Gunther of Pairis shores up the core weakness of his text with direct address. He implies the presence of many miraculous events and sets up the expectation of dramatic moments on the high seas and Alpine passes, but ultimately includes only two visions, one told secondhand. Compared to storms or narrow escapes from pirates or even the traditional heavenly scent of incorruption, this episode lacks drama. Gunther writes that just before Abbot Martin's departure from Constantinople, Aegidius, a Bohemian cleric who had befriended Martin, had the following vision:

> Not while sleeping but while wide-awake—[he] saw very clearly (as he vehemently asserted) two angels at the very spot where the sacred relics were stored. . . . Aegidius, however, was totally ignorant of what was stored there. These angels were seen in the vicinity of the chest in which God's holy gifts were hidden, engaged in a service of wondrous devotion, praising with every reverence God, who had bestowed these articles on His servant. Moreover, when that service of divine veneration ended, with one encouraging the other, they determinedly called upon God to place under His protection that very man to whom He had given such goods, along with all who were attached to him.[25]

The next morning, Aegidius told Martin of the vision, wept, and professed his ignorance of the chest's contents, but vowed not to leave the abbot's side until whatever was in there had been taken back to the West. This way, he would benefit from divine protection on the way home. Martin, in turn, described his own vision from that very same night. He dreamed that he had traveled back to the Holy Land from Constantinople and was in Acre. In the dream, he imagined that between the Levantine city and Sigolsheim, his monastery's village, there was nothing but sea. "However," he continued, "it was so tranquil and trifling that not even a skiff, no matter how small, could fear shipwreck on it. Moreover, there seemed to be constructed overhead, in a straight line from Acre to the aforementioned village, canopied roofs of some sort, so that neither the wind, the rains, nor any other adverse circumstance of sea or ship had the power to harm the abbot in any way while under sail."[26] For any Mediterranean traveler, the idea of a roofed seascape would have been appealing. Storms and other seaborne dangers threatened the crusaders. Both Levantine and Aegean waters were teeming with pirates and privateers.[27] Gunther stresses the dangerous nature of travel in the following lines so as to elevate the impact of these visions. He promises that the next chapters will demonstrate their truth.

Suddenly, in a prose passage, Gunther turns to first-person address. As mentioned above, poems generally serve as his vehicle to instruct and frequently employ first-person verbs, but the sudden appearance of the first-person singular in this moment of prose is stylistically jarring. Gunther writes, "I should like to interject certain things at this point in our narrative. Even if everything else were false, they [the visions] would adequately prove that the things effected through Abbot Martin—both those deeds which we have already narrated and those which still remain to be told—received direction from the font of Divine Providence."[28] This statement, as admitted by the author himself, reads as an abrupt interjection that breaks the flow of the narrative. While calling attention to the visions, it also has a defensive cadence. Gunther acknowledges that some might think "everything else" untrue. Rather than asserting his veracity, he includes a sacral episode to shore up his interpretation and then promises further miracles in the poem that closes the chapter. This verse offers impressionistic images of the seaborne dangers that Martin was about to face:

> Troubling this journey; so many dangers remain
> On the seas and on land. Who can relate them all?
> There are, indeed, winds, exceedingly stormy and violent.
> There are mighty ocean waves and the distant rage of the sea,
> While the wind arouses a hostile tide.
> There are visible reefs, and there are hidden ones,
> And straight ahead Ceraunian shores for incautious sailors to dread.
> Pirates, a race filled with impiety, harass the seas,
> Bandits and other highwaymen [harass] the land.[29]

Gunther concludes the poem by addressing Martin directly:

> You [Martin] do what you do willingly. You embrace the sacred
>   plunder,
> As if it provided you with certain guarantees of your security.
> With it leading you, you will be safe, you will fulfill your vow,
> And you will render thanks to the Lord. So I, the soothsayer, pledge.[30]

Direct address is not unusual for Gunther's poems. They often speak to one of the characters, the audience, scholars, or historical figures long dead. They ring with the author's injunctions. By this point in the text, the reader has encountered Gunther's magnificent, if inaccurate, descriptions of battles and councils. He often specifically invokes medieval stories of travel and tribulation, especially the *vita* of St. Martin of Tours written by Sulpicius Severus.[31] The verses also reference *The Iliad* and *The Aeneid*, two epic poems that together tell of the destruction of an empire and the founding of a new one. Gunther implies that he too is offering a story of war, followed by a story of travel. His account of the siege, conquest, and plundering of a great city in Asia Minor delivers the former. The reader can now expect an account of a heroic journey home, especially after being presented with the above poem and miraculous visions. However, these expectations of imminent dramatic action go unfulfilled.

In describing Martin's journey home, Gunther elides the details. He writes, "It is not easy to recount all the mischances and dangers before which the abbot and those sailing with him in the same vessel repeatedly shrank."[32] Martin, the author relates, was more afraid than anyone (a comic image) because he did not want to lose the relics. The holy items were far more important to him than people's property or lives. Fortunately, we are told, God protected Martin, but Gunther describes this protection only in broad generalities. He summarizes, "Pirate vessels . . . frequently crossed his path. Once his ship was sighted, they turned tame and gentle, hailing it with every peaceful salute. It was not so much that they allowed it to pass by unharmed, as they were compelled to give it leave. For such was God's power, which could restrain pirates and guide Martin's ship to port on a safe course." Gunther wastes this opportunity to relate a stirring tale at sea, a lacuna made even more striking by the exciting seaborne episodes earlier in the narrative. Similarly, he avoids details when talking about the travel overland. He notes the dangers but reassures the reader that Martin knew that "since the same God rules on land and sea, He who had protected him on the sea would also protect him on land." Filled with fear and anxiety nonetheless, Martin set off, and "even though bands of armed men, on the march for nothing less than plunder and rapine, frequently confronted him, they were struck by sudden terror. . . . Moving out of the way, they gave safe passage through their midst to the pack animal carrying the chest with the sacred relics."[33] Again, a more explicit story of miraculous rescue would enhance both the drama and the theological significance of the translatio. God vaguely defended Martin. Where, one might ask, are the saints whose relics he carried? In other texts, the authors explicitly invoke the saints when recounting miracles. Gunther, although he does subtly allude to St. Martin of Tours's vita[34] in the above quotation, curtails the rest of the voyage through "many other dangerous, thief-filled spots," skipping ahead to Martin's arrival in Basel. The interjection "even if everything else were false" stands out as a weak attempt to fill the void, with a direct commandment telling the readers that they must believe in God's hand at work in the translation of Martin's relics.

The two Venetian texts vary in their use of direct address, though both bear connections to the digressions discussed above. The "Translatio Pauli" contains a number of exhortatory statements that command the author's monastic brethren to interpret events correctly. For example, after finishing his account of the Fourth Crusade, the author offers an interesting conclusion that he addresses to his "most beloved brothers." He writes, "And these are the circumstances from which disaster emerges, which all men disdain, for all men are given their power by almighty God. We have had it said to us, my most beloved brothers, that no one should dare to show pride, or show disdain to any other, for God stands above all, and the humble one gives thanks."[35] Like Gunther's poems, the first-person plural address serves as a didactic coda to the section that precedes the main narrative of relic transportation. Pride stands out as the principal sin of the Greek usurper and his entire race. This monastic interpretation of the Fourth Crusade, similar to the argument in the "Translatio Symonensis," argues the standard Venetian interpretation of the religious root causes of the crusade. Although the author of the "Translatio Pauli" acknowledges that the battle for the Holy Land was served by the conquest, he focuses on the sins of the Greeks as causal. They were prideful, and God laid them low by means of the Latin army. Mission accomplished. Thus, the Venetians avoid the trap fallen into by the author from Soissons, who wanted to argue that the redemption of Jerusalem was close at hand, when in fact things seemed grim for the fate of the Latin Holy Land.

The author of the "Translatio Pauli" shifts into the vocative, an even more direct form of address, in an interlude that isolates the moments in which the sailors doubt from the transcendent miracles that save them from the storm. As described previously, the sailors encounter a terrifying storm while off the coast of Cephalonia and lose their oars, mast, beam, and sails. Thinking they are about to die, the men lament their fate, weeping in terror. The author goes on the attack, rhetorically demanding to know why the sailors are afraid, given that their salvation is at hand. Then the tone shifts from exhortation to instruction. The light of Christ, the author claims, cannot be quenched, and only those who have accepted the punishment of death truly revere him faithfully and can shine (*luceat*) with him forever.[36]

The anonymous monk from the Monastery of San Giorgio Maggiore and Gunther of Pairis, both authors of pious-theft narratives, employed multiple modes of direct address in order to convey the central messages of their texts. Less significant use of direct address appears in the "Translatio Symonensis." After the long theological digressions on the seven virtues of the Holy Spirit and the miraculous well at the shrine of St. Simon, the author employs first-person plural verbs (such as *vertamur*) to guide the reader back into the main narrative. The digression on the nature of saintly protection in the "Translatio caput Beati Theodori" from Gaeta begins with the verb *credimus*, a first-person plural statement of belief about the relics of the saints and the power of their patronage.[37] The text concludes with a prayer, in which *imploremus* (to God and the martyrs for their blessings) serves as the principle verb.[38] The two first-person statements bracket the third-person narrative of relic acquisition (confiscation in this case) and translation by Peter Capuano to Gaeta.

Communal Ratification

Although the anonymous monk of Gaeta directs his closing lines to *fratres*, he also draws in the broader community. The brothers are the audience of the source and function as the believers (again, *credimus*) whose prayers are so important, but the city of Gaeta is the one deserving of God's protection (*civitas Caietana munitur*).[39] It is on the city's behalf that the relic of St. Theodore is accepted by the monastery. While the lay citizens of Gaeta do not directly appear in the text, the significance of the translation relies on a dependent relationship between lay and monastic communities. Highly localized communities, in fact, appear in various forms across the corpus of Fourth Crusade narratives in order to ratify or otherwise lend significance to an act of relic translation. As with the Gaetan example, such acts of ratification often overlap with statements of direct address. Upon a new relic's arrival, communities rally to venerate it and experience miracles that affirm the saint's pleasure at the relic's new home. Corrective miracles punish nonbelievers. In the Venetian cases, drawing on long local hagiographical traditions, communities and contracts appear throughout the texts, a subject considered more closely in part III of this book. The general prevalence of communal ratification in the corpus reveals a commonality among otherwise diverse texts. This commonality speaks to the core medieval function of the cult of saints and relics as a creator of communal identity. This, in turn, supports the argument that Fourth Crusade translatio and pious-theft narratives were intended to create or support specific commemorative patterns for the crusade within their specific communities.

In the Soissons narrative, local dissenting voices appear before supportive ones. As discussed in the previous chapter, the text concludes with two cases. First, just after Bishop Nivelon declared the feast day of St. Thomas to be a special holiday, "many persons, inspired by the spirit of the devil, objected."[40] But one woman, driven insane, was brought to church. Her family and neighbors prayed for her and St. Thomas healed her. Not so the unlucky carpenter who was struck dead for daring to work on the feast day, or the many others in the area who "experienced such losses from their work, either corporally or in their affairs, that thereafter they dared nothing of the kind; rather, equally flocking together with the multitude of the people at the church and giving thanks for things seen and heard, they established and made the day solemn by their throngs."[41] This passage begins with the "throngs" resisting veneration of the new saint, but after he cures a sick woman and smites a recalcitrant craftsman, their attitude is transformed. The narrative ends here, with the community safely under the protection of St. Thomas.

For the cathedrals of Amalfi, Langres, and Halberstadt, as well as the parish of St. Simon in Venice, communal ratification depended on preexisting ties between a specific religious house and a saint whose relics had been claimed by a crusader. The texts from Langres and St. Simon make such ties most clear. Walon of Dampierre, throughout his quest for authentication and authorization, bases his claim to the head of St. Mamas on the veneration for St. Mamas already taking place at the cathedral in Langres. The papal legates hand the relic over to Walon on the strength of his historical claim and the great love for St. Mamas expressed by the (absent) citizenry of Troyes. Even the Greek monks from whom the relic was plundered grant permission for the translation, similarly moved by history and love.[42] The unlikelihood of such permission being freely given makes the narrative force of the episode even more significant. The community in absentia enables the translation and is rewarded, promptly, with miracles. The acknowledgment of Langres's rightful possession of St. Mamas by both legates and monks wipes clean any stain of sacrilegious looting. In fact, Garnier of Troyes is elevated to the status of protector of relics for the whole crusade body. Throughout, the text from Langres acknowledges the papal narrative of outrageous pillaging of churches, while making it clear that *its* relic should not be lumped together with the rest. This insistence on a special status for the head of St. Mamas localizes the exculpatory power of the translatio-only narrative. Only Langres is free from blame—not like those other places with their ill-gotten sanctities.

In the "Translatio Symonensis," the parishioners of St. Simon the Prophet repeatedly claim to be acting not just for their fellow conspirators but for the entire parish back home. The author, too, distinguishes the actions of the thieves from other crusaders, but not by appealing to external human authorities. Instead, he assures the reader that while other crusaders lusted only for the gold and silver that could be found in the "fortifications, palaces, and buildings," the seven parishioners of St. Simon were "better men, because of the seven gifts of the Holy Spirit. By these gifts they were driven to hunger and to thirst for justice as The Lord says in the gospel: 'Blessed are those that hunger and thirst after justice, since they etc. [sic].'"[43] "Justice," in this case, seems to indicate the acquisition of the relic of St. Simon for the people who have venerated his name for so many generations. Unlike Walon, the author does not make this case explicitly, but finds various paths to make the communal will behind the relic theft clear. At the very beginning of the text, he writes, "In the aforementioned city, there was a church consecrated to the honor of the blessed Simon the prophet, who was worshiped by the parishioners there with great affection and eagerness. They were most Christian people, filled with the Catholic faith, and most eager to serve the army of Christianity."[44] In conversation, the seven thieves constantly refer back to their parish, drawing links between home and the shrine in Constantinople. Pietro Steno, one of the two originators of the plan to steal the relic, at one point recounts a visit to the shrine with his uncle some years prior to the crusade. Later, Steno reveals his dream of having been back in his parish church and serving Leonardo, the rector. In the dream, he is the only one there to help Leonardo. Steno interprets his solitude not as a sign of dereliction of duty by his fellow parishioners, but as indicating that they need him to act on their behalf, despite his fears.[45] Those parishioners are not physically present at the shrine, so Steno must muster his courage and touch the relic. The text concludes with the great clerics of Venice joining with the parishioners in St. Simon's small church in order to attend the installation of the relic and exalt the occasion with their presence.

The Halberstadt and Amalfi texts note the long-term veneration of St. Stephen and St. Andrew, respectively. As with most other translatio-only narratives, both avoid discussing the process by which the relics were acquired and hence lack the narrative space to draw the ties to communal ratification more firmly. Still, in all four texts, the power of past communal veneration explicitly enables the present acquisition in Constantinople.

Retrospective Prophecy

At the climax of the "Translatio Pauli," in the middle of the storm, the sailors gather round the casket to pray. The author writes that they collectively issue a powerful prayer begging the saint to intercede and free them from the danger of death. Next, the narrator sets the stakes for the success of this prayer. He writes, "Just as the blessed martyr Paul's brother in name and race, the master and blessed apostle Paul said to Caesar . . . that Rome would profit greatly via faith in Christ, so too with this blessed martyr if he allows himself to be escorted to Venice. And if he is escorted to Venice, it is not a prediction, but fact, that similar wonders will be made [here]."[46] The sea and winds, the story continues, calm within the hour.

This passage sets up the key miracle of the text, a miracle that enables the act of translation to go forward. These lines affirm that a successful translation will indicate the saint's pleasure with the "escort" to Venice. The miraculous calming of the sea and wind, along with the triumph of the light over darkness, demonstrates divine approbation for the act of piety. The eventual installation of the relic in San Giorgio Maggiore finalizes the translation and manifests its justification. Note that the supplicants assert that their prayer is not prophetic, but instead it functions as an "if . . . then" statement. If, according to the praying sailors, the saint permits his relic to be translated, then Venice will reap the profit. The author, writing after the fact, uses the present tense of a dramatic narrative to emphasize the significance of this act of translation.[47] But now, with the relic installed, he can confirm that just as Rome rose under Christianity, so too will Venice. Of course, at the time he was writing, it was convenient that the Rome of the East, the city of Constantine, had just fallen to Venetians (and others) and that Venice was newly proclaiming itself "lord of three-eighths of the Roman Empire." From the perspective of a thirteenth-century Venetian monk, the Apostle Paul's prediction to Caesar now signified the imperial legacies that Venice was just beginning to appropriate, a theme explored more thoroughly in part III.

This type of retrospective analysis portrayed as prophetic or prospective vision appears in other spots throughout the corpus of Fourth Crusade hagiographical texts, as well as in the chronicle of Robert of Clari.[48] In the *Historia Constantinopolitana*, Gunther of Pairis relates a similar prophecy about Abbot Martin's safe arrival in Pairis, though he focuses on the man rather than the relic. As noted above, Martin's vision is presented to the reader as the key piece of evidence for divine authorization of relic theft.[49] This ratifying vision specifically promises him a safe journey home. The text, of course, was commissioned by Martin after his successful journey. Thus, the vision functions similarly to the retrospective prophecy in the "Translatio Pauli," with a key difference. Whereas the Venetian text binds its prophecy to the translation of the relic, the text from Pairis focuses on the safe return home of the man.

In the "Gesta episcoporum Halberstadensium," a prophecy turns Conrad's attention from the Holy Land back to the crusade. A hermit in Ragusa predicts the fall of Constantinople as Conrad passes through on his way to Acre. After "divine aid" cures Conrad of malaria, he indeed hears of the victory. Because the prediction had come true, the bishop views it as clear evidence of God's will.[50] The reader, who has been regaled with all the signs of divine grace granted to the persecuted Conrad, is encouraged to do likewise.

Miracles

Miracles provide proof—proof of authenticity, divine favor, the sanctity of a holy person, and the propriety of a relic translation. In the corpus of Fourth Crusade narratives, miracles can either localize or universalize meaning. Authors of translatio narratives traditionally employ miracles to authenticate first, then bind the authenticated relic and saintly presence to the translator. Although the medieval translatio miracles appear in great variety throughout the broader genre, they generally function as one of three types: first contact, travel, or installation. The moment when a would-be translator lays his or her hands on a relic provides a critical narrative junction in which the medieval hagiographer builds suspense and then reveals the relic with rhetorical flourishes and miracles that connote incorruptibility. Once the relic is safely in the possession of the translator, miracles occur to ease the difficult passage across borders and over the water. The saint's in-transit acts specifically ratify the movement of the holy object, especially as natural or human obstacles are brushed aside. Counterexamples, which proliferate in medieval hagiography, reveal the potency of such miraculous interventions. Saints frequently strike down the impious relic thief at the moment of acquisition or in transit, or else compel the sinner to return the relic to its rightful place. But even these miracles could ultimately ratify a translation. For example, during the First Crusade, Gerbault, a priest from Lille, stole an arm reliquary of St. George from a monastery in Asia Minor. He went blind as he fled with it, returned the relic and begged for forgiveness, had his vision restored, and then was given the reliquary by the awed monks. Unfortunately for Gerbault, he failed to pay proper respect to the relic after returning to camp and so fell ill and died.[51] Gerbault's fate is instructive. It follows the traditional conventions of the genre of translatio and places those conventions within a crusade scenario. Few of the texts from the Fourth Crusade cling to these genre norms, with the consequence that the narrative force provided by direct saintly intervention is considerably muted.

Rostang of Cluny repeatedly invokes divine will and sets his text within an apocalyptic framework, as noted earlier. This narrative contains the unusual shift from third person to first person halfway through, as Dalmacius of Serciaco relates his tale directly, but neither the Cluniac monk nor the crusader knight describes any miraculous interventions. The translatio of the head of St. Mamas, translated via Garnier of Troyes and Walon of Dampierre, likewise offers no accounts of miracles at acquisition or in transit. The anonymous canon of Langres included the "Translatio Mamantis" in a larger set of hagiographical texts related to the cult and relics of St. Mamas in Langres. These texts do attest to a history of miracles in the course of the saint's veneration, as one would expect, but the *inventio* itself contains no specific miracles. The text from Gaeta is similarly devoid of miracles, though the prologue on the cult of relics makes it clear that one venerates relics in order to gain their blessings over the community. The author hopes that the presence of St. Theodore will help the people of Gaeta "extinguish the flames of their own defects,"[52] a goal both abstract and monastic. These three texts do not demonstrate the direct linking of relic and saint so common in medieval translatio.

The text from Halberstadt presents much the same type of narrative, as an indirect divine act occurs only in the "strange death" of Philip of Swabia, discussed above. Given that this text is more properly considered *res gesta* (with the *adventus reliquarium de Grecia* as an addendum) rather than strict hagiography, the absence of direct miraculous intervention from the saint is not surprising. And yet the language surrounding the death of Philip alludes to hagiographical concepts. The arrival of the "tokens of saints" in Germany, according to the author, brought "peace."[53] The death of Philip, *mirabili regis Philippi occasu*, is presented as the *mirabili . . . iudicio Dei*. The double *mirabili* and the causal link forged between translation and the wondrous judgment of God permit the reading of the death and subsequent peace as miraculous.

The narrative from Soissons relates a number of direct miracles that provide the occasion for communal ratification of the translation. Both positive (curing) and negative (smiting) miracles reflect standard tropes. That the saint who represents doubt (the Apostle Thomas) is himself doubted offered the anonymous canon the chance to play with hagiographical traditions. Medieval hagiographers frequently introduced doubt only to crush it via miraculous intervention, just as one finds in this text. However, given the author's evident familiarity with hagiographical norms, the lacunae in the text stand out more starkly. For instance, the author provides a stirring account of the final assault on the walls of Constantinople on April 12, 1204. Bishop Nivelon's great ship, the *Paradiso*, provided one of the key routes of ingress onto the walls. One of his men, a *milites* named André d'Ureboise, reached a tower and cleared a space for others to follow. The city belonged to the Latins! The text then abruptly skips the month in which Nivelon presumably took possession of his relics. Instead, we are immediately presented with the coronation of Emperor Baldwin at Nivelon's hand (despite the fact that the bishop was from the other imperial claimant's party) on May 16, 1204, with even the Greek citizens applauding. In the next lines, Nivelon sends relics home with authenticating documents (*cum litteris suo sigilo signatus*).[54] The author thus omits the period between April 12 and May 16—the critical window in which miracles typically associated with relic discovery, or even pious theft or looting, might occur. The miracles begin only once the whole lot of relics has been safely installed in various churches in Soissons and Nivelon begins rewriting the local sacred calendar. The miraculous interventions in "The Land of Jerusalem" therefore serve to localize the newly acquired saintly patronage in Soissons, while avoiding connecting the relics to the Fourth Crusade.

Other than the miraculous vision already discussed, the *Historia Constantinopolitana* lacks miracles. Whereas the Soissons text simply skips the acquisition of relics, Gunther of Pairis creates the expectation of a standard miraculous *translatio* narrative but does not realize those expectations. The voyage home is summarized with a list of potential threats, but no specific miraculous intervention occurs. Gunther also raises the expectation of localizing miracles in Pairis. He begins chapter 24 as follows: "Blessed be God! He alone effects wondrous miracles. In his unspeakable power and mercy, He looked upon and glorified the church at Pairis through certain gifts of His grace, which he deigned to transmit to us through the venerable man, the already frequently mentioned Abbot Martin. The church of Pairis now exults in their presence, and any soul faithful to God is assisted by and profits from their protection."[55] No details follow the setup of the miracles effected by God and the specific profits for those venerating the new relics. The *Historia Constantinopolitana* ends up universalizing its argument for divine sanction instead of localizing, a peculiar twist unique to this text. The arguments for providential blessing are constant, as providential history permeates the source, but Abbot Martin becomes oddly marginalized, lampooned, and even ignored. Miraculous proof of God's blessing is oddly absent.

The text from Amalfi joins both complete and fragmentary texts from Venice in embracing the full potential of translatio as a genre. While weak on providential history (it meekly accounts for the diversion to Constantinople as stemming from either "human or divine leadership"), the narrative concludes with a dramatic account of miraculous intervention at sea. In the midst of a great storm, the frightened sailors pray and St. Andrew appears before them, calling out, "Surge et vade!" He names himself the "apostle whom you called" and calms the sea. Further miracles follow the arrival of the relics in Amalfi, continuing a long tradition of miraculous intercession on-site. The miracle at sea focuses attention on the transit and the saint's approval of both the process of being moved and the men responsible for the deed.[56]

The miraculous acts of saints in transit from Constantinople to Venice occupy a central position throughout the Venetian hagiographical response to the Fourth Crusade. As a group, these texts stand out from the sources examined above. The narratives of St. Paul the New Martyr and St. Simon the Prophet both offer specific miracles. St. Paul calms the sea during a storm. St. Simon's relic emits first a heavenly scent and then a divine light, the latter making its concealment all the more difficult. In the "Translatio Pauli," miracles ratify the theodical predictions of the author. In the "Translatio Symonensis," they exculpate the sins of the seven thieves, who otherwise lack the societal clout to translate the relics of their patron saint. Miracles, for Venice, authorize the act of translation, elevate the status of Venice as host to the saints, and rearticulate the meaning of the Fourth Crusade.

Conclusion

The previous chapters on the textual hagiographical responses to the Fourth Crusade reveal a key commonality. Recipients of relics faced a consistent challenge in promoting their new acquisitions. Some seem to have concealed the provenance of their new saintly patrons, leaving only arguments *ex silencio* as evidence for the meaning of a Fourth Crusade relic to a local community. For example, local Bruges tradition links the relic of the Holy Blood to Thierry of Alsace and the Second Crusade, but no evidence for that attribution has been located. The Fourth Crusade and Baldwin of Flanders make for a more likely provenance, but one erased by local hagiographical tradition.[57] In a similar vein, some of the hagiographers who did link their relics to 1204 still went through rhetorical contortions to exempt these relics from the stain of papal or other condemnation. Through digression, compression of the historical narrative, or deviation from the traditions of pious theft, translatio-only authors attempted to separate their relics from the broader context of the crusade. Given that the crusade in fact enabled the acquisition of the relics, such texts often end up disjointed or riddled with lacunae. The idea of relic theft, for those willing to wield it, transformed the fact of relic acquisition into a tool that not only could repel criticism of the crusade and the looting of churches but could also build an edifice for larger claims of *translatio imperii*. The final section of this book explores one such outcome.

PART III

OUTCOMES

5

Translatio and Venice Before and After 1204

The previous four chapters of this book have examined the translatio narratives of the Fourth Crusade in their immediate contexts and in comparison to one another. But each discrete act of hagiographical memorialization operated within highly localized diachronic cultural systems. Specific cultural norms governed the sites in which hagiographers engaged in contesting the memory of the Fourth Crusade. These localized norms interacted with the pressures from Rome, the stories generated by returning soldiers, and other respondents to the events of 1204. Pull on any narrative thread from any one of the sites that produced translatio texts and you will find long cultural chains connecting a specific narrative to its locality.

In most cases, the interaction between local culture and translatio seems to have been unidirectional. New relics may have reshaped or refocused localized devotional practice, but commemorative practices generally reflected local traditions instead of transforming them. In most cases, we lack evidence that would link the relics of 1204 to broader cultural change. Venice provides an exception. This chapter places the Venetian hagiographical responses to the Fourth Crusade at the heart of Venice's cultural transformation in the thirteenth century. Venetian translatio narratives, for all their paucity and erratic composition, offer a window onto the metamorphosis of Venetian identity that began after the Fourth Crusade. The narratives link the cultural history of the merchant republic of the eleventh and twelfth centuries to the mighty but imperiled maritime empire of the later Middle Ages.

The totality of the way in which late medieval and early Renaissance Venetians integrated their myths into their lives has long impressed scholars.[1] By the late thirteenth century, Venetian "mythmakers," including church and state leaders, artists, and historians, began to reshape cultural narratives based on a new understanding of Venice's unique past. By the fourteenth century, the mythmakers had gone a step further and reimagined their history from the very beginning, inventing new stories when the old ones did not seem to be sufficiently august. Mythographers such as Doge Andrea Dandolo (ca. 1307–1354) subordinated all forms of media to the purpose of reinforcing the Venetian myths. Works of history and art, civic ritual, political posturing, epistolary traditions, architectural choices, and even the explicit policies enacted by the rulers all reflected Venice's constructed self-perceptions. Out of a reimagined glorious past, the mythmakers of Venice hoped to prove the eternal nature of the city's perfection.[2]

By the fifteenth century, the myth and anti-myth of Venice had been firmly established not only in the Veneto but throughout Venetian terra firma and the broader Mediterranean world. The positive view presented a city of free people who had ever protected their independence and whose patriciate was composed of wise and pious rulers who protected the common good, practiced perfect justice, and patronized the arts. To those opposed to Venice, the Venetians were domineering megalomaniacs who cared only for their own power and avaricious gains and would use anyone and any justification to get their way.[3] As James Grubb writes, "Anti-myths have remained within the terms of discourse staked out by the mythmakers and so have actually reinforced the hegemony of the myth. Image and counterimage contend within a single arena."[4] Both popular writers and scholars have often imposed the well-known myth and anti-myth of Venice on the much earlier Venice of Doge Enrico Dandolo.

During the centuries before the Fourth Crusade, Venetian cultural production lacked the monomaniacal totality and emphasis on centrality exhibited in its later mythography. High medieval Venice relied on diversified centers of religious life, political decision-making, and economic activity. Venetian culture prior to 1204 focused on an ongoing contemporary transformation from relatively humble beginnings to regional prominence, rather than a retroactive re-creation of imagined past glory.

Translatio—defined as practice, hagiographic genre, and broader hermeneutic—provides a link between the production of civic identity in Venice before and after 1204. Part III of this book follows the thread of translatio through Venetian culture, beginning with a brief overview of translatio and religious identity in Venice prior to 1204. The heart of chapter 5 links the Venetian hagiographical responses to the Fourth Crusade to the slow transformation of Venetian mythography in the crusade's aftermath. I argue that the post-1204 translatio narratives reveal the application of themes long resident in local Venetian hagiographical traditions to the new regional environment. Chapter 6 then tracks translatio into the last centuries of the Venetian Middle Ages. Even as the Renaissance myth of Venice emerged, echoes of both high medieval and Fourth Crusade translatio informed the cultural mythography of the Most Serene Republic.

Translatio Before 1204

When the seven thieves set out to steal St. Simon's relics on Palm Sunday of 1204, they were imitating the acts of many Venetians before them. Which stories the thieves consumed are unknown, but three stories of relic theft dominated Venice's religious culture, and any medieval Venetian participating in urban life would have had access to them through text, oral transmission, liturgical commemoration, and public visual narrative. The hagiographers and iconographers of early thirteenth-century Venice, including those who commemorated the spoliation of Constantinople, directly echoed earlier translatio narratives in their own creations. Moreover, thief, artist, and hagiographer alike were consumers of a local cultural tradition that prioritized the acquisition and repurposing of foreign sacred objects in order to enhance Venetian power and status.[5]

Translation from the eastern Mediterranean and neighboring Aquileia, in fact, dominates the hagiographical discourse of pre–Fourth Crusade Venice. As Venice emerged from under direct Byzantine control and carved out an independent niche in the northern Adriatic, Venetian leaders, clerics, and artists consciously sought symbols to support the new status. Translatio evolved into the key mode for claiming significance and status on behalf of medieval Venice and its inhabitants. By tracing the trajectory of an object's voyage to Venice, then celebrating its new installation, Venetians used translatio to mark contemporary transformation and growth. While in the era after 1261 Venetians began to glorify their origins and construct elaborate, and false, genealogies for their leading families, the city of the eleventh and twelfth centuries effected no such pretensions.[6] Humble, or at least clouded, origins could be overcome by acquiring greatness in the present moment. That greatness could not be spun out of nothing, but had to be taken from somewhere else. Just as economic exchange brought new families into prominence, the acquisition of sacred items and the use of newly acquired wealth to construct or decorate sacred spaces brought sacred and symbolic prominence to Venice.[7]

The long history of translatio and Venice begins in the Adriatic city of Aquileia. As early as the fourth century, the Aquileans fabricated a relationship between St. Mark and their city. According to local tradition, St. Mark traveled from Rome to Aquileia after composing his gospel in Rome, founded the Aquilean church, consecrated a bishop named Hermagoras (who in turn consecrated his disciple Fortunatus), and then went to Alexandria, where he was martyred. Hermagoras and Fortunatus became the patron saints of Aquileia.[8] The tradition forked when the Lombards invaded northern Italy and the patriarchate of Aquileia fled to the nearby island of Grado, taking the relics of Hermagoras and Fortunatus. Once the Lombards converted to the Latin rite, "old" Aquileia attempted to retake its lost territory and relics from "new" Aquileia on Grado, and the local secular powers became involved. Venice, at the time a mere Byzantine colony, gradually emerged as the major patron of Grado. Over the following centuries, the two rival patriarchates and their various secular allies frequently found themselves in papal courts or in armed conflict over the issues of ecclesiastical jurisdiction and revenues.

When two Venetian merchants stole the relics of St. Mark from Alexandria in 827 C.E., they transformed the Venetian religious landscape and shifted the ecclesiastical balance of power in the northern Adriatic. The arrival of the new relics occurred at a particularly auspicious time for Grado and Venice, as the papacy had recently ruled that Aquileia was the "true" patriarchate and alone could claim apostolic descent from St. Mark.[9] Possession of the relics, however, trumped papal approval in terms of regional sacred prominence. The symbolic translation of St. Mark's legacy to the northern Adriatic led directly to an actual furtive translation of his relics, and by extension St. Mark himself, to Venice. A translatio narrative that recorded the deeds echoed throughout subsequent Venetian cultural production, shaping Venetian mythographic discourse for the next several centuries.

Some form of civic commemoration of the translation must have begun quite soon after the actual event, but the historical record remains clouded until the eleventh century.[10] The earliest surviving Venetian relic-theft text, which likely dates from between 1050 and 1094, marks the beginning of the high medieval period of translatio and its appropriation in Venetian culture.[11] An anonymous author composed the narrative around the same time that the doges of Venice began to transform their private chapel of San Marco into a grander site for all state religious functions.[12] Within the church, mosaics not only depict the translation of St. Mark's relics but also invoke translation in the broader sense. For example, the central mosaic behind the altar depicts St. Peter handing the Gospel of St. Mark to St. Mark himself, who is about to hand it to his Aquilean disciple St. Hermagoras (see fig. 1).[13] In this metaphorical translation, the sacred object is linked visually to the translated relics of St. Mark positioned directly below.

By the time the Venetians constructed their hagiographies of 1204, both the specifics of the story of St. Mark's relics and the ideas that the story engendered permeated Venetian culture. Certain elements of the "Translatio Marci" specifically influenced the later Fourth Crusade texts. The story follows two Venetian merchants, Bonus and Rusticus, who are in Alexandria despite a ducal

Fig. 1   Mosaic of St. Peter, St. Mark, and St. Hermagoras. San Marco, Venice. SM0003, Image Collections and Fieldwork Archives, Dumbarton Oaks, Trustees for Harvard University, Washington, D.C. Photo: Ekkehard Ritter.

embargo against trading with Egypt. An evil Islamic sultan threatens the relics of St. Mark, and the merchants convince the Orthodox priests to let them smuggle the relics out of the city. The author singles out the Venetian people, in their entirety, as especially pious defenders of the saints and Christendom and juxtaposes human weaknesses against divine grace. Each of these elements reemerges in the commemoration of the Fourth Crusade relics.

The doges of Venice quickly associated themselves with the cult of St. Mark. Two later major relic thefts engaged the broader population and other power centers of Venice in the practice of translation and post-translation veneration.[14] In 1100, a Venetian fleet, led by the doge's son and the bishop of Castello (in Venice), embarked for the Holy Land to take part in the late stages of the First Crusade. On their way, they stopped at the shrine of St. Nicholas on the island of Myra.[15] Venice's leaders had coveted the relics of St. Nicholas for some time but knew that the Bariense had stolen the relics from the island of Myra a decade earlier.[16] Still, the two Venetian elites thought they might see if anything could be salvaged. Once on the island, through miraculous intervention, the bishop discovered the "true" bones of St. Nicholas in the tomb of his uncle.[17] While the translatio of St. Mark involved two wayward merchants, the adventure of 1101 established an important example for subsequent generations of Venetian elites. Thomas Madden writes, "Thus began a tradition emblazoned in the service of the faith."[18] Part of this tradition involved translatio. In the wake of 1101, the translatio narratives and related liturgical, visual, and presumably oral traditions directed Venetians to serve the church and Venice's own interests by seizing valuable, meaningful objects from the East. Once brought home, these objects were enshrined in new local practice. This pattern would reemerge after 1204.

The theft of St. Stephen the Protomartyr from Constantinople followed in 1107/8.[19] While in Constantinople, a lone monk of the San Giorgio Maggiore, Venice's principal monastery, stole the relics of St. Stephen. He had to wait out the subsequent tumult in the city resulting from the theft but eventually boarded a ship bound for Venice. No contemporary translatio survives, but both contemporary archival evidence and later tradition places seventy-two members of Venice's leading families on board the ship. A storm threatens, the citizens pray, the ship is saved, and the merchants, many of whom had been newly enriched by trade with Constantinople, form a confraternity in the saint's honor.[20] In this case, merchants and the lone monk of San Giorgio followed the pattern set by Bonus, Rusticus, and those who memorialized the theft of St. Mark.[21]

Thus, all of the classes of Venetian society participated in the acquisition and veneration of the three saints. St. Mark, stolen by merchants, became the ducal patron. St. Nicholas, stolen by a bishop and crusading nobles, operated as the patron of sailors. St. Stephen, stolen by a monk, became the saint of merchants. However, the totality of engagement with translatio belies the relatively small number of saints stolen by Venetians from the East before 1204. To Mark, Nicholas, and Stephen one can also add St. Tarasius in the early eleventh century[22] and perhaps St. Isidore from Chios.[23] Art historians examining eastern influence in Venetian art also consider the many sacred objects and fragments of relics sent to Venice as gifts from Byzantium. In comparison, at least twenty-five relics, some of very important saints, came to Venice between 1204 and 1267, all as a result (to a greater or lesser extent) of the Fourth Crusade. Those relics included fragments of the True Cross, drops of milk from the Virgin, an ampoule of Christ's blood, a piece of the column of the Flagellation, and other relics pertaining to the life of Christ. The fall of Constantinople produced a torrent of translatio.

For Venice, perhaps alone among medieval cities, translatio operated consistently as the dominant mode of mythmaking. Medieval Venice had a unique tradition of using translatio, appropriation, and various forms of transfer to enhance its status. Translatio, as a concept, thus made deep inroads into Venetian identity and prepared the city for the bounty of the Fourth Crusade.

Translatio and Empire

The Fourth Crusade transformed Venice. Translatio provided a hermeneutic through which Venetians developed cultural responses to this transformation. In turn, the growing pains of empire shifted the meaning of translatio for Venetian cultural innovators. The crusade brought Venice mercantile access to the Black Sea for the first time, domination of the Aegean through its acquisition of the Dardanelles, and continued control over the Adriatic through the conquest of Zara, Corfu, and Durazzo. But Venice's leaders initially avoided empire building. Enrico Dandolo could likely have engineered a winning vote for the throne in Constantinople, but Madden persuasively argues that he had no legal authority to do so on behalf of Venice and no personal interest in carving out a new dynasty.[24] Instead, Dandolo acquired Thessalonica and the patriarchate of Constantinople for Venice and then promptly traded the former to Boniface of Montferrat in exchange for Crete as part of a peacemaking deal between Boniface and the new emperor Baldwin.[25] After Dandolo died, the new doge confirmed that the podestà and the Venetian colony in Constantinople, not Venice, would hold three-eighths of the Roman Empire. In any event, neither the colony nor Venice made any initial attempt to subdue Crete.[26] The Genoese then entered Aegean and Ionian waters, took Crete in 1206, and sparked a rebellion against Venice in Corfu.[27] When the potential for Genoese control over Crete threatened Venetian trading interests, the Venetian government dispatched Ranieri Dandolo, son of the late Doge Enrico, to attack Corfu and other Genoese interests. In 1207, Doge Pietro Ziani stripped the podestà in Constantinople of the title of lord of three-eighths of the Roman Empire and assumed it himself.[28] In 1208, he sent a fleet to take Crete, a process that came to a close by 1211.[29] The era of Venetian empire had begun.

When it came to both church property and Constantinople's most important relics, Venetians seemed to follow a similar pattern of protecting their current interests rather than seeking radical expansion. The Venetian government forced the first Latin patriarch, a Venetian named Thomas Morosini, to swear an oath to protect the rights and perquisites of the patriarchate of Grado. Since the days of the alliance between Alexius I and Venice, the Byzantine emperors had allowed Grado to manage most of the Latin churches within imperial domains. Venice's clergy were loath to lose such profitable positions of oversight to a new Latin patriarch. Morosini's appointment led to two decades of arguments among the papacy, French clergy in Constantinople, French clergy in France and Rome, Venetian clergy in Venice, Venetian clergy in Constantinople, and the secular patrons for all of these groups. Instead of viewing Morosini as a symbol of Venetian aggression, greed, and colonial ambitions, however, we should regard his appointment as conservative. Venice wanted to maintain the rights and privileges that had brought it such wealth.

Similarly, Dandolo and elites back in Venice were careful not to let the relics taken from Constantinople erode Venetian hagiographical traditions. This was not a new concern. When the relics of St. Nicholas were brought to Venice, they were isolated on the Lido, so that they might not rival St. Mark. In other sites in the Latin West, new relics from Constantinople wholly transformed local devotional practice. Troyes's cathedral gained great wealth through its possession of the relics of St. Helen of Athyra.[30] Fragments of the True Cross

from Constantinople became focal points of religious devotion in many locations.[31] Patrick Geary suggests that the sheer bulk of relics from Constantinople devalued all but the greatest of holy items in the eyes of the devout. In
many cases, a focus on the Passion (represented by the cross fragments) and
the Eucharist replaced traditional intense veneration of a local saint.[32] The
acquisition of the relics of the Passion in 1239 transformed French royal iconography.[33] Nivelon of Soissons encountered resistance in trying to promote
the veneration of St. Thomas and had to use his position of authority to overcome that resistance.[34] Venice had staked its identity on its relationship to St.
Mark; therefore, all future relics, no matter how desirable, had to fit into an
appropriate relationship to the evangelist. In 1238, for example, Venice briefly
possessed the Crown of Thorns, but made no attempt to keep it. Venetians
sought new sacred items that would enhance, but not preempt, existing devotional traditions. The authors of the translatio narratives of 1204 walked this
fine line through careful use of the preexisting tropes of translatio, even as
they responded to the challenges of a new age.

"Translatio Symonensis" and "Translatio Pauli"

The translatio narratives from the Fourth Crusade reveal the development of
Venetian myths in the following categories: invocations of Venice's sacred
past, characterizations of Venetians as a race, discussions of Venice's relationship to the sea, explications of the fall of Constantinople and the Fourth Crusade, and connections drawn by the authors between the people and their
church.

The first category, invocation of the sacred past, is evident in both explicit
prose and the ways in which thirteenth-century writers structured their compositions to mimic the foundational translatio narratives of Venice. The city's
mythographers met the challenges of the Fourth Crusade by drawing on three
distinct types of relic-stealing narratives extant in the Venetian cultural lexi-
con. The identities of the protagonists provide the crucial distinctions among
the "Translatio Marci," the "Translatio Stephani" (as reconstructed from later
accounts), and the "Translatio Nicolai." The first text relates the story of two
common merchants who defied their doge. The second contains a story in
which a monk works with elite merchants. The third depicts a theft by a doge's
son and the bishop of Castello. The "Translatio Symonensis" replicates the

first. The "Translatio Pauli" has a nearly identical narrative pattern to the second. No extant text conforms to the third, but thanks to the chronicle of Andrea Dandolo, one could easily imagine that the lost stories of Enrico Dandolo, translator of relics, were similar.

By mirroring the narrative structure of Venice's foundational stories of sacred theft, the authors of the Fourth Crusade translatio texts could invoke the widely available exculpatory force of pious thievery while building upon specific Venetian traditions. While Geary's work demonstrates that some relic thefts were memorialized in the face of oppositional voices, the translation of St. Mark to Venice was a generally well-accepted tale, devoid of controversy or doubt, throughout the Latin world by 1204. If a Venetian author could demonstrate that the theft of St. Simon the Prophet was just like the theft of St. Mark, then the later translation would also become unimpeachable. To do this, the author of the "Translatio Symonensis" borrowed content, phrasing, and organizational strategies from the "Translatio Marci."

Consider the following story stripped of its details. An important saint's relics languished in a dangerous city. Christians still controlled the relics, but evil men were threatening them and the safety of the sanctuary. Secular moderate-status Venetians were driven to this locale by the will of God and discovered that the relics needed rescuing. Because they were already devoted to this saint's veneration, they decided to act. These Venetians believed that great benefit would accrue to both the relics and Venice if the theft was successful. Upon acquiring the relics, the sweet aroma coming from the saint's body miraculously informed the thieves that they had been found worthy and the saint had forgiven them for any transgressions. Upon returning home, with some difficulty, the thieves feared that they would be punished for breaking the law, but received only praise and absolution from the city's leaders. Mutatis mutandis, the above paragraph could contain an outline for either the "Translatio Marci" or the "Translatio Symonensis."

That the later author would structure his tale to parallel Venice's foundational myth is not surprising, but perhaps it should be. The actual thefts, as opposed to their portrayals in the sources, had very little in common. In the former, Bonus and Rusticus, two merchants, defied a ducal edict and took their single ship to trade in Alexandria, a Muslim city. In the latter, Venetians from St. Simon's parish were part of an enormous naval expedition that conquered Constantinople, a Christian city. Bonus and Rusticus took the relics of St. Mark with the permission of the Greek guardians and evaded the Egyptian

(Muslim) customs officers. The seven thieves stole the relics from a Greek crypt and evaded their own officials. The only Greek with whom they spoke was the old woman they paid to look after the chapel on the Bosphorus, although they never told her what was inside it. Bonus and Rusticus had to sneak out of a hostile pagan city and did so with two Greek clerics in tow. The men of St. Simon spent the six months after the theft waiting to leave Constantinople in relative comfort. The "Translatio Marci" thus tells the story of a quick, surreptitious extraction of a relic with the aid of the proper guardians, whereas the "Translatio Symonensis" relates an episode of carefully planned looting in the aftermath of a conquest—very different indeed.

The thirteenth-century author's decision—and ability—to reshape the Fourth Crusade tale in order to match the structure of Venice's founding myth reveals the extent to which translatio had permeated Venetian society. The "Translatio Symonensis" is a profoundly local story. It focuses on relatively insignificant secular men. The text ascribes meaning from the theft to the parish, and only to Venice by implication. When the text explicitly addresses Venice's sacred past, it does so in a way that heightens the importance of the theft and the parish. The author writes, "The amount of rejoicing and praise that filled the city of Venice, and the number of seaborne miracles that God had judged them worthy to be shown, not one man in any tongue has the ability to describe. The lord Leonardo, rector, and other clerics and parishioners all took up the relics, and they asked lord Benedetto Faletro, then the patriarch of Grado, and lord Marco Nicola, bishop of Castello, whether they might come and recognize the precious gifts."[35] The phrase "seaborne miracles," or *mirabilia in mari veniendo*, connects the arrival of St. Simon to the arrival of other saints by means of the sea. God had judged the Venetians worthy of more miraculous events than the author could relate, and Simon belonged within that pantheon. The author might also be referring to the general blessings brought to Venice by the sea: trade, food supply, and protection from the mainland. These maritime blessings had a divine sponsor in St. Nicholas, the patron saint of sailors, whose (alleged) relics also came to Venice by means of the sea in the twelfth century. The author of the "Translatio Symonensis" directly connected his text to the larger history of translatio on the Venetian lagoon and then demonstrated that the parish of St. Simon was as worthy as any other part of the city. The greatest religious dignitaries in Venice came to the parish in order to authenticate and authorize the new relics. Thus, with bishop and patriarch looking on, no one could argue with the "Translatio Symonensis" taking its place among the other miracles of the sea.

The "Translatio Pauli" is even more explicit. When the prior Marcus approaches the podestà Marino Storlato, his reasons for seeking help with the relic theft are given as follows: "He asked [for help] so that the precious gem might be brought to the abbot, in order that it might adorn not only the monastery, but all of Venice. For just as innumerable men and women come from all parts to visit the blessed Mark, so too it will become the glorious custom to see the blessed Paul."[36] Just like the author of the "Translatio Symonensis," the monk of San Giorgio Maggiore wanted to connect his monastery's gain to the city of Venice and tie that city's history to the new relic. He argued that everyone should help with the theft because this deed would not only enrich the cloistered brothers of San Giorgio but bring spiritual and tangible wealth to all. The author linked the theft of St. Mark to the theft of St. Paul by comparing both the type of action (relic theft) and the resulting benefits.

Although he invoked the Marcian myth in the above passage, the monk of San Giorgio did not rely on the "Translatio Marci" as his template for the Fourth Crusade composition. Instead, he drew on the story of St. Stephen. The choice is not surprising, as both narratives feature a monk of San Giorgio taking a relic from Constantinople. The author of the "Translatio Pauli" references the translation of St. Stephen's relics explicitly, writing that all of the monks and nuns rejoiced at the arrival of St. Paul's relics, just as they had at the arrival of the relics of "St. Stephen the Protomartyr, the relics of the martyrs Cosmas and Damian, Cosmas the holy confessor," and many others. The author names some of the other relics housed in San Giorgio and alludes to still more "martyrs and virgins" than he has time to describe.[37] Although St. Stephen is the only "stolen" martyr on his list, the relics of Cosmas and Damian, a fragment of a larger set of relics,[38] were licitly translated from Byzantium in 1154. The key, therefore, was not theft but the acquisition of a new object of value from the East.

Acquisition figures prominently in the "Translatio Pauli." In the central theological discussion, the narrator reminds the reader to obey scripture and "acquire wisdom as if it were gold."[39] He adds that "knowledge is ornate."[40] These phrases were calculated to appeal to a devout mercantile audience. The writer does not imply that the acquisitive (that is, mercantile) nature of the Venetian economy is sinful, but instead that one should apply that nature to holy endeavors with the same zeal as one pursues secular wealth.[41] As a result of a holy translation, in fact, secular wealth might follow. Not only does the author mention the benefits that could accrue to Venice as a result of increased pilgrimage, but he also refers to Rome's past glory at just the moment of the miraculous calming of the winds. As discussed in chapter 4 under "Retrospective Prophecy," after describing the devout sailors' prayer for deliverance from the storm, the narrator links the positive outcomes for Christianized Rome to a similar imperial future for a Venice that receives the relics of St. Paul. This passage sets up the key miracle of the text and establishes that a successful outcome will signal the approbation of the saint. The eventual installation of the relics in San Giorgio finalized the translation. Thus, just as Christianity brought greatness to Rome, St. Paul the New Martyr will do likewise for Venice. Indeed, from the perspective of the Venetian monk writing in the thirteenth century, the Apostle Paul's prediction would appear to signal the imperial legacies that Venice was then appropriating. Notably, St. Paul the Apostle referred to Nero, the emperor of pagan Rome. It was Constantine's Byzantium that would embrace imperial Christianity, and Venice had helped conquer Constantine's city in 1204. The author of the "Translatio Pauli" forced his story into the context of the Fourth Crusade although the theft took place in 1222, involved no danger, and had nothing to do with the conquest of Constantinople. Through the reference to the Apostle Paul's prediction, the author was claiming that Venice had acquired not only a relic but also a destiny similar to the one that the apostle had predicted for Rome. The translation of a relatively minor relic signified a form of *translatio imperii*.

As a concept, translatio imperii dates back to at least Vergil[42] but found frequent expression in the Middle Ages by political thinkers who saw their civilization as an heir to the Roman Empire.[43] Moreover, by the time of the Fourth Crusade, Western ideas about the East, including their projections upon the Islamic and Byzantine worlds, the Roman past, and the Holy Land, shaped the discourse about Westerners' own identity.[44] Literary sources apply the concept of translatio imperii to signify not only the transfer of secular power but also the knowledge and learning of the ancient world (thus *translatio imperii et studii*).[45] Political theorists on both sides of the debates between the Holy Roman emperors and popes invoked the concept to bolster their respective causes.[46] Innocent III did this in his letters after the Fourth Crusade. For example, he wrote to the crusader clergy in Constantinople, "Constantinopolitanum imperium a Grecis transtulit ad Latinos."[47] Propagandists for Michael VIII Palaiologos promoted the related concept of *renovatio imperii* when he retook Constantinople in 1261, claiming that Constantine had come again.[48] Frederick II, who rose to power after the Latin conquest of Constantinople, sought to pattern his court after Caesar's, and the Holy Roman emperor's propagandists rose to the task. Frederick attempted to use "the desired halo of historical legitimacy" as a tool in his conflicts with the papacy and in positioning himself as the defender of Christianity.[49] When Frederick came to Venice in 1232 in order to visit the shrine of St. Mark, the Venetians treated him coolly. The Grand Council debated whether to allow a Venetian goldsmith to make him a crown, because it did not want to permit Frederick, a master of ritual and ceremony, to stake any kind of symbolic claim over the Republic of St. Mark. The Venetians feared that Frederick wanted to be caesar, lord over all the Romans. They wanted their *quartae et dimidiae parties totius Romaniae* (one quarter and a half of a quarter of the Roman Empire, or three-eighths) and feared that Frederick would try to deny them their due.[50]

The translation of the relics of the Passion to Sainte-Chapelle in Paris stands out as the thirteenth century's most famous case of relic-based translatio imperii and provides a useful comparative note. For Louis IX and his supporters, the great translation of relics cast France as the new Holy Land, a land chosen by God to house the Crown of Thorns. The acquisition of Christ's relics bolstered claims that the French kings had superseded the ancient role of the emperor as the defender of the faith. With the relics of the Passion, Louis had concrete evidence of his status as the "most Christian" of kings.[51] For example, he patterned his entry into Sens after the story, as recorded in *The Golden Legend*, of Heraclius's return of the Holy Cross to Jerusalem in 630 C.E.[52] French writers supported the king's conceit and, in literary compositions, linked the concept of translatio imperii to the recovery of the Holy Grail and its translation back to France.[53] However, the French had no choice but to acknowledge the newness of the relics of the Passion in France. Lacking long-standing ties to ancient Rome and Constantinople, the French monarchy and its supporters invented new ties and argued that this new status would result in many benefits for the kingdom.[54] Writers tried to make Paris into Jerusalem.

Venice, unlike France, could draw on a long-established legacy of the translation of religious symbols from east to west in the early Middle Ages. Venice also had a unique dual connection to Rome and Byzantium. Throughout Italy, city leaders in the late Middle Ages and Renaissance claimed the status of "new Rome" for their respective cities, but Venice was able to argue that it had conquered Constantinople, the "true" second Rome.[55] The author of the "Translatio Pauli" recognized the potential gain for Venice in the perceived collapse of Byzantium and sought to appropriate the prophetic promise of St. Paul the Apostle. Although the theft of St. Paul's relics took place in 1222, the author related the story as if it had taken place in the immediate aftermath of the crusade. He could have presented the relic translation as a simple bureaucratic transfer. After all, the abbot had ordered his prior to translate a relic from one religious house under his control to its mother house in Venice. Instead, the author cast the narrative as a peril-filled story of relic theft. He understood that the Fourth Crusade and the sack of Constantinople enabled his greater claims of significance for Venice and his monastery, and a theft allowed him to make stronger statements regarding the saint's preference for a new Venetian home.

Despite all these invocations of Venice's imperial heritage and hints at her destiny, neither the "Translatio Pauli" nor the "Translatio Symonensis" overstates the case for Venetian prominence, at least as compared to later medieval mythologizing of the Fourth Crusade. As chapter 6 will show, Venetian chroniclers and artists would claim that the purpose behind the crusade was to enhance Venice's glory. They suggested that God wanted to liberate the city from imperial oversight and used the holy war as the vehicle to do so. Louis IX's propagandists likewise argued that "the true meaning of the fall of Constantinople to the crusaders in 1204 lay in the chain of events it unleashed which allowed Louis to obtain relics of the Passion."[56] But neither Venetian translatio text approaches this level of audacity.

Instead, the two authors focus on the sins of the Greeks and argue that God used the crusade to punish them. The message is essentially negative. The later text, the "Translatio Pauli," contains a fuller account of the crusade, which the monk follows with a homily on pride. He writes that disaster occurs whenever men show pride; man should be humble because God is the source of all power.[57] The "Translatio Symonensis," on the other hand, focuses on the interfamily violence of the usurpation in Constantinople. The anonymous author writes that God "punishes the iniquities of fathers unto sons. He thus hated the kingdom of the Greeks on account of their iniquities. God, therefore, incited the Doge of Venice and the Count of Flanders to go against them in war, so that He might put down their arrogance and lift up their humility, and so that He might destroy the malignant and bring peace to the benign."[58] Although it presents slightly different sins as the cause of God's wrath toward the Greeks, the essential characterization of the wars remains the same. The "Translatio Pauli" mentions the war for the Holy Land, but only in passing, focusing instead on the conflict in Constantinople. The "Translatio Symonensis" ignores the greater crusade entirely. As noted above, this characterization served the apologetic purpose of the narratives, because one could argue that a holy war waged to punish the Greeks had been successful, whereas invoking Jerusalem just drew attention to the continued plight of the holy city. Discussing the conquest of Constantinople also gave the authors an opportunity to weigh the sinful Greeks against the pious Venetians, one *gens* against another. The "Translatio Symonensis" follows the model of the "Translatio Marci," beginning with a general characterization of the Venetians as a pious and good people. However, it does not particularly castigate the Greeks as a people, only blaming the "kingdom of the Greeks," as noted above. The "Translatio Pauli" praises all of the Venetians who enter the text in some detail and contains a general criticism of the Greek race at the very beginning. It states, "The Greek people, who ruled over the Empire of Constantinople, were despised and loathed by nearly all people who were in both the secular and spiritual worlds."[59]

Both texts elevate the Venetians, denigrate the Greeks, present the conquest of Constantinople as divinely ordained, and claim that the conquest was the entire point of the crusade. Each then focuses on a single relic. Through the theft of that relic, the author shifts the reader's attention from Constantinople to Venice and argues that the saint wished to leave the fallen city and take up residence in the glorious city on the Rialto. Both authors tie the thirteenth-century thefts to earlier relic thefts by mimicking the narrative structure of a preexisting translatio and by making explicit references to Venice's sacred past. Appropriating items of value from Byzantium and the East was a long-standing, venerated tradition in Venice; war and the conquest of Constantinople allowed that tradition to take on new meaning.

Fragments and *Perdita*

The medieval chronicles, inscriptions, artwork, and summaries of translatio stories in later compositions, as well as the surviving material record— reliquaries and precious objects—allow one to tease out hints of a greater discussion on the relics of 1204 in Venice. The most significant lacuna in the Venetian hagiographical records on these relics pertains to Enrico Dandolo's translation of relics. How did Venetians portray this aspect of their most famous doge? After Ranieri Dandolo died fighting the Genoese in Crete in 1208, Venice honored the family. Thomas Madden suggests that the ensuing permanent exemption from taxation was meant to reward both the fallen father, Enrico, and his son Ranieri.[60] Contemporary Venetian sources praise Enrico fulsomely.[61] In Constantinople, where, of course, many Venetians were in residence, Dandolo was laid to rest with great honor in what became a chapel of the Venetians and perhaps was even celebrated by Hagia Sophia's famous *deesis* mosaic.[62] Did Venice also glorify Dandolo as the greatest translator of relics since the thieves in Alexandria, or at least since the bishop and prince claimed the relics of St. Nicholas? In 1205, how did Venice celebrate his role in the conquest of Constantinople?[63] Specifically, does the tradition of Dandolo as relic translator, documented in the fourteenth century, extend back to the early thirteenth century? According to that tradition, Dandolo sent more sacred items back to Venice than any other person in its history. And yet no contemporary translatio exists.

One can gain some sense of the local traditions surrounding Dandolo through the Venetian chronicles. In ways that echo the arguments built into the translatio narratives, the chroniclers of Venice used the writing of history as a tool to justify their particular political viewpoints and to argue for Venetian superiority.[64] In the *Chronica per extensum descripta*, Andrea Dandolo wrote,

> The princes came upon hidden relics of saints . . . and the doge [Enrico Dandolo] obtained a marvelous cross laden with gold, which Constantine had carried in battle after the intervention of his mother, and the miraculous blood of Jesus Christ in an ampoule, and the arm of Saint George the martyr, with part of the head of Saint John the Baptist. The doge sent them to Venice and ordered them to be placed in his chapel. . . . Similarly, the bodies of Saints Agatha and Lucy, virgins, which Basileus and Augustus Constantine[65] had ordered brought from Sicily to Constantinople, were discovered. The doge obtained the body of Saint Lucy for Venice, and sent it to the monastery of Saint George, where, dedicated in his name, it was deposited. The body of the blessed Agatha the Sicilian was relinquished to certain other pilgrims.[66]

The phrase *sanctorum occultatas reliquias tamdem inveniunt* evokes the language of *furta sacra, inventio,* and *translatio.* It makes Dandolo the human agent of divine will behind the translation of relics. Given Venetian cultural history, the passage is suggestive of a lost translatio tradition. Another passage in the *Chronica* mentions the acquisition of gems and pearls for the altar table of San Marco by Angelo Faledro, a procurator of San Marco, in 1207.[67] Further entries describe, briefly, the acquisition of St. Simon the Prophet; the body of St. Helen (allegedly), taken to Venice by a canon in 1211; and the relics of St. John the Martyr (1214), St. Paul the Martyr (1222), St. Paul the First Hermit (1239), St. Theodore the Martyr (1257), and St. Barbara (1258).[68] In cases where we have extant translatio narratives or other contemporary documentation to compare to Andrea Dandolo's work, his chronicle is largely reliable, if abbreviated. He includes no details disproved by more complete sources, but he often omits information that is preserved elsewhere. For example, Dandolo names only two of the seven thieves from St. Simon's parish.[69] Out of all the people discussed in the "Translatio Pauli," the chronicler only mentions the podestà Marino Storlato and Abbot Paul of the San Giorgio Maggiore, the two highest-ranking figures.[70] Whether these omissions signify Dandolo's ignorance or his attempts at summary is unclear.

Two abbreviated chapters from a vast fourteenth-century legendary—a collection of saints' lives and miracles associated with their relics—by the Venetian Dominican Pietro Calò provide further examples of communal ratification and clerical memorialization of relic translation.[71] Calò's legendary contains more than 850 entries (standard editions of *The Golden Legend,* in comparison, tended to contain fewer than 200), many of them pertaining to specific hagiographies from the Veneto and Venice itself.[72] He was an abbreviator of local legends, but not a merger. Simon Tugwell argues that Calò "does not generally attempt to merge his sources, he prefers to respect their separate existence and he probably used them successively rather than simultaneously."[73] If this is correct, the friar's "Translation of St. John the Martyr" and "Translation of Santa Barbara" both reflect *perdita* in our record of relic memorialization in post-1204 Venice. Calò's "Translation of St. John the Martyr," though abbreviated, applies the narrative structure of the "Translatio Pauli" (itself patterned after St. Stephen's translatio) to this later event.

According to the friar, the Monastery of San Daniele received the Monastery of the Psychosostria as a gift from the brothers Marco and Martino Zorzi.[74] Prior Robaldus traveled to Constantinople in 1214 in order to take possession of it, and while there saw a large throng gathering at the church of the Theotokos. He heard that people were coming to venerate the relics of St. John the Martyr (also called "of Alexandria" or "the almsgiver").[75] Deciding to steal it, Robaldus took a monk, a priest, and a Greek servant, and "led by the zeal for God" they broke into the church through a window.[76] They took the saint's body and left via the same window. They wrapped the body in "clean muslin,"[77] hid it in Robaldus's new monastery, and subsequently shipped it off to Venice inside a casket without insignia, so that the sailors would not interfere. "Thus," we are told, "it was conveyed to Venice and deposited in the monastery of San Daniele."[78] Here is another case of a monk who, having acquired new ecclesiastical territory in Constantinople, used his position to enrich the relic treasury of his home church. Although the secular elite were not explicitly involved with the theft, Robaldus did travel to Constantinople to meet with the Zorzi brothers, who had donated the site. Just as with St. Paul's relics, the prior who acquired the corpse did not travel back to Venice with it, but attempted to ship it incognito.

Calò's text begins with a compressed account of the Fourth Crusade that focuses on the conversion of the Greek church to Latin worship as the key rationale. It concludes with a compressed account of a sea voyage. In terms of the raw narrative structure, the story closely mimics the form of the "Translatio Pauli." One can imagine the contours of a fuller translatio filled with digressions and high drama, now tragically lost, and from there wade into the hazardous waters of conjecture, imagining a fuller corpus of Fourth Crusade Venetian translatio narratives. If, in fact, a Venetian canon did bring the body (or a fragment of the body, more likely) of St. Helen to Venice, this event that Andrea Dandolo disposes of with a few terse lines would have provided another opportunity for the construction of such a translatio.[79] Although detailed records of this translation do not exist, a cross "of St. Helen" survives in the treasury of San Marco. This relic of the True Cross once belonged to the empress who converted Constantine and recovered the entire True Cross at Jerusalem. The Venetian fragment figured prominently in local political iconography during the mid-thirteenth century.

A single manuscript preserved in the Marciana Library in Venice contains a fragmentary account of the translation of St. Lucia to Venice.[80] Its provenance is uncertain; the manuscript is from the sixteenth century and the story is heavily abbreviated.[81] Given that it mentions the relic's translation from the Monastery of San Giorgio Maggiore to a new church dedicated to St. Lucia in

1280, the original source was not contemporary with the Fourth Crusade. The narrative names Enrico Dandolo, Baldwin of Flanders, and Boniface of Montferrat and omits any mention of the crusade for the Holy Land or the three Alexii. Instead, the text simply states that the Latins took Constantinople, named Baldwin emperor, and divided up the spoils. Venice received "half the city,"[82] and the Venetian citizens who lived there were often called "Venetians in name only."[83] The text then rehearses the history of the relic of St. Lucia and how it came to Constantinople, where the Latins found it, and states that Baldwin gave it to Venice.[84] The story concludes with a brief summary of the decision to build a church for St. Lucia in 1280. This manuscript therefore offers little of interest, other than noting that Baldwin himself gave the relic to Venice.

The immediate and continued veneration of St. Lucia serves as a final piece of evidence for the importance that the Venetians immediately ascribed to the new relics from Constantinople. Of all the relics translated to Venice after 1204 for which there was not already an indigenous cult, the veneration of St. Lucia seems to have found the most traction in Venetian society. Every source mentions the relic's multiple translations and takes pride in the fact that Venice became her final resting place. Lucia died in Sicily, and a Byzantine emperor claimed her corpse as plunder for Constantinople while fighting the Muslims. Then the Latins who overthrew Byzantium took the body, and Enrico Dandolo sent it home (meaning back to Italy, where she had lived). The chain of transmission from the emperor's recovery to the doge's decision would have been clear to all. A Venetian could make the connection between the first translation of the saint—taken from Italy to Greece during a war between (Greek) Christians and Muslims—and the second. In the second, the relic returned to Italy as a result of a crusade, even though no Muslims were involved.

Furthermore, St. Lucia became the most important female saint in Venice. According to Gino Damerini, visitations to her shrine became an important part of regular religious practice within the city and the region—a practice that would culminate with a great festival on her holy day, December 13. Because she was housed on the island of San Giorgio Maggiore, many Venetians would sail the short distance from San Marco to the island en masse.[85] Alas, in 1279, a winter storm suddenly blew in during the mini-pilgrimage across the canal of San Marco (where the mouth of the Grand Canal meets the lagoon). It capsized many boats and caused a number of would-be celebrants to drown. In 1280, to forestall a similar tragedy, St. Lucia was given her own church connected to the convent of the Annunciation in Cannaregio, in part because there was some fear that the storm was a result of her anger at being housed with so many other saints. As a pamphlet from 1617 records, this was her third translation. D. Giorgio Polacco, the author, wrote *Della triplicata traslazione del corpo della gloriosa Vergine, & martire S. Lucia* in order to celebrate the renaming of the Chiesa D'Annuciata as the Chiesa di Santa Lucia.[86]

In the initial aftermath of the Fourth Crusade, the stories and veneration of the relics of 1204 quickly proved important to Venice. The Venetians, particularly the conservative oligarchy who had weathered so many crises in the previous generation, were trying to figure out how best to maintain a prosperous course in an uncertain future.[87] The authors of the translatio narratives sought to find a greater meaning for Venice in the translation of relics and did so by invoking the local traditions of memorializing relic theft that had already come to define the Venetian sacred landscape. As the century continued, however, the relics of 1204 provided material for the creation of new stories, new myths, new rituals, and new claims about Venetian destiny. Thus, the reinvocation of translatio that resulted from the Fourth Crusade permeated Venetian society. Translatio became the hermeneutic used not only to interpret the past but also to seize new meaning for Venice. To some extent, all of the ways in which Venetians would invoke translatio—whether with regard to the relics of 1204, or to St. Mark, St. Nicholas, and St. Stephen, or to the more abstract translatio imperii—stemmed from the actual translation of relics and other material remnants of conquest in the aftermath of the Fourth Crusade.

6

Translatio and the Myth of Venice

On January 13, 1231, a fire ripped through the treasury of San Marco. It burned for almost a day, feeding on the wood of the inner sanctum. The fire should have reduced everything to ash. But, according to a letter sent by Doge Ranieri Zeno (r. 1253–68) to the pope in 1265, three relics survived: a piece of the True Cross, an ampoule containing the blood of Christ, and the skull of St. John the Baptist, which had been in a wooden box. Considered a miracle, the alleged survival of these relics inspired Zeno to create a new feast day in its honor. He also sent various friars and state ambassadors to Rome along with the letter describing the miracle in order to gain papal recognition. Assuming that the miracle would be recognized (it ultimately was not), the friars planned to spread the word of it in their sermons.

The thirty-four-year gap between the fire and the letter demonstrates the challenge in determining when, exactly, Venetians began using relics to bolster the myth of Venice. Does this episode reflect innovation in the 1260s, or is it just the earliest evidence for an ongoing celebration of a miracle? The move to widely promote the miracle certainly reflects change. Zeno reigned as the Latin Empire collapsed and Venice faced threats from a resurgent Byzantium and Genoa. He employed religious symbols connected to the crusades in order to boost locale morale, insult Genoa, support Venetian claims to regional dominance, connect traditions of militant Christianity to Venice's battles, and promote the power of his state. He, along with the artists and authors he patronized, created new legends, modified old ones, and did everything he could to fight Venice's enemies conceptually, even as he fought them militarily and economi-

cally. The chronicler Martin da Canal, who began writing toward the end of
Zeno's life, offers the earliest evidence for many new myths and modes of
Venetian self-representation. Over the following century, historians, artists,
and civic leaders replicated and expanded upon these myths.[1] During this for-
mative period, the Piazza San Marco was paved and the famous bronze quadriga took its august position on San Marco. The piazza became an imperial
setting for state rituals.[2] Venice began to transform from a city with wooden
houses, grass, animals, dirt paths serving as back alleys for the canals, multiple shipbuilders, and decentralized economic activity to the centralized, rig-
idly stratified city of stone streets, great *palazzi*, the Arsenale, and the market
at the Rialto.

Translatio and the relics of 1204 became central to this cultural transformation. This chapter traces the cultural aftermath of the Venetian hagiographies of the Fourth Crusade from the 1230s to the last centuries of the Middle
Ages. It extends the analysis to visual fields in which *spolia* and references to
looted relics emerge as particularly important. The key distinction between
earlier and later mythography lies in the narrative relationship to time, as
mythographers transitioned from constructions of translatio imperii to renovatio imperii. The former tracks the shift in power from the East to Venice.
The latter claims that Venice had always, at least in the eyes of God, possessed
imperial grandeur. In both cases, the movement of sacred and other material
objects functioned as a signifier for the transformation of culture.

Before 1261

The types of activities and narrative interpretations of activities from the
immediate postcrusade environment seem to have continued from the 1230s
to the 1260s. In 1258, according to Pietro Calò, a Venetian merchant named
Raphael Basilius acquired the relics of St. Barbara from Brother Simon, the
prior of the monastery where they had been kept. Having a "secret wish" to
send the relics to Venice, Simon and Raphael effected the translation. Calò's
account is devoid of all the details one might wish to know about the translation, but as before one can perceive the existence of a pattern that followed the
"Translatio Stephani" and the "Translatio Pauli": a Venetian monk in Constantinople allied with a Venetian merchant in Constantinople in order to
translate a Constantinopolitan relic back home.[3]

In 1240, Iacobo Lantzlo, yet another Venetian merchant, worked with Peter, the abbot of Santa Maria Pervilepsi, to acquire the relics of St. Paul the Hermit for the church of San Giuliano in Venice. We have two fragmentary texts from St. Julian. One is a translatio of uncertain origin. It briefly mentions the first translation of St. Paul's relics to Constantinople by Emperor Manuel Comnenus in 1169. Then the text describes Lantzlo sailing to Constantinople to acquire the relic, his receipt of the item and verifying documentation from Abbot Peter, and his return to Venice. There, everyone rejoices and worships the saint appropriately.[4] Although the translatio is preserved only in a Renaissance copy, a liturgical reading from San Giuliano also survives. Someone from the church wrote it for use on November 14, St. Paul's day of translation. It recounts the same story, from Manuel to Lanzio (Lantzlo) to the installation at San Giuliano.[5]

In 1257, a Venetian noble named Jacobo Dauro acquired the body of St. Theodore in Mesembria after defeating the Vlachs.[6] According to an anonymous translatio, Dauro led an army against enemies of both Constantinople and the faith, defeated them, and claimed the relic as a trophy. He took it to a Venetian church in Constantinople, and Marco Dauro, a relative (*consanguineus eiusdem Iacobi*), carried it to Venice a decade later. The relic was subsequently kept in the church of San Nicoló on the Lido. In this text, therefore, a noble family continued the Venetian tradition of serving the state militarily and claiming relics for the city in the process.[7] This translatio includes several post-translation *miracula*. The first is "a miracle during a tempest at sea by St. Theodore," and it follows, albeit in compressed form, exactly the same pattern as the "Translatio Pauli." According to the account, near Ithaca and Kefalonia in the Ionian Sea, in the precise spot where St. Paul the New Martyr saved the ship in the legend from 1222, St. Theodore protected the sailors carrying his relics from a storm. The men, who were desperate and afraid, begged the saint for protection, showed him all due reverence, and rejoiced in the tranquil seas that he brought as a result of their prayers.[8] His second miracle was likewise maritime in nature, as he saved a boy who fell overboard. He also, we are told, healed many people at his shrine in Venice. This was a saint whose miracles followed in the previously established Venetian tradition and whose relics had been taken as the spoils of war. In fact, Byzantium had installed St. Theodore as Venice's first patron saint when the city was established as a colony, although the Venetians muted the response to the arrival of his relics in 1267.[9] As before, in order to avoid threatening the preeminence of St. Mark, Venice's clerics sent St. Theodore's relics to the church of San Salvatore. Moreover, the images of St.

Theodore from the thirteenth century and earlier in Venice all emphasize his role as a martyr, not as a warrior saint.[10] He rarely appears alone, but is usually grouped with other saints and martyrs, especially St. George.[11] It was not until 1329 that the Venetians set up an armed and armored statue of St. Theodore next to the winged lion on the columns of the Piazzetta San Marco.[12]

Two other military saints featured in a set of relief icons neatly illustrate a mode of visual commemoration of translatio and spoliation. At some point between 1230 and 1267, six relief icons were placed on the west facade of San Marco.[13] Two of them, a relief of Heracles and one of St. Demetrios, were spoils of the Fourth Crusade. Inspired by the plunder, a single artist or workshop likely made three of the others—another Heracles, a relief of St. George, and a relief of the Virgin. As he worked, the artist's craft evolved from mere copying of the Byzantine pieces toward the genesis of an independent Venetian style reminiscent of Greek antecedents (figs. 2–5).[14]

One could take the creation of these reliefs as a metaphor for the development of post-1204 Venice in general, but there is a more specific detail pertinent to the discussion of the letter with which this chapter began and a related artwork, another relief plaque, discussed below. The two warrior saints, Demetrios and George, take pride of place in the middle of the set and control the program of the interlinked icons.[15] The production of this set suggests a new focus on placing Byzantine models into a Venetian program, as inspired by the acquisition of tangible Greek objects. St. Demetrios had been the most widely venerated warrior saint of the Greek empire and is often shown in the folding chair of the "Strategos," or Byzantine general. Of particular interest is the Greek myth that John the Vlach, the first great enemy of the Latin Empire, died in his tent while besieging the Greek city of Thessalonica (Salonica), presumably of some illness. Thessalonica possessed the primary pilgrimage shrine to St. Demetrios's relics, held in a tomb in the city. A legend quickly developed that the warrior saint had ridden out from his tomb and lanced the Vlach king. The legend appears in many thirteenth-century Greek histories,[16] as well as in the chronicle of Robert of Clari. One can assume, therefore, that the Venetians knew of it. Clari writes, "Now there lay in this city the body of my lord St. Demetrios, who would never suffer his city to be taken by force. And there flowed from this holy body such great quantities of oil that it was a fair marvel. And it came to pass, as John the Vlach was lying one morning in his tent, that my lord St. Demetrios came and struck him with a lance through the body and slew him."[17] St. Demetrios thus had particular importance in the

Fig. 2 Marble relief of St. Demetrios. San Marco, Venice. 166 × 99 cm. Photo: Cameraphoto Arte, Venice / Art Resource, N.Y.

Fig. 3 Marble relief of St. George. San Marco, Venice. 165.5 × 94 cm. Photo: Cameraphoto Arte, Venice / Art Resource, N.Y.

Fig. 4 Marble relief of Heracles and the Erymanthian boar. San Marco, Venice. 159 × 88 cm. Photo: Cameraphoto Arte, Venice / Art Resource, N.Y.

Fig. 5 Marble relief of Heracles and the Lernaean Hydra. San Marco, Venice. 174.2 × 93.5 cm. Photo: Scala / Art Resource, N.Y.

world of the new Latin Empire. John the Vlach had captured Baldwin of Flanders, who died in captivity. Enrico Dandolo had died upon returning from the disaster at Adrianople, during which John trounced the crusaders. John's death, recounted here as a miracle, spared the empire from further trauma.

St. Demetrios's ancient Byzantine pedigree was bolstered by this recent miracle story of relevance to the Venetians. The cult of St. George, on the other hand, had long been part of life in Venice, as evidenced by the principle monastery's dedication to San Giorgio Maggiore. Enrico Dandolo had acquired an arm reliquary of St. George in Constantinople, about which more will be said below.[18] The saint's "other" arm had figured prominently as a powerful relic during the First Crusade and had been translated to the West. St. George had thus operated as a patron of holy military activity for the Latins in the East since the beginning of the crusades, a significance that would not have been lost on the relic-savvy Venetians.[19] Now, Venice appropriated both Demetrios and George. Otto Demus writes, "Demetrios and George were, for Venice as well as for Byzantium, a pair of Dioscuri, of heavenly twins. Having found a relief of St. Demetrios in the booty from Constantinople, the Venetians would, almost as a matter of course, link the Warrior Saint with their own protector, St. George. . . . Demetrios and George were, then, important tutelary saints, holy protectors of the doge and the state." The six relief icons functioned as an apotropaic set, with the Virgin and Angel unusually relegated to the edges so that the military figures could dominate.[20]

Heracles, clad in a lion skin and thus associated with the lion of St. Mark, played a multilayered iconographic role. He at once represented classical Rome and the abstract concept of *virtus*.[21] As the half-human son of the god Jupiter, Heracles could be seen as prefiguring the coming of Christ. The icon looted from Constantinople displays Heracles carrying the Erymanthian boar—a fierce creature that Eurystheus had ordered the hero to bring back alive for his fourth labor.[22] The Venetian artist, in making his own version, chose to display Heracles trampling the Lernaean Hydra. A hydra, viewed as a serpent, can represent Christ's victory over evil. For a Venetian, Heracles's name could also refer to the city of Eraclea, the first site of political power on the Venetian lagoon and the city that crowned the first doge.[23] This is a compelling interpretation, since it would enable a reading of the reliefs as an invocation of both Romes, Venice's local history, and Venetian hopes for the future. Whereas St. George is shown sitting, sword bare, ready to leap out of his general's chair and engage the enemies of Christ (or of Venice), Heracles tramples a draconian creature. The classical Greek demigod, made by the same Venetian artist who produced the sitting saint, invokes the story of George and the dragon that would become so popular in the following decades.[24]

Within these icons are all the themes of thirteenth-century Venetian cultural development: Christian militarism from the East and the West in St. Demetrios and St. George, the celebration of local origins and the protection of St. Mark, and the appropriation of the glory of three different Roman empires—classical pagan, Constantine's Christian empire, and the recently fallen Byzantium. The acquisition, or translation, of two Greek icons became the enabler of new mythmaking.

The Doge and the Chronicler: Ranieri Zeno and Martin da Canal

Venetians continued to acquire relics long after the conquest, and Ranieri Zeno and his mythmakers continually found new ways to use the spoils of 1204 to justify Venetian aspirations for both internal and external audiences.[25] Debra Pincus has linked Zeno's letter to a relief plaque that still hangs in the hallway between San Marco and the Palazzo Ducale (fig. 6).[26] The letter, the plaque, and the commissioning of public preaching worked collectively as a mythographic response by Zeno to new external threats. These actions combined in a single episode of shrewd "propagandizing of relics," in ways that extend beyond the more subtle messaging of the external relief icons.[27]

The plaque dominates the hallway through which the doge and his court would have passed on their way to all-important ceremonial occasions in the church. It depicts five relics, each of which had a specific purpose. Three of them are the relics saved from the fire in San Marco. Four were later listed by Andrea Dandolo as having been sent specifically to Venice by Enrico Dandolo.[28] The reliquary at the center contains the blood of Christ. On either side are two crosses, one of which belonged to the Empress Irene Doukas (1066–1123); the other served as the coronation cross of Henry of Flanders. According to Venetian tradition, Henry employed a relic of the True Cross once carried by Constantine and then gave it, in a new gold reliquary, to Dandolo, who sent it to Venice.[29] The two lesser relics are the arm of St. George and the head of St. John the Baptist. All five relics point to a new stage in representations of Venetian glory.

Fig. 6   Marble relief of relics from the treasury of San Marco. Corridor to Palazzo Ducale, Venice. Photo: author.

The designer of the plaque chose the relics carefully. Although Christological relics never dominated in Venice as they did in other Italian cities in the twelfth and thirteenth centuries, the Holy Blood did have a connection to the doge.[30] Pincus notes that the *corruccio*, a special red woolen robe worn by the doge during Holy Week, represented Christ's blood.[31] The crosses not only refer to the crucifixion, of course, but "have an additional overlay as ruler reliquaries with impeccable pedigrees, and moreover ruler reliquaries signifying imperial power."[32] Irene ruled as the Byzantine empress before abdicating in 1118. She, Alexius I, and her son John II probably all appeared on the Pala d'Oro in the 1260s, although their images are now covered by a dedicatory plaque installed by Andrea Dandolo.[33] Since Venice's commercial greatness came as a result of its citizens' military and economic dealings with Alexius I, a cross associated with Irene might well have served as an imperial relic for the doge. The cross of Henry of Flanders and allegedly of Constantine offered an even more potent symbol for the merger of eastern and western imperial traditions in the form of the Latin Empire of Constantinople. By the 1260s, with the Latin Empire fallen, Venice was claiming that legacy for itself. The relics of

St. George and the Baptist point more toward Venice's rivalry with Genoa than to the former city's claims of imperial prominence. Both saints figured prominently in Genoese iconography. Genoa had acquired the relics of the Baptist in 1098 or 1099 and made the veneration of those relics the centerpiece of its sacral calendar. St. George protected the Genoese in military matters. Since Latin Christians viewed him as the "commander of Christ's armies," he provided a particularly potent symbol of militant Christendom. According to legend, he interceded to aid the crusaders during the First Crusade, and thus, by 1242, the Genoese were bearing the *stendardo di San Giorgio* in their war against the Pisans. The chief officials of the city would donate golden spheres to the two saints' altars on their feast days, singling them out and connecting them ritually. If Venice's chosen saints were Mark and Nicholas, then Genoa's were George the aggressor and John the Baptist the defender.[34] In the 1260s and 1270s, at the same time that Venice was asserting *its* claims over the relics of St. George and the Baptist, the Genoese cleric Jacopo da Voragine was popularizing the story of St. George and the dragon and glorifying Genoa's possession of the two major relics. He also wrote a chronicle of the city and a translatio about the Baptist's relics.[35]

The 1260s was a rough decade for Venice. Although it had defeated Genoa at Acre in 1258, the loss propelled Genoa into an alliance with the Palaiologoi. On July 10, 1261, Michael VIII Palaiologos and the Genoese signed the Treaty of Nymphaion, agreeing to a "permanent" alliance of Byzantium and Genoa against the Venetians. Over the next two centuries, Genoa and Venice fought over Byzantium, drew Byzantium unprofitably into their other conflicts, and made dominance over Byzantine trade their most important goal. As Donald Nicol states, "After 1261, the trade and economy of Byzantium was to be at the mercy of not one Italian republic, but of two."[36] Nicol generally views the Italians as predatory; in the long run, intra-Italian conflict was unhealthy for Byzantine stability.[37] In the short term, however, the alliance benefited Michael Palaiologos greatly. He recaptured Constantinople. The Genoese created their colony at Pera. The Venetians, meanwhile, suffered both loss of life and territory. In this context, it is no wonder that Ranieri Zeno sought to undermine Genoese sacral power, even as the Venetians fought Genoa in other ways.[38]

At the same time that Genoa and the Palaiologoi were threatening Venice, the fall of Latin Constantinople created an opportunity for Venetians interested in enhancing their city's imperial stature. The last Latin emperor fled on a Venetian ship, and Venice did not recognize Michael as a valid emperor until

1267, when the two sides reached an accommodation.[39] Venice never gave up its claim to three-eighths of Romania. Thus, when Zeno sent his emissaries to Rome and likely commissioned the relief plaque, Venice recognized no legitimate eastern emperor with whom it might compete or whom it worried about offending. The door was open for Venice.

The door, however, was also open for Michael Palaiologos to reassert his status as a "new Constantine." Translatio imperii, as a concept, had long been part of Byzantine society. Constantine's transfer of the Roman capital to Constantinople was arguably the most tangible imperial translation, and thirteenth-century Byzantines expressed pride in their Roman heritage in their iconography, art, and diplomacy. Greek writers referred, pejoratively, to the pope as the ruler of "old Rome," as opposed to the "new Rome" in which they now lived.[40]

These grave conflicts between the powers of the Mediterranean provided the context in which Zeno commissioned the plaque and wrote the letter to Rome. These actions were designed to promote Venetian imperial aspirations while undercutting Genoa's special relationship with its patron saints. The head of St. John the Baptist, because of its biblical prominence, in some ways trumped Genoa's possession of the saint's ashes. As Pincus says, "In announcing its possession of the head of the Baptist, Venice would seem to be outbidding the power conferred on Genoa by its own patron saint."[41] St. George, the soldier, offered a link to imperial military Christendom. The arm of a soldier is a particularly potent symbol; St. George's arm gave Venice a claim to the saint's strength.[42]

Zeno wrote his letter to the pope in 1265. By 1267, circumstances had changed, and Emperor Michael and Venice found a common foe in Charles of Anjou. The Greek ruler feared that Charles would ally with Venice against Genoa and Constantinople. Venice would never peacefully accept being closed out of the Eastern market that had so long sustained its economy, and thus could have made common cause with the Angevins. Charles, however, was threatening Venice's Adriatic dominance, so the city's leaders were more than willing to discuss an alliance with Michael. In 1267, therefore, Michael and Venice came to terms. The emperor reopened Constantinople to the Venetians and commerce resumed.[43] Settling into a simmering conflict rather than open hostilities, Genoa and Venice maintained a "fragile equilibrium" until 1291.[44] When the Mamluks closed the ports of the Levant to Italian merchants, Mediterranean commerce no longer provided the means for either city to triumph, and war began anew.[45] The two cities would battle, off and on, for the next century.[46]

In scale, novelty, and audacity, Zeno's claims about Venice differed from those of the Fourth Crusade translatio texts. After the Fourth Crusade, Venice built on its long-standing traditions to enhance its current position. However, when the Latin Empire fell, Venice made claims about its heritage and legacy more directly. Enrico Dandolo had taken the relics of St. George and the Baptist, but it was Zeno who promoted their presence to a broader European audience. This was something entirely new, though it did not indicate a full break with the past. In Zeno's letter to Rome, after listing all the relics that would be commemorated on the new holiday, the scribe notes that "Jesus himself wished [the relics] to be collected in the city of Venice with the body of the blessed Mark, his Evangelist."[47] By seeking a papal blessing, Venice protected itself from charges (from Genoese clerics, for example) of impropriety concerning the relics' acquisition. Furthermore, the above quote explicitly links the early pious theft of St. Mark's body to the more recent translations effected by Dandolo. Zeno thus drew a neat line from the origins of the Venetian church to the ritual he wanted to create. He sought continuity with the past even while creating a new iconography for imperial Venice.

Ranieri Zeno would do much to promote Venice's greatness, but many secular and clerical citizens joined him in the effort. As the centuries continued, Venetians kept acquiring relics from the East and telling their stories in the same manner. The enemies from whom the relics needed protection changed—Muslims, Greeks, Vlachs, and finally Turks—but the translatio narratives, in structure if not in detail, remained constant.[48]

"New Wine in Old Bottles": Translatio and Rewriting the Past

Although thirty-four years had elapsed since the fire of 1231 inside the treasury of San Marco, Zeno made it clear to the pope that he was requesting recognition of a *new* ritual of celebration for the survival of the relics. From 1230 to 1261, Venetians claimed new relics from the declining and then collapsing Latin Empire. The maker of the new relief sculptures created a new style with a new message. In each case, Venetians—the clerics, the doge, his supporters, the soldiers who acquired relics, the artist—followed preexisting traditions in their actions and used those traditions to strengthen their claims. They never pretended that their creations were ancient. Venetians gloried in the foreign legacy of their plunder. That a relic had been just recently taken from Constantinople, or once taken from Alexandria, was not a source of shame. Instead, the foreign origin made that item more important. Venice's possession of a storied piece from a once-potent realm signified the translation of some of that old site's power to the lagoon.

During the latter half of thirteenth century and moving into the fourteenth, however, a new rhetoric evolved in addition to the local Marcian legend and elaborations on Venice's past. The chroniclers, artists, and politicians who invoked and depicted these new traditions all insisted that they had been in existence for generations, sometimes since the birth of Venice. This rewriting of the past often still depended on episodes of translatio, but the argument that emerged was different: instead of recently acquiring the right to rule from Constantinople, Venice had always had that right. Venetians then created "traditions" to justify this audacious stance.

Translatio provided the means to develop material symbols in support of such re-creations.[49] For example, the civic ritual of the *sposalizio del mar* became linked to a fabricated myth based around a series of translated items with sacral implications (gifts, rather than loot or stolen items). The doges and people of Venice had given formal annual thanks to the sea since at least around 1000.[50] This ritual had military overtones, because it commemorated Doge Pietro II Orseolo's conquest of much of Dalmatia, a campaign that secured Venetian dominance of its local waters.[51] The transition from an annual blessing to a formal marriage ceremony between the doge and the sea is harder to date. The first concrete evidence, though, can be found in da Canal's chronicle, dated to sometime in the 1260s.[52] Whether da Canal was responding to ritual innovation or an ongoing practice that had developed sometime closer to 1204, it is clear that by the 1260s the ritual functioned as one means by which Venice claimed increased imperial status after the fall of the Latin Empire.

While the marriage did not specifically invoke Constantinopolitan relics or the Fourth Crusade, links to Venice's relic history remain. Just as the author of the "Translatio Symonensis" gave thanks for the *mirabilia in mari veniendo*,[53] the *sposalizio* ritual served simultaneously to give thanks and to assert dominion. The gendered relationship between Venice and the sea proliferated throughout the cultural productions of the city.[54] The anonymous monk of the Lido who composed the "Translatio Nicolai" names Venice as the daughter of St. Nicholas, patron saint of sailors.[55] Images of Venus—naked, beautiful, and spawned from the sea—signify Venice in the art of the Serenissima.[56] Renaissance artists sought other classical motifs, rendering Venice as Neptune's city, for instance.[57] The doge married the sea just offshore from the church of San Nicolò of the Lido. St. Nicholas served as Venice's intercessor with the sea. The church had been built to house relics stolen by a doge's son and a bishop—relics that the Venetians wanted badly enough to create the most improbable of their relic-theft narratives (claiming that the Bariense accidentally stole Nicholas's uncle, while the Venetians got the real item). The acquisition of St. Nicholas's relics had provided Venice with a tangible symbol of the sea, and the creators of the *sposalizio* employed that symbol admirably.

The *sposalizio* offers an early example of the new Venetian willingness to put "new wine in old bottles." The new ritual obscured the history of Sensa festivities in preceding centuries. No clear decree or account of when or how the ritual started exists, although it must have been enacted deliberately and consciously; no one would have accidentally flung a ring into the water and proclaimed the sea to be his bride. But once Venetian mythographers began to reshape their rituals, an entirely new imperial iconography began to emerge. For example, the ring from the marriage rite became associated with the *trionfi*, seven gifts presented by Pope Alexander III to Doge Sebastiano Ziani in the legend of the Peace of Venice.

This story is a rewriting of the famous peace treaty signed by Frederick Barbarossa and Pope Alexander III in 1177. The two rulers met in Venice, a useful neutral site, and both offered minor useful privileges to the Venetians in thanks. But the legend tells a wildly fictionalized version of events leading up to the peace treaty, casting Venice as the savior of Italy, defender of the papacy, and recipient of august trophies of Venetian piety and might. Each of these gifts—a candle, lead seal, sword, ring, umbrella, banners, and trumpets—possessed a specific meaning associated with imperial Christianity. One can read this story, which exists in poetry, prose, and multiple image cycles, as a form of translatio. The gifts provide permanent symbols of the momentary heroism and piety in 1177 and carry privileges forward into the "present" moment for each author or artist. The sacred items travel from the hands of the pope to the doge, and thus to the government, of Venice. Just as relic thieves received their bounty by expressing and demonstrating their unworthiness, piety, and charity, Doge Ziani received his seven symbols because of his piety, humility, and generosity toward Alexander. The Venetians, as a *gens*, receive praise for their piety.[58] The umbrella, lead seal, banners, and trumpets function as both papal and imperial insignia. The ring is a link to the sea. The sword reflects the "two swords" of the Gospel of Luke.[59] The papal blade was given to Venice, according to various fourteenth-century versions of the legend, because of the city's commitment to justice. In the fourteenth century, the sword of justice had become a symbol of the crusades and papal militarism. Indeed, the military component of this story comes to operate as an imaginary political crusade.[60] Venice stands as the imperial defender of the Roman papacy, which is fighting the Holy Roman emperor. The story of the *trionfi* thus operates as a story of translatio imperii, with an imagined translation of key objects from Rome to Venice driving the transfer of empire.

Retroactive prophecy, by its nature, relates knowledge of the contemporary in the voice of the past. We have seen the use of such prophecy in the "Translatio Pauli" already. By the late thirteenth century, retroactive prophecies extended into the heart of the Venetian sense of self. To the local *vita* of St. Mark was added the *praedestinatio*, according to which the saint's final resting place was divinely ordained back in the first century C.E. The *titulus* on a mosaic depicting the episode reads, "While he [St. Mark] was sailing across the area where the church of San Marco now stands, an angel announced that at a certain time after his death, his body would be interred here with great honor."[61] The *acta* of the relics in Venice were likewise transformed to fit this new element of the story. When the church of San Marco was renovated in 1094, the relics of San Marco were brought out of storage and ceremoniously reinstalled.[62] By the era of da Canal, however, this event had been retold as a story of *apparatio* and miraculous *inventio*. In the story, the relics were lost, the leaders of the city prayed and processed, and a column miraculously opened to reveal the lost sacred items.[63] Da Canal claims that Doge Zeno merely renewed the old festival of the *apparatio*—a fabrication. The chronicler is doing more than just pouring the wine of innovation into an old bottle; he has fabricated a new bottle that looks old.

How much of the transition in the mythmaking of Venice can be attributed to da Canal and Zeno is difficult to assess. The chronicler often provides the earliest written record, but many earlier historical texts from Venice have been lost. Rather than an originator, da Canal's *Les estoires de Venise* could be only the first extant compilation of preexisting legends. Zeno, on the other hand, ruled during a difficult time. He seems to have sought both offensive and defensive reinforcement in the power of myth and legend. Although he was operating in a culture in which translatio already had extraordinary power, he may have personally triggered the shift in Venetian mythmaking from translatio imperii to renovatio imperii. The former celebrated the movement of the empire from abroad to Venice, whereas the latter pretended that Venice had always been the imperial center of the Christian world.

Sources become more prevalent, or at least more survive, from the period after 1261. Historians of Venice in the late thirteenth and early fourteenth centuries increasingly rewrote the city's past. As they did so, the process begun by Zeno intensified, and translatio gave way to an imaginary renovatio as the dominant mode of Venetian mythmaking. Presupposing a prior origin for the greatness acquired by Venice was no longer enough for the Venetians. Instead, Venetian chroniclers employed local traditions in constructing new and bolder claims. The Trojan origin myth for Venice crystallized in local chronicle traditions, placing the founding of Venice by Antenor prior to Aeneas and Rome.[64] Andrea Dandolo invented new privileges, allegedly given to Venice by Charlemagne, in order to solidify the city's Western pedigree.[65] A chronicle from 1292 contains a retroactive prophecy predicting the fall of Constantinople in 1204. The author used the prophecy to find meaning in an accidental conquest, turning the haphazard—as the conquest of Constantinople surely was—into a sign of predestined greatness.[66] One can extract similar messages from the chronicles' approach to all the conflicts and treaties with Byzantium, including the Fourth Crusade.[67] The crusade influenced the historical presentation of other events. For example, when the Venetian chronicles describe the crusade of 1122–26,[68] they emphasize that the soldiers were crusading against Islam, yet were forced to fight the heretical Greeks. Thus, they use this campaign to prefigure the events of the Fourth Crusade.[69] Like Andrea Dandolo's chronicle, many of these chronicles proudly list the relics taken from Constantinople.[70]

Dandolo may have gone further than others by adding a relic theft to the story of the 1122 campaign. His promotion of the cult of St. Isidore provides one final example of how translatio remained important even as Venetians reconstructed their identity. According to the chronicle, documents on the celebration of the saint's translation,[71] and a full translatio narrative,[72] Doge Domenico Michiel seized the relics of St. Isidore in 1125, while wintering on Chios.[73] On the surface, this episode appears to provide a fourth archetypal translatio that one could group with the stories of Mark, Nicholas, and Stephen. But regarding Isidore, Demus writes, "Not much was made of the relics of St. Isidore, taken from Chios in 1125; it is even likely that they were kept hidden and were found again only under Andrea Dandolo (r. 1343–54), when they were exposed to public veneration in the newly built Cappella di S. Isidoro in San Marco."[74] Perhaps, but Venetians in the late thirteenth and fourteenth centuries constantly invented new stories and claimed that they were old stories. No records of St. Isidore's translation or veneration prior to Dandolo's reign exist. While Michiel perhaps did snatch the relics of St. Isidore, it seems just as likely that Dandolo felt that Michiel *should* have snatched the relics and so generated the appropriate myth.

Although St. Isidore's main connection to Venice is that he came from Alexandria (St. Mark's city) before being martyred on Chios, the island itself became newly relevant as of 1345, just when Dandolo began the design and construction of the chapel in San Marco. In 1204, Chios briefly belonged to Venice. In the early fourteenth century, a Genoese adventurer, Benedetto Zaccaria, established a brief lordship there. Local unrest forced his son, Martino Zaccaria, to flee from the island. Martino then asked the pope to let him use crusader forces to take it back. In 1344, around the time that Dandolo "rediscovered" the relics of St. Isidore, Venice joined a new crusading effort aimed at Smyrna, just across the water from Chios. An illustrious Venetian admiral, Nicolà Pisani, traveled to Constantinople as part of Pope Clement VI's efforts to persuade Empress Anna of Savoy to let the fleet use Chios as a naval base. According to papal records, this plan met with favorable reception in Constantinople, but just then a Genoese privateer fleet arrived in the area, declined to join the crusade, and instead reconquered Chios. Not long after, Empress Anna lost Constantinople to Emperor John VI.

John soon declared war on Genoa and lost, but the Genoese offered peace terms in order to keep business running smoothly. Among the agreements, they promised to pay rent for Chios for the next ten years and then give it back. In 1350, however, Venice declared war on Genoa. Throughout the subsequent battle in the Aegean, Chios remained a key holding for the Genoese and a prize most desired by John, who sided with the Venetians in order to regain the island and other lost territory. The Genoese won that round and ruled Chios until 1566.[75]

At the very least, Dandolo promoted the story of St. Isidore's relics anew. He endowed a chapel dedicated to St. Isidore and had it decorated with mosaics depicting a wartime relic theft. To Dandolo's mind, any crusade against the

Greeks should include the taking of relics for Venice in order to enhance the sacred status of the city. If the legend of the Peace of Venice includes an imaginary crusade, then the story of St. Isidore offers an imaginary relic theft.

One can find other events and images that demonstrate the continued importance of pilfered relics to Venetian identity. The thirteenth-century mosaic cycle of the theft of St. Mark on the facade of San Marco, now mostly destroyed, retold the story with contemporary Venetian dress and contemporary personalities.[76] A Venetian purchased relics in Constantinople from an empress in 1359. One of these relics was a piece of the famous girdle of the Virgin, the most important relic stored in St. Mary Chalkoprateia—the same church where seven Venetians stole the relics of St. Simon the Prophet.[77] As the Ottoman Turks extended their reach into the islands of the Aegean and Mediterranean, Venetians often claimed relics out of the endangered territories just ahead of the invasion. They acquired, in the fifteenth century, the relics of St. Luke Stiroto, who they tried to claim was Luke the Evangelist. They also acquired the relics of St. Athanasius of Constantinople (1230–1310), claiming that he was the more famous St. Athanasius of Alexandria (296–373), and later the relics of St. Rocco.[78] As late as 1617, Venice held a grand celebration of the relics in San Marco. Eyewitnesses recorded the items, relic by relic, as they were paraded from the treasury through the Piazza San Marco. Relics claimed from Constantinople during the Fourth Crusade dominated the first and second ranks (the relics were grouped into three ranks, by importance). Thus, the use of the relics of 1204 remained central to state ritual more than four centuries after the city's fall.[79]

Conclusion

Several critical questions remain. Why did Venetians in Constantinople continue to steal relics and produce these narratives long after 1204? What do their actions tell us about Venetian faith and identity? More importantly, why did a society in the midst of political, economic, and cultural transformation turn to the relatively outmoded practice of relic theft and the composition of translatio narratives? By the thirteenth century, Venice had long since left Patrick Geary's world of *furta sacra* behind. And yet Venetians continued to steal relics and write narratives.

It is far too easy to focus on elite actors such as Ranieri Zeno and Abbot Paulus of San Giorgio Maggiore, or highly educated authors such as Martin da Canal. The myths are evident on the golden mosaics of San Marco, but the people we can identify are either saints or the most elite citizens of the Rialto. When we find depictions or written descriptions of less elite people, they are too often mere throngs who venerate a relic at a shrine, attend a festival, or are otherwise reduced to anonymity.

But students of the history of Venice know the power and importance of Venice's citizenry, even though the social order became increasingly stratified as the Middle Ages waned. In the twelfth century, the *arengo*—the assembly of all the people (citizens) of Venice—theoretically provided the only legitimacy for the government's authority.[80] In times of crisis, doges could appeal to the arengo for help. At times, the people formed angry mobs and wreaked violence upon the leaders of the state. When the crusaders were stranded on the Lido and could not pay the Venetians for the construction of their fleet, Enrico Dandolo feared that just such a fate awaited him. In 1172, as he well knew, Doge Vitale II Michiel's failure to handle the conflict with Byzantium resulted in his death at the hands of the mob.[81] When Dandolo needed to unify his people behind a new bargain with the Franks—the agreement that Venetians would suspend repayment of the loan until Egypt fell in exchange for help from the Franks against Zara—he turned to the arengo.[82]

What did the people think when Venetians returned from the East bearing relics, precious objects, and tales of new opportunity?[83] Did the doges' adoption of new imperial titles and regalia transform what the citizens of Venice thought about their leader? Even more importantly, did the arrival of new relics and the subsequent innovative mythography change what the citizens thought about themselves? To answer these questions, we must largely turn to indirect evidence, at least until the fourteenth century. The glorious golden mosaics were accessible to all inhabitants, whereas chronicles, monastic writing, and diplomatic missives were not. The hints that mendicants were preaching in the 1260s about the miraculous survival of the relics in the treasury of San Marco offer some evidence of the dissemination of translatio stories. Citizens sailed in great numbers to see the relics of St. Lucia and to witness the *sposalizio*.

To understand the common citizen of postcrusade Venice, one must link the city's centers, such as San Marco and eventually the Palazzo Ducale, to the parishes. The parishes of Venice offered key points of identification for the citizens of the lagoon.[84] When the Dandolo family wanted to distinguish itself from the throng of midlevel merchant families, it allied with like-minded families and established the parish of San Luca.[85] The notaries of twelfth- and thirteenth-century Venice were typically parish priests who identified themselves and their clients by parish. As water distribution was organized around neighborhoods, the very liquid that sustained life emerged from one's local relationships.[86] Eventually, Venice would stratify and centralize, but not until long after 1204. Before the fall of Constantinople, trade took place in many little markets, not the big Rialto. Countless small *squeri* built the merchant vessels and warships of the republic, not the great Arsenale of the Renaissance.[87] The "city of wood," even as it transformed itself into the "city of stone," began at the parish level.

We have little information about the beliefs of the *populari* because the sources privilege the elites. But we can tease out some clues by returning to the seven men from the parish of St. Simon the Prophet—Andrea, Pietro, Angelo, Nicola, Marino, Leonardo Steno, and Leonardo Mauro—and to the translatio that describes their deeds. Although this source puts their actions into the larger context of Venetian sacral history, the men focused resolutely on their parish. At considerable risk to themselves—in defiance of leaders who had not only ordered capital punishment for anyone who concealed loot but also specifically ordered crusaders to swear not to despoil churches— these seven found the resolve to claim a relic for themselves, their parish, and their city. And despite the many relics potentially available for plunder, they specifically sought the body of their patron saint. At their core, the deeds of these seven Venetians were audacious acts of devotion—devotion to St. Simon the Prophet, devotion to the parish of St. Simon the Prophet, and, finally, devotion to Venice.

However, while these men cared about Venice, they were not seeking city-wide glory. St. Zachary's relics rested in the very same crypt as St. Simon's. In Venice, the convent dedicated to St. Zachary was filled with women from the most important families in the city, and the seven thieves could have brought that patron saint home instead, or in addition. But they chose only St. Simon. The seven focused on elevating their parish's status within the city by means of a sacred theft. They sought glory as members of a community and within that community. Perhaps bringing St. Simon's relics home to his parish created both political and economic opportunities. Pietro Steno's dream about being the only person to aid his parish priest implies the potential to gain local prestige, a useful commodity for a businessman or politician. But the language of the translatio, a text almost certainly produced within the parish, focuses on the fraternal ties among the band. They are brothers, comrades-in-arms, fellow devotees to the parish, and dutiful assistants to Father Leonardo. When they shirk from danger, others chide them to be "men" and to work together in order to do their duty.

The seven may have been exceptional, but they acted in accordance with their culture's traditions. They thought of themselves as crusaders, although they never saw a Muslim. They thought of themselves as brothers from the parish of St. Simon and were proud of their community's position within the Venetian milieu. They had their gaze firmly on Venice's sacred history, but not on a history that claimed august origins in Troy. They saw a past in which merchants who had descended from salt farmers and refugees built a great city based on trade and then seized eastern symbols of power whenever and however they could. The Fourth Crusade's shocking success opened up new opportunities, and created new hazards, for Venice. These seven Venetians, themselves merchants, had no delusions of grandeur. They saw a new opportunity, and like their forebearers, they seized it. The merchants who stole the body of St. Mark, also in defiance of their doge, were immortalized on the walls of San Marco in gold. The seven who stole Simon would have seen those mosaics repeatedly throughout their lives; the sight would have indoctrinated them with a particular brand of acquisitive piety. "Acquire wisdom as if it were gold," commands the "Translatio Pauli."[88] By extension, one should pursue relics, too, with the same verve of Venetians who sought secular wealth. Such characteristics of Venetian faith do not indicate a lack of piety, but instead a seamless integration of the principles of everyday existence into the religious culture of Venice. The seven thieves from the parish of St. Simon, like the anonymous author of the "Translatio Symonensis," knew that miracles, like wealth, came to Venice by means of the sea—*mirabilia in mari veniendo*—and from the East. But miracles, like gold and silver, did not arrive on their own accord. Rather, the medieval Venetian had to seize the opportunities that presented themselves.

The actions of the men who stole the relic of St. Simon, as well as the messages contained in the text recording those actions, suggest that the transformation of Venice from a merchant republic to a maritime empire was not purely a top-down development. Citizens took an active role, creating their own minor, neighborhood-level myths. The Venetians who became involved in the translation of relics from Constantinople and the East after the Fourth Crusade included common merchants, crusaders of all social strata, low-ranking monks, priors, ship captains, the podestà of Constantinople, the abbot of San Giorgio Maggiore, the bishop and patriarch who oversaw the installation at St. Simon, and even the doge himself. First they translated relics. Then they assigned meaning to the events that enabled these translations. Finally, Venice tried to appropriate not just the symbols of Christian rule, but an empire—or at least a quarter, and half of a quarter, of one.

Epilogue

Although I have emphasized distinctions among the various narrative sources, they are more similar than dissimilar in comparison to the rest of the primary record for the crusades—even in other cases where relics were prominently featured. These similarities beg the question: Why did so many medieval people react to the Fourth Crusade by writing translatio narratives? The answer lies in turning to the memorializing contexts in which these relics, their bearers, and their recipients found themselves. The pope and others criticized the crusaders on moral grounds. The critics focused consistently on the looting as the moment in which God turned from the Latins, and then tried to leverage such criticisms to serve economic, military, and political goals. Translatio offered a counternarrative, relying on the manifest absolution and justification inherent in the theological underpinnings of the practice and memorialization of pious relic theft. All sins, if any were committed, could be washed away in the newfound glow of saintly approbation.

Other questions remain. Did the pope and other critics find such counternarratives persuasive or at all concerning? Why did Latin authors outside of Venice stop writing translatio narratives on the crusade? The "Narratio exceptionis apud Cluniacum capitis beati Clementis," written in Cluny sometime around 1208, is the latest non-Venetian text to make even the most tenuous invocation of sacred theft. We have seen Venice's reasons for maintaining its traditional approach to translated relics, but why the change in the rest of Europe? Pilgrims still went to and from Latin Constantinople; some acquired relics. Emperor Henry, his successors, the prelates of the Latin East, and the rulers of Frankish Greece continued to dole out relics as they saw fit. Further military campaigns into Greek, Bulgarian, and Muslim territories may have occasioned the acquisition of new relics, although this has not yet been studied. Papally sponsored campaigns into Egypt, the Levant, northern Europe, Spain, and southern France would have put victorious crusaders in positions where they might have claimed relics. But translatio never became a widely used form of memorializing the late crusades. What changed?

As of 1204, canon law defined only a limited number of conditions under which one could legally move a relic. If one could argue, however, that the relic was threatened by persecutors, that the site was unworthy because sinners possessed the relic, or that the new site would have fewer "difficulties" for people wanting to venerate the relic, then one could take it without breaking the law of the Church.[1] These loopholes had long allowed the authors of relic-theft narratives to claim that the translation of pilfered relics occurred in accordance with canon law, because the relics had not been safe or properly venerated, or had been kept in disadvantageous locations. The Fourth Crusade texts generally depict the Greeks harshly in order to demonstrate their unfitness to serve as guardians of relics, while emphasizing the benefits that would accrue to the relics in their new locations. Thus, the post-1204 translations were technically canonical.

Innocent III responded to the translation of relics from Constantinople to the West with Canon 62 of the Fourth Lateran Council, held in 1215. The council was an extraordinary event. The pope and his curia spent years planning this gathering, which would be the first true general assembly of the church since at least the Second Council of Nicaea in 787, with the intention of fixing the major problems that they perceived in Christendom. Innocent wanted to reform ecclesiastical organization, deal with heretics, continue the crusading effort against heretics known as the Cathars, end civil war in the Holy Roman Empire, alter the practice of the sacrament of confession, and otherwise purge the Christian world of its errors and sins. Only then, Innocent believed, would God allow the Christians to retake the Holy Land.[2]

In order to make sure that everything went as planned, Innocent tried to leave no detail to chance. He sent summonses to the delegates two and a half years before the intended commencement date. He had chosen a time in late autumn so that people could travel throughout the summer months. He arranged for pomp and visual splendor that would match the import of the legislative activities that he had planned. He ensured that adequate copies of the constitutions of the council would be prepared for all delegates, and for anyone who could not attend.[3]

One can safely argue that Innocent regarded each canon as the solution to a crucial problem. Canon 62 addressed relic trafficking. According to the canon, no one, for any purpose, could sell a relic, take a relic out of its vessel, or venerate a new relic without papal permission. It railed against forgeries and people who deceived the devout with false documents and "worthless fabrications."[4] The canon focused on the basest form of relic trafficking but also prohibited the types of arguments made by the authors of narratives about relic theft. At the very least, this canon somewhat closed the loophole left open by Gratian's writing on relics and canon law. All future translations of any important relic had to go through the pope.

But in the final moments of the council, as recorded in the sole known account of the closing ceremonies, Innocent made a surprising choice.[5] According to an anonymous monk of Aulesburg who witnessed the entire council, the pomp of these ceremonies trumped all the wondrous days of the two weeks that had come before. On Monday, November 30, Innocent began with a sermon on the Trinitarian Creed and then had the entire throng recite both the creed and articles of faith along with him. This was the feast day of St. Andrew, from whom the patriarchs of Constantinople marked their apostolic descent—a fact that emerges as relevant given the ritual links to Constantinople that follow.[6] Next, the gathered dignitaries and their associates heard all of the new canons read aloud, bearing witness to this important legislative moment. After the reading, Innocent personally led the closing ceremonies, which concluded with an exposition and adoration of a relic of the True Cross. He then used that relic to give his final blessing.[7] As historian Brenda Bolton stresses, Innocent had the scene choreographed down to the specific moment of commencement. He began the final blessing "at the ninth hour of the day," the hour of Christ's crucifixion on the very wood that he now held up before the throng.[8] With it in hand, he demanded devotion to Rome, commitment to crusade, and diligence in reforming all of Christendom. It was Innocent's finest hour.[9]

In this ultimate moment of the council, the pope chose to use a newly acquired relic from Constantinople. Although the reliquary no longer survives, a 1311 inventory of the Holy See's treasury records its inscription: "This [reliquary] contains the wood of the living cross translated from Constantinople to the city in the time of lord Innocent the Third."[10] The monk of Aulesburg wrote that Innocent exposed "a large part of the wood of the sainted cross that had been brought from Constantinople" and that everyone fell to their knees in awe.[11] Bolton describes the appearance of this relic as Innocent's "master stroke," but Stephan Kuttner, a celebrated scholar of medieval canon law, disagrees.[12] Kuttner writes, "Less than an hour earlier Innocent had enacted a conciliar constitution (c.62) against the trafficking in relics: as is well known, they flooded the West as a result of the Crusades, especially after the sack of Constantinople. It is therefore somewhat surprising that at this solemn moment he would expose for adoration, and give his final blessing with, a relic of the True Cross that had been brought recently from the imperial city; for many may have asked themselves by what means it had been acquired."[13]

Kuttner continues by listing all the other relics of the True Cross that were easily available to Innocent at that moment. The pope could have used a relic that Constantine (according to tradition) had given to Rome, one sent to Rome by Emperor Justin II (r. 565–78), or even a fragment of the relic found by Emperor Heraclius in Jerusalem in 628.[14] Innocent easily could have linked this last piece to his crusading agenda, because Heraclius recovered the cross in his war against the Persians, and the emperor's reconquest of Jerusalem often figured as a proto-crusade in the West. If none of these relics seemed appropriate to Innocent, he also could have employed the relic of the True Cross that popes almost always used in their formal liturgy. Pontiffs carried this fragment, known as Pope Sergius's Cross, during the procession from the Lateran to Santa Croce on Good Friday, but returned it to the Lateran on September 14 (the Feast of the Exaltation of the Cross). Thus, in November, the fragment was easily at hand in the Lateran.[15] In fact, of all the relics of the True Cross available to the pope, the relic from Constantinople was the *least* used by later pontiffs. The 1311 inventory, cited above, is the only other textual record of the relic that has been found. Kuttner concludes, based on this scarcity, that "the testimony of G [the monk from Aulesburg] thus acquires a particular significance for the liturgical use of this relic soon after its arrival from Constantinople."[16] Taking Bolton's emphasis on Innocent's fanatical micromanaging of every detail along with Kuttner's analysis of the many relics of the True Cross available to Innocent, one can make a strong case that Innocent's choice must have been conscious and significant.

Kuttner wrote that "many may have asked themselves by what means it [the relic] had been acquired."[17] Kuttner was aware of Innocent's long-established pattern of condemning the looting of Constantinople's churches and that the gathered dignitaries might link the relic before them to that condemned prac-

tice. But perhaps making such a link before the elite of Christendom was precisely Innocent's plan. Innocent and his lawyers designed Canon 62 to shut
down relic trafficking and to legislate the concept of *furta sacra* out of existence. "Sacred theft" would become mere theft. One could not avoid papal
criticism by seeking the manifest justification of pious thievery. Still, many
relics had been translated out of Constantinople and would not be returning.
With the ritual, therefore, Innocent tried to seize control over the *meaning* of
the relics of 1204.

Innocent's reaction to the Fourth Crusade consistently displayed ambiva-
lence. On the one hand, he deplored the diversion of the crusaders from Cairo
to Constantinople. On the other, he applauded the chance to bring the Greek
church under Roman control. He condemned the atrocities of the sack but still
sought to use Constantinople as a base of operations against the Muslims. He
fought against the expropriation of sacred relics by secular soldiers and wayward clergy, but demanded that Genoa send to Rome the pirated relics that
had been expropriated on his behalf. By bringing out the piece of the True
Cross that had been removed from Constantinople, Innocent was activating
Canon 62, not, as Kuttner thought, working against it. His display of the fragment argued that control of the relics belonged to Rome, no matter what sinful
processes had removed them from Constantinople and scattered them across
Western Christendom. By featuring this relic, Innocent III was telling his own
story of pious theft.

But the story of the relics of 1204 did not end in 1215. Whereas other sites
had created new traditions of pious thievery to respond to the plunder of
1204, the Venetian pattern was too long established to be altered by Innocent's actions. As late as 1669, the Senate of Venice ordered its *capitano da
mar* to strip the Cathedral of St. Tito in Candia, Crete, of its relics. For twenty
years, Venice had fought the Ottomans over Crete, seeking to hold on to the
island that Enrico Dandolo had bought and for which Ranieri Dandolo had
died. The Venetians managed to keep a few fortresses but otherwise ceded
Candia and the majority of the island. Thus, the *capitano* needed to acquire
the head of St. Tito, the head of St. Barbara, a bone from St. Saba, and a phial
containing the blood of Christ.[18] Venice had once ruled Crete as a direct
result of the Fourth Crusade, and these would be the last relics of the crusade
translated to Venice.

Today, the many relics of 1204 are scattered. Most of the Venetian relics
that survive occupy later medieval or baroque reliquaries. The fall of the

republic to Napoleon was not kind to the treasure of the Serenissima. Napoleon even removed the bronze horses from San Marco for a time, although after the emperor's death Venice reclaimed them. St. Lucia and St. Barbara lie in baroque cases, the former in her third Venetian site. St. Athanasius likewise rests in a baroque case, and the inscription misidentifies him as an earlier saint. St. Simon's tomb now possesses a fifteenth-century effigy, but at least the inscription on the wall has remained undisturbed since 1318. The monasteries of San Giorgio Maggiore and San Nicolò on the Lido are long gone, their treasuries mostly lost.

Anti-Catholic sentiment drove participants in the French Revolution to damage the treasures of Sainte-Chapelle badly, although a recent exhibition at the Louvre has shown us the many objects that remain.[19] Work remains to be done on the relics of 1204 in northern France, Flanders, and especially Champagne. As Alfred Andrea's research in Halberstadt has shown, future examinations of these relics may prove revelatory.[20]

But as the exchange and dispute between the Vatican and Patriarch Bartholomew has demonstrated, the stories of these relics never necessarily end. For believers, the power of the saint to intercede in its location renders relics permanently alive with narrative possibility. In November 1981, two gunmen broke into the church of San Geremia, the final resting place of the oft-translated relics of St. Lucia. They made the priest and a young couple lie down on the floor, then grabbed the body and made off with it. Some initial suspicion fell on the Sicilian city of Syracuse, St. Lucia's point of origin.[21] Could this have been a relic theft aimed at repatriation, much as the Venetian merchants claimed that Venice was the first home of St. Mark and thus he belonged there? The story gets stranger. A month later, on December 13, 1981, Lucia's feast day, the relics were found in a nylon bag in a building outside of Venice. As reported by the *Catholic Herald*, "The discovery was made on the saint's feast day as thousands of Faithful were paying their respects to the relics left behind by the robbers."[22]

Despite the firearms, the narrative contours of this modern story of relic abduction and recovery resonate with echoes of the Middle Ages. While the medieval hagiographers might never have imagined such a strange place as modern Venice, they knew that the relics of 1204 could, in theory, last forever. And so they wrote stories, memorializing journeys through space, from east to west, and attempting to shape the meaning of the longer trip into perpetuity.

NOTES

Unless otherwise noted, English translations of foreign-language sources are my own.

Introduction

1. Queller and Madden, *Fourth Crusade*, 181–86.
2. Riant, "Dépouilles religieuses à Constantinople."
3. The second volume of Riant's *Exuviae sacrae Constantinopolitanae* (hereafter abbreviated *ESC*) was published in 1878. In 2004, as a commemoration of the eight hundredth anniversary of the Fourth Crusade, the Comité des travaux historiques et scientifiques in Paris published facsimile editions of the two volumes with a preface by Jannic Durand. See Durand's preface for details on Riant's construction of the *ESC* (1:7–10).
4. Wortley, review of *Exuviae sacrae Constantinopolitanae*.
5. Geary, *Furta Sacra*, 9–27.
6. Riley-Smith, *First Crusade*, 91–119; Morris, "Policy and Visions"; Murray, "'Mighty Against the Enemies of Christ.'"
7. Whalen, "Discovery of the Holy Patriarchs," 142–44.
8. "Narratio quomodo relliquiae martyris Georgii."
9. Hahn, *Strange Beauty*, 165.
10. Heinzelmann, *Translationsberichte und andere Quellen des Reliquienkultes*.
11. Geary, "Sacred Commodities," 208.
12. Buc, "Conversion of Objects," 99–100; Remensnyder, "Legendary Treasure at Conques," 884–85.
13. Carruthers, *Book of Memory*.
14. Fentress and Wickham, *Social Memory*, 177.
15. See, for example, Spiegel, *Past as Text*.
16. See, for example, Gabriele, *Empire of Memory*, esp. 4–9 and 69, and Paul and Yeager, "Introduction," 5–9.
17. Gaposchkin, *Making of Saint Louis*, 33–36, offers an analogous study of hagiographical sources composed shortly after the events in question by authors focused on shaping memory.
18. "Greek Orthodox in Turkey Celebrate Return of Relics Stolen 800 Years Ago," *Agence France-Presse*, November 27, 2004.
19. "Row as Vatican Returns Relics," *The Hindu*, November 29, 2004, http://www.hindu.com/2004/11/29/stories/2004112902411100.htm.
20. Ibid.

Chapter 1

1. Queller and Madden, *Fourth Crusade*, 197–200.
2. Robert of Clari, *Li estoires*, 69: "Et se leur fist on jurer seur sains, que il main ne meteroient seur moine, ne seur clerc, ne seur prestre, s'il n'esoit en desfense, ne qu'il ne froisseroient eglise ne moustier."

3. *Die Register Innocenz' III*, 8:127 (hereafter abbreviated *Reg.*). I have used Andrea's translations of this text when they are available. See Andrea, *Contemporary Sources*, 166.

4. Niketas Choniates, *O City*, 314-15. These descriptive passages recall John 19:1-4, 23-24, 34.

5. Angold, *Fourth Crusade*, 116-19.

6. Runciman, *History of the Crusades*, 123, 480.

7. Queller and Madden, *Fourth Crusade*, 194.

8. Angold, *Fourth Crusade*, 111-13, 116-17.

9. Joranson, "Problem of the Spurious Letter."

10. Robert of Clari, *Li estoires*, esp. 81-82.

11. Queller and Madden, *Fourth Crusade*, 82. Alexius had promised one hundred thousand marks in order to pay off the Venetian debt, a vow that the crusaders felt should accrue to whoever held the throne of Constantinople after Alexius, in theory. See also Madden, "Vows and Contracts."

12. Queller and Madden, *Fourth Crusade*, 123-24.

13. Ibid., 186-89.

14. *Reg.*, 7:205; Andrea, *Contemporary Sources*, 142.

15. Wolff, "Organization of the Latin Patriarchate."

16. Queller and Madden, *Fourth Crusade*, 199; Geoffrey of Villehardouin, *Conquête*, 2:52.

17. Robert of Clari, *Li estoires*, 96.

18. Andrea, "*Devastatio Constantinopolitana*," 126.

19. Madden, "Outside and Inside," provides a useful overview. Queller and Madden, *Fourth Crusade*, 199-200 and 294-95n60, provides the best accounting of the total loot.

20. McCormick, *Eternal Victory*, 82-83.

21. Niketas Choniates, *O City*, 316.

22. Niketas Choniates, *Historia*, 575-76.

23. Angold, *Fourth Crusade*, 112.

24. Ibid., 111-13; Harris, "Distortion, Divine Providence, and Genre"; Simpson, "Before and After 1204."

25. Angold, *Fourth Crusade*, 112.

26. I have used McNeal's translations of this text. See Robert of Clari, *Conquest of Constantinople*, 101.

27. Ibid., 101-2. Robert of Clari, *Li estoires*, 81: "Et chil meïsme qui l'avoir devoient warder, si prenoient les joiaus d'or, et chou que il voloient et embloient l'avoir."

28. See, for example, Clari's section on the division of the empire. Robert of Clari, *Li estoires*, 81, 96.

29. Geoffrey of Villehardouin, *Conquête*, 2:76. I have used Smith's translations of this text. See Geoffrey of Villehardouin, *Chronicles of the Crusades*, 51.

30. Geoffrey of Villehardouin, *Conquête*, 2:253; Geoffrey of Villehardouin, *Chronicles of the Crusades*, 85.

31. Andrea, "*Devastatio Constantinopolitana*," 123-29.

32. Andrea, *Contemporary Sources*, 262.

33. Ibid.

34. Andrea, "Conrad of Krosigk," 64-65.

35. Klein, "Eastern Objects and Western Desires," 283-314.

36. In "Conrad of Krosigk," 65-69, Alfred Andrea argued that the relics were stolen, but he has since concluded in an unpublished lecture that some of the material evidence supports the gift claim. See Andrea, "What Remains to Be Said About Relic Thievery."

37. Angold, *Fourth Crusade*, 232–33.

38. Andrea, *Contemporary Sources*, 62.

39. Andrea and Rachlin, "Holy War, Holy Relics."

40. Geoffrey of Villehardouin, *Conquête*, 2:3, 68.

41. Andrea, *Contemporary Sources*, 224–25.

42. Wortley, "Marian Relics."

43. Andrea, *Contemporary Sources*, 227.

44. Queller and Madden, *Fourth Crusade*, 201.

45. *Reg.*, 7:205; Andrea, *Contemporary Sources*, 142.

46. Queller and Madden, *Fourth Crusade*, 194.

47. Canon of Langres, "Historia translationum reliquiarum," 22.

48. Gunther of Pairis, *Capture of Constantinople*, 109–11.

49. Andrea, *"Historia Constantinopolitana,"* 296.

50. Perry, *"Translatio Symonensis"*; Chiesa, "Ladri." On the Chalkoprateia, see Matthews, *Byzantine Churches*, 319–20. Cyril Mango, in "Notes on Byzantine Monuments," discusses the twelfth-century pilgrims' accounts that reference the relics of Simon the Prophet.

51. The sole manuscript copy of the "Translatio Symonensis" is Biblioteca Nazionale Braidense, Milan, MS Gerli 26, fols. 71r–74v. Geoffrey of Villehardouin, *Conquête*, 2:54, sec. 251, confirms that the army paused in its postconquest activities to celebrate Holy Week.

52. MS Gerli 26, fol. 74v. No other confirmation of this lottery exists in contemporary texts, though the use of lotteries at other moments during the campaign did occur.

53. Mango, "Notes on Byzantine Monuments."

54. Madden, *Enrico Dandolo*, 174–200; Jacoby, "Latin Empire of Constantinople."

55. Andrea Dandolo, *Chronica*, 280.

56. Pincus, "Christian Relics," 39.

57. See "Corporis beate virginis ac martiris Lucie."

58. Perocco, *Horses of San Marco, Venice*, 56–64. The horses were not actually mounted on San Marco until the 1260s.

59. Schulz, "Piazza medievale"; Madden, *Enrico Dandolo*, 174.

60. Robert of Clari, *Conquest of Constantinople*, 126.

61. Klein, "Eastern Objects and Western Desires."

62. Fotheringham, "Genoa," 42–44.

63. In his letter (*ESC*, 2:56), Innocent lists the gifts as follows: "Carbunculum unum emptum, ut afferit, mille marcas argenti, unum anulum pretiosum, examita quinque, palliumque peroptimum ad altaris ornatum; et per eumdem ad opus Templi transmitterat: duas iconas, unam habentem tres marcas auri et aliam decem marcas argenti, cum ligno vivifice Crucis et multis lapidibus pretiosis, duas cruces aureas, et inter topazios, smaragdos et rubinos pene ducentos, unam crystallinam ampullam, et duos scyphos argenteos, unam sacellam desuper deauratam, duas capsellas, et unam ampullam argenteas, et insuper quinquaginta marcas argenti."

64. Fotheringham, "Genoa," 44.

65. Ibid. *Annali Genovesi di Caffaro*, 2:93, reads, "[A certain ship from Porto Veneris] ceperunt magnum peccunie quantitatem, et multas reliquias sanctorum et cruces dominicas. . . . Ianuam adducta fuit, et per ecclesias, prout uocabula sanctorum errant, diuisa."

66. Fotheringham, "Genoa," 44. The cross is currently on display in the Museum of the Treasury in the Cathedral of San Lorenzo in Genoa.

67. Ibid.

68. *Annali Genovesi di Caffaro*, 2:93.

69. Andrea, *Contemporary Sources*, 98.

70. Brown, "Cistercians." See also Andrea, "Cistercian Accounts," 8. There were six Cistercian abbots who participated in the crusade, and probably many other brothers did as well.

71. *ESC*, 2:61.

72. Ibid., 1:196; Klein, "Eastern Objects and Western Desires," 302, esp. n. 107.

73. *ESC*, 2:64. See also Mark 15:17 and John 19:2, 5.

74. Angold, *Fourth Crusade*, 236.

75. Queller, Compton, and Campbell, "Fourth Crusade"; Kedar, "Second Front."

76. Angold, *Fourth Crusade*, 229.

77. *ESC*, 2:178; Constable, "Troyes"; Durand, "Fragments"; Geary, "St. Helen."

78. *ESC*, 2:109–11.

79. Janin, *La géographie ecclésiastique*, 69.

80. *ESC*, 2:111: "Cum aliis reliquis sanctorum."

81. Ibid.: "Idem vero archiepiscopus magnam contulit portionem illus partis capitis ecclesie Beati Victoris, prece domini Iohannis Teutonii, tunc eisdem ecclesie abbatis."

82. Ibid. Peter does not list the year of the translation.

83. Canon of Langres, "Historia translationum reliquiarum," 29.

84. St. Mary of Egypt Orthodox Church, "Byzantine Monastic Foundation Documents," http://stmaryofegypt.org/typika/typo43.html#page2 (accessed August 29, 2006). Anthony of Novgorod's pilgrim book states that the Byzantine emperor Isaac Angelos (r. 1185–95) restored the Monastery of St. Mamas in Constantinople, which was located in the southwestern portion of the city near the Xylokerkos Gate. It was founded in 527 C.E. Angelos also brought St. Mamas's head from Cappadocia to the monastery to celebrate its restoration.

85. Canon of Langres, "Historia translationum reliquiarum," 28–29: "Cum capta esset Constantinopolis, exultabant victores Latini capta preda, sicut qui invenerant spolia multa. Sed ceca cupiditas, que facile persuadet, ita manus eorum victrices victas tenuit, ut non solum ecclesias violarent, immo etiam vascula, in quibus sanctorum reliquie quiescebant, impudenter effringerent; aurum inde & argentum & gemmas turpiter evellentes, ipsas vero reliquias pro nihilo reputabant. Quo audito, seniores exercitus doluerunt valde, timentes ne talis victoria eis in exitium verteretur; habito igitur consilio, legatus, qui vicem apostolici gerebat, cum archiepiscopis & episcopis, sub districti anathematis interminatione precepit, ne quis sibi retineret reliquias, sed omnes in manu bone memorie Guarneri, tunc Trecensis episcopi, libere resignarent. Inter quas inventum est caput gloriosi martyris."

86. Angold, *Fourth Crusade*, 170, 229; Longnon, *Compagnons*, 219.

87. Ricardus de Gerboredo, "De capta et direpta a Latinis Constantinopoli," 37.

88. Riant, "Dépouilles religieuses à Constantinople," 32.

89. Geary, "St. Helen," 222; Angold, *Fourth Crusade*, 228; Jones, "Constantinople," 32.

90. Rostang of Cluny, "Narratio exceptionis."

91. Ibid., 133: "Valde litteratus."

92. Gill, *Byzantium and the Papacy*, 39.

93. Rostang of Cluny, "Narratio exceptionis," 134–40.

94. *Reg.*, 8:56; Wolff, "Politics in the Latin Patriarchate," 234–36.

95. There is some disagreement about when this happened. Andrea, *Contemporary Sources*, 165n640, argues for March 1205. Madden, *Enrico Dandolo*, 192n127, argues for March 1206. In a letter, Innocent accuses Capuano of having lifted the crusading vow for those who had stayed from "the preceding March to the next," but whether that refers to March 1205 or 1206 is difficult to say (*Reg.*, 8:126).

96. Rostang of Cluny, "Narratio exceptionis," 134: "Angustia ventorum compulsi."

97. Benedict sent a relic shrine, including a piece of the True Cross, to Rome, but it was waylaid by Hungarian pirates. As with the Genoese case, Innocent intervened. See Klein, "Eastern Objects and Western Desires," 303, esp. n. 117.

98. Maleczek, *Pietro Capuano.*

99. Matthew of Amalfi, "Translatio corporis S. Andree," 174–75.

100. Anonymous of Gaeta, "Qualiter caput S. Theodori," 154: "Neapolim vero de aliorum sanctorum reliquiis."

101. *ESC,* 1:ic–c.

102. Ibid., 2:87. The document is a grant from Henry of Ulmen gifting the relic on his behalf and the behalf of his ancestors.

103. Klein, "Eastern Objects and Western Desires," 300–301; Ševcenko, "Limburg Staurothek."

104. Ricardus de Gerboredo, "De capta et direpta a Latinis Constantinopoli," 36–44; Angold, *Fourth Crusade,* 230.

105. Angold, *Fourth Crusade,* 230; Wormald, "Rood of Bromholm"; Andrea, *Contemporary Sources,* 288–89.

106. Klein, "Eastern Objects and Western Desires," 304.

107. Robert of Clari, *Conquest of Constantinople,* 5–6.

108. Ibid., 7–9.

109. Nicolaus Hydruntinus, "Tractatus de Communione," in *ESC,* 2:233–34: "Ὁ Ἀλβετανιασ επισξοποσ, ξαι ο τησ βψλεευ υποψηθιοσ . . . κατακρυψαι."

110. Andrea, "Conrad of Krosigk," 65n229.

111. Lateran IV, Canon 62, in *Conciliorum oecumenicorum decreta,* 263–64; Klein, "Eastern Objects and Western Desires," 300–303.

112. Klein, "Eastern Objects and Western Desires," 302.

113. Jacoby, "Venetian Quarter," 160–64.

114. *ESC,* 2:81.

115. Ibid., 2:83.

116. Ibid., 2:99–100.

117. Ibid., 2:100–101.

118. Ibid., 2:104–5.

119. Ibid., 2:107.

120. William I of Champlitte ruled until 1209. Geoffrey I Villehardouin, who ruled from 1209 to 1228, had two sons. The first, Geoffrey II Villehardouin, ruled from 1228 to 1246, and William II Villehardouin, his brother, ruled from 1246 to 1278. The attribution to "Guillemi de Villa-Harduini, principis Achaiae," is probably a scribal error. Lock, *Franks in the Aegean,* 362.

121. *ESC,* 2:113: "Credimus esse de illo pretioso Sanguini, qui de latere Domini in cruce pro salute fidelium emanavit."

122. Ibid., 2:114–15.

123. Geary, "Sacred Commodities."

124. Hahn, *Strange Beauty,* 223–24.

125. On the Pantepoptes, see Janin, "Les sanctuaires de Byzance," 175–76.

126. Monk of Saint George, "Translatio corporis Beatissimi Pauli Martyris."

127. Mercuri, *Corona di Cristo,* 97–148.

128. Durand, "La translation des reliques"; Mercuri, *Corona di Cristo,* 111–15.

129. Angold, *Fourth Crusade,* 236–40.

130. Klein, "Eastern Objects and Western Desires," 305–6.

131. Rostang of Cluny, "Narratio exceptionis," 134–35.

132. Lateran IV, Canon 62, in *Conciliorum oecumenicorum decreta*, 263–64.

133. Macrides, "New Constantine"; Majeska, "St. Sophia"; Majeska, "Relics of Constantinople."

Chapter 2

1. Madden, "Vows and Contracts," 441.

2. *Reg.*

3. *Deeds of Pope Innocent III*, xiii–xvii.

4. Queller and Madden, *Fourth Crusade*, 66–67, 74–75, 79–82, 85–93, 179–81.

5. Angold, *Fourth Crusade*, 50–74.

6. Gill, *Byzantium and the Papacy*, 28–33.

7. Fotheringham, "Genoa," 43–44.

8. Andrea, *Contemporary Sources*, 114. *Reg.*, 7:153: "Magnifica tecum miracula dignatus est operari ad laudem et gloriam nominis sui, ad honorem et profectum apostolice sedis et ad utilitatem et exaltationem populi Christiani."

9. Andrea, *Contemporary Sources*, 114. *Reg.*, 7:153: "Unde tam te quam terram et hominess tuos sub principali beati Petri speciali nostra protectione suscipimus, dantes firmite in preceptis universes archiepiscopis et episcopis nec non aliis ecclesiarum prelatis, regibus terras et hominess tuos manuteneant et defendant nec eos ipsi molestent nec ab aliis faciant molestari."

10. Andrea, *Contemporary Sources*, 114–15. *Reg.*, 7:153: "Per cuius subventionis auxilium Terra sancta facilius poterit de paganorum minibus liberari."

11. Andrea, *Contemporary Sources*, 115. *Reg.*, 7:153: "Postquam regnum Grecorum ab obedientia sedis apostolice deviavit, de malo simper declinavit in peius, donec a superbis ad humiles, ab inobedientibus ad devotos, a scismaticis ad catholicos iusto Dei iudico est translatum, ut per obedientie virtutem resurgat ad bonum, quod per inobedientie vitium defluxit ad malum."

12. Andrea, *Contemporary Sources*, 115. *Reg.*, 7:153: "Que sunt Cesaris, Cesari et, que sunt Dei, Deo sine confusione reddantur."

13. The relevant scriptures appear in the *Biblia sacra vulgatae editionis* as follows. Matthew 22:21: "Reddite ergo quae sunt Caesaris Caesari et quae sunt Dei Deo." Mark 12:17: "Reddite igitur quae sunt Caesaris Caesari et quae sunt Dei Deo." Luke 20:25: "Reddite ergo quae Caesaris sunt Caesari et quae Dei sunt Deo." Scriptural references throughout the notes are to this edition of the Vulgate.

14. Andrea, *Contemporary Sources*, 142. *Reg.*, 7:205: "Sciendum etiam, quod clerici, qui de parte illa fuerint, de qua non fuerit imperator electus, potestatem habebunt ecclesiam sancte Sophie ordinandi et patriarcham eligendi ad honorem Dei et sancte Romane ecclesie et imperii. Clerici vero utriusque parties illas ecclesias ordinare debent, que sue parti contigerint. De possessionibus vero ecclesiarum tot et tantum clericis et ecclesiis debent provideri, quod honorifice possint vivere et sustentari. Relique vero possessions ecclesiarum divide et partiri debent secundum ordinem presignatum."

15. *Reg.*, 7:205: "Si aliquis contra hanc institutionem ire temptaverit, sit excommunicationis vinculo innodatus."

16. Madden, *Enrico Dandolo*, 176–77.

17. Andrea, *Contemporary Sources*, 61. Andrea notes that in one letter Innocent compares the Venetians to the thieves in the parable of the Good Samaritan and in a later letter links Dandolo to the pharaoh of Exodus. He writes, "We do grieve . . . [that] you follow

Pharaoh, who strives, under a certain semblance of necessity and the veil of piety, to subject you to ancient servitude beneath the yoke of sin."

18. Wolff, "Politics in the Latin Patriarchate."

19. Andrea, *Contemporary Sources*, 142.

20. Janin, *La géographie ecclésiastique*, provides an overview of church property prior to the siege.

21. Andrea, *Contemporary Sources*, 140.

22. Ibid., 107.

23. Ibid., 126n502, suggests that Baldwin had composed his letter in July 1204.

24. Andrea, *Contemporary Sources*, 127–28.

25. Gerland, *Geshichte des lateinischen Kaiserreiches*, 10–13.

26. Madden, "Venetian Version," 317–22.

27. Andrea, *Contemporary Sources*, 129. *Reg.*, 7:202: "Superveniente autem inspiratione divina magis quam humanu, ut opinamur, consilio, superveniente Alexio filio quondam Ysachi." Andrea (129nn511–12) suggests that "superveniente," used twice, reinforces the notion that no person had initiated these unpredictable events. Instead, God had intervened directly.

28. On King Emeric of Hungary from the Venetian perspective, see Queller and Madden, "Some Further Arguments," 449–50. Dandolo wrote in regard to Emeric, "I do not think that you [Innocent] or your predecessors would protect those who only assume the Cross in order to wear it, not even to complete the journey for which pilgrims normally assume the Cross, but to acquire the possessions of another and to criminally hold them." *Reg.*, 7:202; Andrea, *Contemporary Sources*, 129n509.

29. *Reg.*, 7:202.

30. Andrea, *Contemporary Sources*, 130.

31. Madden, *Enrico Dandolo*, 135–36.

32. Ibid., 133–35.

33. Madden, "Venetian Version."

34. Andrea, *Contemporary Sources*, 129.

35. Queller and Madden, *Fourth Crusade*, 190–92.

36. Andrea and Rachlin, "Holy War, Holy Relics," 149–50.

37. For the development of Innocent's apocalyptic interpretation of the Fourth Crusade and the influence of Joachim of Fiore over the pontiff, see Whalen, "Joachim of Fiore," 105–6.

38. Andrea, *Contemporary Sources*, 116–26. See also Whalen, *Dominion of God*, 125–28.

39. Andrea, *Contemporary Sources*, 116–26.

40. *Reg.*, 7:203.

41. Andrea, *Contemporary Sources*, 138. *Reg.*, 7:203: "Cum ad imperii regimen et subventionem Terre sancte ac unitatem ecclesie conservandam utilis et necessaria esset societas eorundem."

42. Andrea, *Contemporary Sources*, 221n93.

43. Rousseau, "Papal Matchmaker."

44. Andrea, *Contemporary Sources*, 139. *Reg.*, 7:203: "Verum cum personarum delictum in dampnum ecclesiarum non debeat redundare, nec idem subdiaconus in aliquot deliquisset."

45. Andrea, *Contemporary Sources*, 139. *Reg.*, 7:203: "Que non solum utilitatem, verum etiam necessitatem."

46. *Gesta Innocentii*, 180–82.

47. *Reg.*, 7:208. The papal scribe enregistered the entirety of the letter to Baldwin, as well as the additional passages from Dandolo's letter, and then remarked that the others received a letter written "in eundum modum" as the one addressed to Baldwin.

48. Andrea, *Contemporary Sources*, 149. *Reg.*, 7:208: "Quam pro eisdem pactionibus confirmandis nobis porrigere procurasti, non duximus admittendam. In eis namque continebatur expresse, quod inter Francos et Venetos divide debent possessions ecclesiastics reservata clericis portione, de qua possint honorifice sustentari. Cum igitur hoc attemptari non posset sine iniuria Creatoris, iuramentum super hoc prestitum illicitum penitus appareret et posset periurium potius appellari, nisi 'salvo apostolice sedis honore' in eodem iuramentio fuisset adiectum."

49. Andrea, *Contemporary Sources*, 151. *Reg.*, 7:208. Referring to anyone who might have tried to take property already, the text reads, "Si fuerit attemptatum, illud faciant per districtionem eandem in statum pristinum revocari."

50. Carile, "Partitio terrarum imperii Romanie."

51. Wolff, "Politics in the Latin Patriarchate," 255–74, addresses the attempts at a settlement process.

52. Janin, "Les sanctuaires de Byzance," 130–76.

53. Andrea, *Contemporary Sources*, 158–60. Kalojan had been crowned by a papal legate in November 1204. He posed a considerable risk to Boniface's agenda.

54. *Reg.*, 8:127: "Ecce etenim, quod cum merore referimus et rubore, unde videbamur hactenus profecisse deficimus, et angustamur unde credebamus potissimum dilatari."

55. *Reg.*, 8:59 (58); Andrea, *Contemporary Sources*, 161.

56. *Reg.*, 8:59 (58), n. 1.

57. Ibid., 8:59 (58); Andrea, *Contemporary Sources*, 158–60.

58. On the circumstances of Dandolo's absolution, see Madden, *Enrico Dandolo*, 178–79.

59. Andrea, *Contemporary Sources*, 158–60. *Reg.*, 8:59 (58): "Gladios, quos exerere debuerant in paganos, Christianorum sanguine cruentantes nec religioni nec etati nec sexui pepercerunt."

60. Andrea, *Contemporary Sources*, 158–60. *Reg.*, 8:59 (58): "Et tam matronas quam virgins etiam Deo dicatas exponentes spurcitiis garcionum." See also Angold, *Fourth Crusade*, 111–12.

61. Andrea, *Contemporary Sources*, 166. *Reg.*, 8:127: "Nec suffecit eisdem imperials divitias exaurire ac diripere spolia principum et minorum, nisi ad thesaurus ecclesiarum et, quod gravius est, ad ipsarum possessions extenderent manus suas, tabulas argenteas etiam de altaribus rapientes et inter se congringentes in frusta, violantes sacraria et cruces et reliquias asportantes."

62. *Reg.*, 8:133: "And thus [the Greeks] rightly detest [the Latins] more than dogs." The phrase appears in both letters, but is placed more powerfully in the letter to Boniface (who was, after all, one of the Latins whom the Greeks now hated).

63. Wolff, "Organization of the Latin Patriarchate," 34.

64. See Andrea, *Contemporary Sources*, 168–69, for this interpretation.

65. Ibid., 175–76. *Reg.*, 8:134: "Ut sub timore Domini et spe venie terram divino iudicio acquisitam teneas et defendas et tenendam ac defendendam acquiras, populos tibi subiectos in iustitia regens, sub pace conservans et religioni conformans, ita ut ecclesiastica bona restituas secundum propriam facultatem."

66. Andrea, *Contemporary Sources*, 161n588.

67. Ibid., 164, esp. nn. 633–35.

68. Ibid., 164–65.

69. Andrea, *Contemporary Sources*, 165. *Reg.*, 8:127: "mittentes vos [Peter Capuano] non ad capescendas temporales divitias sed promerendas eternas."

70. For conflicting views on Venice and the conflict over the patriarchate of Hagia Sophia, see Wolff, "Politics in the Latin Patriarchate," 232, and Madden, *Enrico Dandolo*, 183.

71. Richard, "Latin Church in Constantinople," 55–58.

72. Andrea, *Contemporary Sources*, 147. *Reg.*, 7:206: "Cumque dilectus filius T(homas), Constantinopolitanus electus, in proximo Constantinopolitane ante adventum ipsius aliquid disponendum a laicis vel confirmandum a nobis, quod posset in iuris eius iniuriam et ecclesie sue dispendium redundare."

73. Madden, *Enrico Dandolo*, 181.

74. Ibid., 182.

75. Wolff, "Politics in the Latin Patriarchate," 233.

76. Gill, *Byzantium and the Papacy*, 30–33.

77. Hamilton, "Latin Church in the Crusader States."

78. Wolff, "Politics in the Latin Patriarchate," 255–61.

79. *George Akropolites: History*, 84–85 (text) and 254–55 (commentary). Akropolites, writing in the latter half of the thirteenth century, relates that Pelagius imprisoned and threatened Greek clerics with death. Gill, *Byzantium and the Papacy*, 39, suspects that the story is an exaggeration based on a real conflict.

80. Wolff, "Politics in the Latin Patriarchate," 262–63.

81. Niketas Choniates, *Historia*, 314–15.

82. Geoffrey of Villehardouin, *Chronicles of the Crusades*, 68. Geoffrey of Villehardoiun, *Conquête*, 2:253: "Li uns aporta bien et li autres mauvaisement: que covoitise, qui est racine de toz mals, ne laissa; ainz comencierent d'enqui ennavant li covetous a retenir des chose, et Nostre Sire les comença mains a amer. Ha! Diex, cum s'estoient leialment demené trosque a cel point! Et Dam le Diex lor avoit bien mostré que de toz lor afaires les avoit honorez et essauciez sor tote l'autre gent; et maintes foiz ont domage li bon por les malvais."

83. Robert of Clari, *Conquest of Constantinople*, 100–101. Robert of Clari, *Li estoires*, 79–80: "Et puis aprés fist on crier par l'ost que nus ne presist ostel devant la que on aroit atirè comment on les prenderoit. Adont si s'asanlerent li haut homme, li rike homme, et prisent consel entr'aus que le menue gent n'en seurent mot ne le povre chevalier de l'ost, que li prenderoient les meilleurs ostex de le vile; et tresdont commenchierent il a traïr le menue gent, et a porter leur male foi et male compaingnie, que il comperent puis molt kier, si comme nous dirons aprés."

84. Robert of Clari, *Conquest of Constantinople*, 126. Robert of Clari, *Li estoires*, 106: "Ensi faitement se venja Damedieus d'aus, pour leur orguel et pour le male foi qu'il avoient portee a le povre gent de l'ost, et les oribles pekiés qu'il avoient fais en le chité, aprés chou qu'il l'eurent prise."

85. On the authorship of this text, see Andrea, "*Devastatio Constantinopolitana*," 125.

86. Andrea, *Contemporary Sources*, 221. Andrea, "*Devastatio Constantinopolitana*," 125: "Interea ceperunt communia dividere, et quasi quedam preludia."

87. Translation from Gunther of Pairis, *Capture of Constantinople*, 15–16; see 137nn54–55. See also Swietek, "Gunther of Pairis," 70–71. Burchard of Ursperg, *Chronicon*: "Quidam etiam abbas . . . qui vocatur Parisius . . . plurimus reliquias ad monasterium suum detulit, quae adhuc retinentur ibidem; an furtivae sint, iudicet qui legit. An videlicet domnus papa talem rapinam in populo christiano factam potueri iustificare, sicut furtum Israelitici populi in Aegypto iustificatur auctoritate divina."

88. *De doctrina Christiana*, book 2, sec. 40.

89. Robert of Clari, *Conquest of Constantinople*, 59. Robert of Clari, *Li estoires*, 32: "Or y eut il aucuns qui ne s'acorderent mie a aler en Coustantinoble, ains disoient: 'Ba! que ferons nous en Coustantinoble, nous avons no pelerinage a faire et ausi pourposement d'aler en Babyloine ou en Alexandre.'" See also Siberry, *Criticism of Crusading*, 172.

90. Throop, *Criticism of the Crusade*, 30; Siberry, *Criticism of Crusading*, 174–75. See also Guiot de Provins, *Les œuvres*, 34: "Je di que ce seroit raisons / c'on destrusce la covoitise / qui en Rome s'est toute mise, et l'orguel, et la felonie: ou mont n'ait tant de trecherie."

91. Throop, *Criticism of the Crusade*, 30–31.

92. *Deeds of Pope Innocent III*, xi–xiii, offers an informed speculation that the author was Peter of Benevento. Peter compiled Innocent's decretals in 1209, around the same time that the *Gesta* was composed. The attribution is logical. If it was not Peter, it most certainly was a cleric inside the curia who knew Innocent and his advisors personally.

93. *Reg.*, 8:127 (my translation): "Cruces et reliquias asportantes."

94. *Deeds of Pope Innocent III*, 172.

95. *Reg.*, 8:126: "viris et viribus . . . destituta."

96. *Reg.*, 8:226; see the comments of Hageneder et al.

97. *Deeds of Pope Innocent III*, 172–73.

98. Angold, *Fourth Crusade*, 114, 127n15; *History of the Albigensian Crusade*, 56–59, lines 104–6. This passage occurs within a description of the many heroic qualities and exemplary history of Simon de Montfort. This section also mentions how Abbot Guy of Vaux-de-Cernay always agreed with papal policy, read the letters from Innocent to the crusaders, and refused to be involved with the attack on Zara or the diversion to Constantinople.

99. Angold, *Fourth Crusade*, 114.

100. Pryor, *"Eracles"*; Edbury, "Lyon *Eracles*."

101. Angold, *Fourth Crusade*, 114–15.

102. Ibid.; Robert of Auxerre, *Chronicon*, 265.

Chapter 3

1. See Siberry, *Criticism of Crusading*, 81–84, for the "purging of sin" in crusade and anti-crusade narrative.

2. Murray, "'Mighty Against the Enemies of Christ.'"

3. Andrea and Rachlin, "Holy War, Holy Relics," 172–73.

4. Anonymous of Halberstadt, "De peregrinatione in Grecia," 15. Andrea, *Contemporary Sources*, 255: "In the end, once the city was captured, Alexius, put in the place of Alexius, was put to flight and was blinded by Alexius, the paternal uncle of Alexius."

5. Matthew of Amalfi, "Translatio corporis S. Andree," 166–71.

6. Andrea, *Contemporary Sources*, 224.

7. Geoffrey of Villehardouin, *Conquête*, 1:40–44.

8. Andrea, *Contemporary Sources*, 224. Although Innocent entrusted the bishop with letters forbidding the diversion to Constantinople, Nivelon instead took part in keeping the news of the pope's disapproval from the rank-and-file crusaders.

9. Schmandt, "Fourth Crusade and the Just War."

10. Geoffrey of Villehardouin, *Conquête*, 2:66; Robert of Clari, *Li estoires*, 93.

11. Andrea, *Contemporary Sources*, 226–27.

12. Ibid., 235. Lock, *Franks in the Aegean*, 206. Innocent granted Nivelon permission to serve in both Soissons and Thessalonika simultaneously. *Patrologia Latina*, 215:1037–38.

13. Geoffrey of Villehardouin, *Conquête*, 2:388.

14. Andrea, *Contemporary Sources*, 225.

15. Originally titled "De terra Iherosolimitana et quomodo ab urbe Constantinopoli-tana ad hanc ecclesiam allate sunt reliquie."

16. Andrea and Rachlin, "Holy War, Holy Relics," 152.

17. Ibid., 155–56.

18. Ibid., 165: "Peccatis exigentibus."

19. Andrea, *Contemporary Sources*, 224, argues that the text must have been written before Nivelon died on September 13, 1207, because it refers to the bishop as still living.

20. Andrea and Rachlin, "Holy War, Holy Relics," 171.

21. The connection between the finger of Thomas and the belt of the Virgin Mary extends well beyond this document. See Most, *Doubting Thomas*, 155–213, and MacClan-nan, "Bulgarini's Assumption with Doubting Thomas," 65–67.

22. Andrea and Rachlin, "Holy War, Holy Relics," 172–73.

23. Ibid., 172.

24. Ibid., 173n56. Andrea cites Josephus's *Antiquities* on the death of the Baptist. The Soissons text claims that both his head and arm were delivered to Soissons, but the head also appears frequently in other Fourth Crusade relic inventories.

25. Andrea and Rachlin, "Holy War, Holy Relics," 174n65.

26. Ibid., 157, 173.

27. Ibid., 174.

28. Ibid., 174–75.

29. See Reynolds, *Kingdoms and Communities*, 79–100, for the power of lay collective action within a parish, despite the overt hierarchies present.

30. Andrea, "Conrad of Krosigk."

31. Ibid., 21. On Philip and Otto, see Winkelmann, *Philipp von Schwaben und Otto IV.* Andrea, "Conrad of Krosigk," 21nn35–36, has disagreed with a number of Winkelmann's conclusions as regards the papal legates and Conrad.

32. Andrea, "Conrad of Krosigk," 21–26.

33. Ibid., 60. Conrad managed to get a protégé elected as his successor and so had some continued influence.

34. Ibid., 63.

35. Andrea, *Contemporary Sources*, 241–43.

36. Ibid., 254.

37. Riant, in *ESC*, 1:iv, argued that the section on relics operates as a distinct text, but Andrea, *Contemporary Sources*, 240, sees the entire account of the crusade, including the arrival of its sacred spoils, as a single *apologia*.

38. Andrea, *Contemporary Sources*, 254.

39. Ibid., 256 and 256n92. The church was supposedly built by Peter and Andrew, and it is well attested to in medieval pilgrimage texts.

40. Andrea, *Contemporary Sources*, 257.

41. Ibid., 239–64.

42. Ibid., 255. Anonymous of Halberstadt, "De peregrinatione in Grecia," 15: "Quam prodigiosa autem per exercitum tam humilem quam despectum, dominus operatus sit miracula."

43. Andrea, "Conrad of Krosigk," 67 and 67n236; Burchard of Ursperg, *Chronicon*. Although the author of the "Gesta" was a canon of the Cathedral of Halberstadt, Conrad had entered the Cistercian monastery at Sittichenbach. Burchard and Abbot Martin were both Cistercians as well.

44. Andrea, *Contemporary Sources*, 260.

45. Ibid., 260–61. Anonymous of Halberstadt, "De peregrinatione in Grecia," 19: "Et merito venerandum antistitem qui venerat conclamabant in nominee Domini benedictum: ipse enim secum sanctorum pignora apportavit, cum quibus indubitanter pax et salus patrie sunt illata."

46. Andrea, *Contemporary Sources*, 261. Anonymous of Halberstadt, "De peregrinatione in Grecia," 19: "Nam in serenissimo eorumdem sanctorum adventu."

47. Andrea, *Contemporary Sources*, 261 and 261nn115–17.

48. Ibid.

49. "Iustum deduxit Dominus." Andrea, *Contemporary Sources*, 261 and 261n121. Andrea notes that this chant was generally reserved for unjustly persecuted martyrs and discusses how its use liturgically reinforces the author's theme.

50. Andrea, "Conrad of Krosigk," 65–66; Konrad von Krosigk, *Urkundenbuch der Familie von Krosigk*, 401, no. 499.

51. Longnon, *Compagnons*, 219.

52. Queller and Madden, *Fourth Crusade*, 3; Geoffrey of Villehardouin, *Chronicles of the Crusades*, 29.

53. Queller and Madden, *Fourth Crusade*, 69, 181. See also Pryor, "Transportation of Horses."

54. Queller and Madden, *Fourth Crusade*, 255n141; Queller, Compton, and Campbell, "Fourth Crusade."

55. Queller and Madden, *Fourth Crusade*, 180.

56. Ibid., 201; *Reg.*, 8:152.

57. See *ESC*, 2:109–11, for the letters regarding the translation of the head of St. Victor.

58. Angold, *Fourth Crusade*, 229. See Lock, *Franks in the Aegean*, 57–60, for the formation of the Frankish states, and 193–217 for the Latin secular church.

59. The historiography of Langres and its cathedral has focused on the position and rights of its bishop. As early as 967 C.E., the bishop obtained nominal lay oversight of the region, and by 1179 possessed the title of Count of Langres and all its rights. By 1356, the position had been augmented to a duchy and had become the third "ecclesiastical peer of the realm." See Constable, "Disputed Election at Langres," 119–20; Claudon, *Histoire de Langres*, 32–39; and Daguin, "Les évêques de Langres." With regard to the early cult of St. Mamas in Langres, Didier has published an edition of a charter from 893 that established the annual celebration of St. Mamas's day ("La pluralité des archidiacres," 275–76).

60. See, for example, Geary, "St. Helen," 149–68. St. Helen was a relatively insignificant saint who nevertheless captured the imagination of the local clerics and ultimately their followers and proved very useful in mid-thirteenth-century fundraising. Troyes, a city near Langres, unleashed a major publicity campaign for Helen and over time raked in vastly increased donations.

61. Riant suggests that the author inserted the Fourth Crusade story into a preexisting textual tradition, adding a new prologue and a new section. *ESC*, 1:lx–lxiii and 22–28.

62. See, for example, Ricardus de Gerboredo, "De capta et direpta a Latinis Constantinopoli," 37.

63. Canon of Langres, "Historia translationum reliquiarum," 29: "AGIOS MAMAS."

64. Ibid.

65. Ibid.

66. Ibid., 31.

67. Longnon, *Compagnons*, 219.

68. Angold, *Fourth Crusade*, 170, 229.

69. Canon of Langres, "Historia translationum reliquiarum," 31–33.

70. On Gaeta, see Abulafia, *Frederick II*, 94–102. Skinner, *Family Power in Southern Italy*, emphasizes the rise of merchant families within the city. Fiengo, *Gaeta*, 59–105, discusses the churches.

71. *ESC*, 1:c.

72. Anonymous of Gaeta, "Qualiter caput S. Theodori," 150: "Sicut enim stele in cello, ita sancti lucent in ecclesia Dei, ad quorum claritatem . . . id est a Christo."

73. Ibid., 150–51.

74. See Angold, *Byzantine Empire*, 295–315, on the "failure of the Comenian system." See also Magdalino, *Empire of Manuel I Komnenos*.

75. Anonymous of Gaeta, "Qualiter caput S. Theodori," 153: "Quod Terre Sancte succurrerent."

76. Ibid.

77. *Deeds of Pope Innocent III*, 155.

78. Anonymous of Gaeta, "Qualiter caput S. Theodori," 153–54: "Sicut decebat, est reverenter susceptus, et cum modo civitas Constantinopolitana spoliata erat, et ecclesie violate."

79. Ibid., 154: "Rebus sanctis."

80. Ibid.: "Qui siquidem, utpote cautus et circumspectus, reliquias occultavit, et occulte illas ad civitatem nativatis sue . . . properavit."

81. Ibid., 154–55: "Ita nos vitiorum flammas, miserante Domino, extinguentes." St. Theodore of Amasea was burned at the stake in 306 C.E.

82. *ESC*, 1:c.

83. Niketas Choniates, *O City*, 298–99.

84. Robert of Clari, *Li estoires*, 31.

85. Maleczek, *Pietro Capuano*, 214, 240; Del Treppo and Leone, *Amalfi medioevale*, 20, 36; Dvornik, *Idea of Apostolicity in Byzantium*, 181.

86. Maleczek, *Pietro Capuano*, 235–36. There remains some confusion about the precise date of composition of this manuscript. Maleczek asserts that Riant and various later scholars misdated and misidentified the "Translatio corporis S. Andree de Constantinopoli in Amalphiam." Riant states that it is a fourteenth-century text ordered by Peter Capuano of Amalfi, who served as archbishop from 1351 to 1360, to lionize his ancestor. Maleczek argues that Matteo of Amalfi (d. 1229), also archbishop, wrote the text. Riant identifies an archdeacon of the same name. There are two manuscripts, each varying slightly from the other, both quite late. No reliable connection to the thirteenth century exists. See ibid., 230–33nn10–15.

87. Matthew of Amalfi, "Translatio corporis S. Andree," 166–71.

88. Ibid., 174–75.

89. Janin, *La géographie ecclésiastique*, 246–51.

90. The date in the title is based on the Venetian calendar. Using the modern Gregorian calendar, the date of the theft was April 18, 1204 C.E. See Chiesa, "Ladri," 446–48, and Perry, "*Translatio Symonensis*," 102.

91. Biblioteca Nazionale Braidense, Milan, MS Gerli 26, fols. 71r–74v; quotes on 71r. A full English translation is published in Perry, "*Translatio Symonensis*," 107–12. See Chiesa, "Ladri," for another edition.

92. MS Gerli 26, fol. 71r.

93. Ibid.

94. Isaiah 11:2–3: "Et requiescet super eum spiritus Domini spiritus sapientiae et intellectus spiritus consilii et fortitudinis spiritus scientiae et pietatis et replebit eum spiritus timoris Domini non secundum visionem oculorum iudicabit neque secundum auditum aurium arguet."

95. See Perry, "*Translatio Symonensis,*" 93–95, 106, for the names.

96. MS Gerli 26, fol. 72r: "predestinatum."

97. Ibid., fol. 74r.

98. *Uxeria* were designed to be beached on the shore so that knights could ride their horses directly out of the hold and onto the deck, then charge down a ramp into battle. Pryor, "Transportation of Horses," 21–23.

99. MS Gerli 26, fol. 74v.

100. Crouzet-Pavan, *Venice Triumphant,* 69–70; Wolff, "Politics in the Latin Patriarchate," 234; Powell, *Anatomy of a Crusade.* For post-Damietta criticism of the Fifth Crusade, see Throop, *Criticism of the Crusade,* 31–34, and Siberry, *Criticism of Crusading,* 63–66.

101. Robbert, "Venetian Participation," 33–34.

102. Pride as a cause for losing God's good will is a common theme in contemporary crusading literature. See, for example, Oliver of Paderborn, *Die Schriften des Kölner Domscholasters,* 277–78.

103. Monk of St. George, "Translatio corporis Beatissimi Pauli Martyris," 141–42.

104. Ibid., 142: "Nos hec diximus, fratres mei dilectissimi, ut nemo superbire audeat, vel aliquem habere despectui: quia Deus superbis resistit, humilibus autem dat gratiam." See 1 Peter 5:5.

105. Ibid.: "Grecorum imperium ex tunc in antea factum est Latinorum."

106. Wolff, "Politics in the Latin Patriarchate," 227–44.

107. On this church and Venice, see Ousterhout, "Some Notes," 47; Matthews, *Byzantine Churches,* 59–70; and Wolff, "Politics in the Latin Patriarchate," 255–74.

108. The text is referring to Paolo Venier, who was abbot from 1220 to 1234. Damerini, *L'isola e il cenobio,* 188–89.

109. Monk of St. George, "Translatio corporis Beatissimi Pauli Martyris," 143.

110. Ibid.: "Tanti vero thesauri, quem reliquerat, non immemor."

111. Ibid.

112. Wolff, "New Document," 544–47; Thiriet, *La Romanie vénitienne,* 92–93. See Madden, *Enrico Dandolo,* 196–97 and 226n3, on the office of the podestà.

113. Wolff, "New Document," 561 and 561n3, lists Storlato as podestà from August 27, 1222, to "as late as 15 April 1223." Storlato had risen from *iudex* (judge) in 1195 to councillor by 1219, and was alive as late as 1231.

114. Monk of St. George, "Translatio corporis Beatissimi Pauli Martyris," 144.

115. Ibid.: "Nam, sicut b. Marcum pene de universsis partibus visitare adveniunt innumerabiles viri & femine, ita beatum Paulum facta est gloriosa consuetudo videndi."

116. Ibid.

117. Ibid., 147: "Sed sicut confors nominis et gentium magister beatus apostolus Paulus Cesarem appellaverat . . . se Rome in fide Christi multis profuturum."

118. Ibid.

119. Riant drew his edition of this text from a seventeenth-century publication of the manuscript. By Riant's time, the original manuscript had already been lost. *ESC* 1:xciv–xcv.

120. Rostang of Cluny, "Narratio exceptionis," 128: "Urbanus . . . vir religiosissums et reverendissimus, quem divina disposition de claustro Cluniacensi elegit in sacerdotem sibi."

121. Ibid.: "Nunc vero ad modernos, et ad moderna tempor stylum vertamus, brevite intimantes . . . a quibus caput S. Clementis a Constantinopoli Cluniacum translatum est."

122. Whalen, *Dominion of God,* 142.

123. Rostang of Cluny, "Narratio exceptionis," 130–32.

124. Ibid., 132.

125. Ibid., 133: "Huic sacro comitatui iunxit se quidam miles, nominee Dalmacius de Serciaco, vir nobilis et valde litteratus, qui sibi affociavit quondam militem nominee pocium de Bufferia, virum fidelem et bonum socium." See Longnon, *Compagnons*, 219–21.

126. Rostang of Cluny, "Narratio exceptionis," 133: "Qui transitum eis neque naulo neque aliquot pretio ex longo tempore concedere voluerent."

127. Ibid.: "Tandem a laburintho eorum liberati." The labyrinth refers to the impasse at Venice, although it was really the agreement to attack Zara that liberated the crusade.

128. Ibid.: "Greci vero divino nutu terga vertentes."

129. Ibid.: "Quapropter idem predictus Dalmacius, eo quod Hierusalem adire non poterat, deliberavit cum socio suo qualiter caput beati Clementis pie furari posset. Quot caput audierat a quodam imperatore a mari Constantinopolim esse translatum. . . . Quod quomodo Deo concedente Dalmacius predictum Sancti caput Clementis obtinuerit, ipso narrante audite."

130. Ibid., 133–34: "Ego, Dalmacius de Serciaco, et socius meus Poncius de Busseria . . . proposueramus terram Hierosolymitanam visitare."

131. Ibid., 133.

132. Ibid., 134: "Exaudivit Dominus vocem fletus mei."

133. Ibid.: "Ut undecumque possem habere sanctorum reliquias absque venalite, quia lex inhiber ut nemo martyres distrahat, nemo mercetur." *Distrahat*, from *distraho* (to distract or disassemble), can mean to sell off in parcels.

134. Ibid., 135. The actual transliteration of the Greek should be "O Agios Clementios," or "'Ο ΑΓΙΟΣ ΚΛΕΜΕΝΤΙΟΣ." A lowercase gamma (g) looks a lot like the Latin "y," and presumably neither Rostang nor Dalmacius were literate in Greek.

135. The head of St. Clement was kept in the Monastery of St. Mary Peribleptos in the southwest corner of the Golden Horn. Angold, *Fourth Crusade*, 229.

136. Rostang of Cluny, "Narratio exceptionis," 136–38.

137. Ibid., 139. The pun works in Latin as in English: "Ut confugeremus ad sanctum Clementem, cuius reliquias portabamus, eiusque experirmur clementiam."

138. Ibid., 139–40.

139. Gunther's work has been well studied. See Alfred J. Andrea, "Essay on Primary Sources," in Queller and Madden, *Fourth Crusade*, 305. Andrea first published on the *Historia Constantinopolitana* in 1980, almost two decades before he published his translation and commentary. I have used Andrea's translations of this text. See Gunther of Pairis, *Capture of Constantinople*.

140. See Gunther of Pairis, *Capture of Constantinople*, 5–14, for Gunther's career as a writer.

141. Ibid., 5.

142. Andrea, in Gunther of Pairis, *Capture of Constantinople*, 38–44, links Gunther to Robert of Rheim's prosimetrical *Historia Iherosolimitana* and Boethius's *Consolation of Philosophy*. Robert uses poetry as mere ornament, whereas both Boethius and Gunther use it more centrally. On the genre, see Swietek, "Gunther of Pairis," 59–62.

143. Gunther of Pairis, *Capture of Constantinople*, 65n1.

144. Ibid., 64.

145. Martin has been remembered by historians as a simple, almost clownish, greedy person. See, for example, Queller and Madden, *Fourth Crusade*, 195. One must wonder what the abbot, as patron, thought of his caricature.

146. Gunther of Pairis, *Capture of Constantinople*, 64.

147. Ibid., 44.

148. Ibid., 66: "Quia sine me nihil potestis facere." Presumably this is a reference to John 15:5. Note that in the "Translatio Symonensis" Andrea Balduino prayed the same prayer before first setting out to find the relics of St. Simon.

149. Ibid., 75–76. Gunther does admit that his Martin is, perhaps, "the lesser" of the two.

150. Andrea, "Cistercian Accounts," 27. See also Brown, "Cistercians," 75–76.

151. Swietek, "Gunther of Pairis," 78–79.

152. Gunther of Pairis, *Capture of Constantinople*, 89.

153. See Swietek, "Gunther of Pairis," 50–55, and Gunther of Pairis, *Capture of Constantinople*, 56–58.

154. Gunther of Pairis, *Capture of Constantinople*, 91.

155. Swietek, "Gunther of Pairis," 65.

156. Harper, "Turks as Trojans," 154–56, notes that whereas ancient Romans tended to Orientalize all depictions of the Trojans except for Aeneas, medieval artists and authors "tended to deprioritze both the chronological distance and the easternness of Troy." Thus, Gunther's portrayal of the Latins as "Hellenes" and the Greeks as "Trojans" is unusual. That said, Robert of Clari also identified Constantinople as Troy, so one could speculate that this analogy was prevalent within the Latin army.

157. Gunther of Pairis, *Capture of Constantinople*, 109.

158. Ibid., 111.

159. Andrea, in Gunther of Pairis, *Capture of Constantinople*, 173n241, suggests that the author could have selected the more neutral verb *caparet* (to seize) had he wanted to.

160. Ibid., 112.

161. Ibid., 128.

Chapter 4

1. Geary, *Furta Sacra*, 9–14. See also Andrea's introduction to Gunther of Pairis, *Capture of Constantinople*, 17.

2. Gunther of Pairis, *Capture of Constantinople*, 65.

3. Ibid., 91.

4. Ibid., 93.

5. Jacoby, "Venetian Quarter," map on 154; see also 160–62. In 1223, Marino Storlato, podestà, formed a commission with Emperor Robert of Courtenay (r. 1219–28) to resolve the commercial and territorial arguments between the Venetians and the Franks that still lingered up to that point.

6. Cracco, "Chiesa e istituzioni," 17–18 and 28n27.

7. Andrea and Rachlin, "Holy War, Holy Relics," 154. Riley-Smith, *First Crusade*, 108, also emphasizes the relic-like qualities of the Holy Land for Latin crusaders.

8. Whalen, *Dominion of God*, 142.

9. See Isaiah 11:2–3.

10. Biblioteca Nazionale Braidense, Milan, MS Gerli 26, fol. 72r.

11. Ibid.: "Sed ad ea que gesta sunt vel facta ab illis de translatione corporis sancti Simeonis prophete vertamur stillum."

12. Ibid., fols. 72v–73r. The final sentences read, "In hoc enim, karissimi, considerare possumus quam grave delictum est periurum. Caveamus ergo nos, dilectissimi, a periurio et ab omni peccato, ut digni simus videre speram claritatis eius."

13. Matthews, *Byzantine Churches*, 319–20; Mango, "Notes on Byzantine Monuments."

14. Monk of St. George, "Translatio corporis Beatissimi Pauli Martyris," 144: "Sunt qui nequiter humiliant se, et interiora eorum plena sunt dolo et fallacia." See Ecclesiasticus 9:23: "Et est qui emittit verbum certum enarrans veritatem est qui nequiter humiliat se et interiora eius plena sunt dolo."

15. Ibid.: "Accipite sapientiam, sicut aurum." See Proverbs 8:10: "Accipite disciplinam meam et non pecuniam doctrinam magis quam aurum eligite."

16. Ibid.: "Ideo sapientia etiam eum dicimus ornatum."

17. Ibid., 145. The monk quotes James 3:17 from the Vulgate word for word here: "Quae autem desursum est sapientia primum quidem pudica est deinde pacifica modesta suadibilis plena misericordia et fructibus bonis non iudicans sine simulatione."

18. Ibid.: "Dei, cecus passus est . . . cecitatem. O mira! O stupenda!"

19. Ibid., 146: "O naute, cur timebatis perire? Portabatis portantem, et nesciebatis; habebatis salvantem, et ignorabatis."

20. Ibid.

21. Andrea, *Contemporary Sources*, 261 and 261n121.

22. Andrea, "Anonymous Chronicler of Halberstadt's Account," 447–69.

23. Whalen, *Dominion of God*, 142.

24. MS Gerli 26, 71r; Monk of St. George, "Translatio corporis Beatissimi Pauli Martyris," 149.

25. Gunther of Pairis, *Capture of Constantinople*, 120–21.

26. Ibid., 121.

27. Ibid., 123n305.

28. Ibid., 120.

29. Ibid., 122.

30. Ibid.

31. Andrea notes that correlations between St. Martin and Abbot Martin appear frequently in the text and has detected numerous places where Gunther clearly drew from the former's *vita*. Gunther of Pairis, *Capture of Constantinople*, 147; Sulpicius Severus, *Writings*, 79–254.

32. Gunther of Pairis, *Capture of Constantinople*, 122.

33. Ibid., 123.

34. Ibid., 123 and 178n308.

35. Monk of St. George, "Translatio corporis Beatissimi Pauli Martyris," 142: "Fratres mei dilectissimi."

36. Ibid., 146.

37. Anonymous of Gaeta, "Qualiter caput S. Theodori," 150.

38. Ibid., 154.

39. Ibid.

40. Andrea and Rachlin, "Holy War, Holy Relics," 174.

41. Ibid., 174–75.

42. Canon of Langres, "Historia translationum reliquiarum," 31.

43. Perry, "*Translatio Symonensis*," 107. See Matthew 5:6.

44. Ibid.

45. Ibid.

46. Monk of St. George, "Translatio corporis Beatissimi Pauli Martyris," 147: "Beatus martyr Paulus sed sicut confors et gentium magister beatus apostolus Paulus Cesarem appellaverat, sciens per Spiritum, se Rome in fide Christi multis profuturum: ita beatus iste martyr, deduci se sinebat Venetias, et si, non predicatione, miraculis similia multis

facturus." The Monk of St. George might be referring to Acts 25:11, in which Paul says, "Caesarem appello," or perhaps to an unknown medieval *vita*.

47. On the practice of retrospective prophecy more generally, see Otter, *"Prolixitas Temporum,"* 47–49. On the predictions in the "Translatio Pauli," see Perry, "Paul the Martyr."

48. Robert of Clari, *Li estoires*, 89–90.

49. Gunther of Pairis, *Capture of Constantinople*, 120.

50. Ibid.

51. Riley-Smith, *First Crusaders*, 150–52. For the translatio from Anchin, see "Narratio quomodo rellquiae martyris Georgii."

52. Anonymous of Gaeta, "Qualiter caput S. Theodori," 154–55.

53. Anonymous of Halberstadt, "De peregrinatione in Grecia," 19.

54. Andrea and Rachlin, "Holy War, Holy Relics," 171.

55. Gunther of Pairis, *Capture of Constantinople*, 125.

56. Matthew of Amalfi, "Translatio corporis S. Andree," 177.

57. Vincent, *Holy Blood*, 73–74.

Chapter 5

1. One must disentangle the Renaissance myth of the perfect republic from the medieval city. To approach this large subject, begin with Fasoli, "Nascita di un mito"; Benzoni, "Venezia: Tra mito e realtà"; Dale, "Inventing a Sacred Past"; and Muir, *Civic Ritual*, esp. parts 1 and 2. Muir's chapter on the relationship between the creation of rituals and the creation of myths, "From Myth to Ritual or from Ritual to Myth," is especially relevant (*Civic Ritual*, 55–64). See also Pincus, "Venice and the Two Romes." Demus's vital work on San Marco (*Church of San Marco in Venice*) included a section on "mythogenesis," a term he coined. As regards various aspects of Venetian myth, see the essays in Martin and Romano, *Venice Reconsidered*, especially the editors' introduction, "Reconsidering Venice." Finally, see Crouzet-Pavan, *Venice Triumphant*.

2. Pincus, "Andrea Dandolo"; Grubb, "When Myths Lose Power," 44. Also see all of Maguire and Nelson, *San Marco, Byzantium, and the Myths of Venice*.

3. For the negative perspective, see Rubenstein, "Italian Reactions to the Terraferma Expansion," and Grubb, "When Myths Lose Power," 44n4.

4. Grubb, "When Myths Lose Power," 44.

5. Perry, "Material Culture"; Barry, *"Disiecta Membra."*

6. For the development of the origin myths of Venice, see Carile, "Le origini di Venezia."

7. Madden, *Enrico Dandolo*, 1–19; Dale, "Cultural Hybridity," 151–53.

8. Demus, *Church of San Marco*, 11–16.

9. Tassini, *La questione storico giuridica*, 45.

10. For references to the translation before 1050 c.e., see Tramontin, "Realtà e leggenda," 53; Niero, "Questioni agiografiche," 18–27, esp. 20; Geary, *Furta Sacra*, 92; Tobler and Molinier, *Itinera Hierosolymitana*, 311; Cracco, "I testi agiografici," 923; and Demus, *Church of San Marco*, 9–10.

11. McCleary, "Note storiche," 223. McCleary provides the critical edition of the translatio text. A tenth-century version of the narrative also exists.

12. Cracco, "I testi agiografici," 950–52.

13. Demus, *Mosaics of San Marco*, 1:30–33. Perry, "Material Culture," 15 and 24.

14. Niero, "Reliquie e corpi di santi," 195–96.

15. Pertusi, "La contesa per le reliquie di S. Nicola." For the translatio narrative, see Monk of the Lido, "Historia."

16. Pertusi, "Venezia e Bisanzio," 6–7, suggests that the bishop of Castello may have sought an appropriate elite saintly patron, though the translatio focuses on a possible resting place in San Marco.

17. Monk of the Lido, "Historia," 266–67.

18. Madden, *Enrico Dandolo*, 11.

19. Niero, "Reliquie e corpi di santi," 197.

20. *San Giorgio Maggiore*, 2:504nCXLIV.

21. Cracco, "I testi agiografici," 951: "Un santo per i vinti." In Cracco's conception, Mark was the saint of the doges, Nicholas the saint of the commoners (the sailors), and Stephen the saint of the merchants.

22. Madden, *Enrico Dandolo*, 8; Andrea Dandolo, *Chronica*, 217.

23. Chiesa, "Santità d'importazione."

24. For example, Dale, "Cultural Hybridity,"

25. Madden, *Enrico Dandolo*, 189–90.

26. Ibid., 195–99.

27. Fotheringham, *Marco Sanudo*, 50–55; Madden, *Enrico Dandolo*, 198.

28. Madden, *Enrico Dandolo*, 200n26; Lazzarini, "I titoli dei dogi di Venezia," 300.

29. Fotheringham, *Marco Sanudo*, 80–85.

30. Geary, "St. Helen."

31. Angold, *Fourth Crusade*, 235.

32. Geary, *Furta Sacra*, 29–30.

33. Angold, *Fourth Crusade*, 237–40.

34. Andrea and Rachlin, "Holy War, Holy Relics," 162–63.

35. Biblioteca Nazionale Braidense, Milan, MS Gerli 26, fol. 74r: "Quanti tripudii quantique gaudii repleta sit civita Venetorum, quantaque mirabilia in mari veniendo Dominus dignatus est ostendere, nullus hominum nulla lingua valeret annuciare. Suscepto itaque corpore reliquiis omnibus domino Leonardo plebano ceterisque clericis et convicinis, rogaverunt dominum Benedictum Faletro tunc Gradensem patriarcham et dominum Marcum Nicolam Castellanum episcopum ut venirent et reconderent preciosa pignora."

36. Monk of St. George, "Translatio corporis Beatissimi Pauli Martyris": "Hunc rogavit, ut pretiosam gemmam suo abbati deferret, que non solum monasterium, sed & totam Venetiam sua presentia decoraret. Nam, sicut b. Marcum pene de universsis partibus visitare adveniunt innumerabiles viri & femine, ita beatum Paulum facta est gloriosa consuetudo videndi."

37. Ibid., 148.

38. Corner, *Notizie storiche*, 474. See also Damerini, *L'isola e il cenobio*, 245, for a 1362 inventory of the contents of the treasury.

39. Monk of St. George, "Translatio corporis Beatissimi Pauli Martyris," 144: "Accipite sapientiam, sicut aurum." See Proverbs 8:10: "Accipite disciplinam meam et non pecuniam doctrinam magis quam aurum eligite."

40. Ibid.: "Ideo sapientia etiam eum dicimus ornatum."

41. Perry, "Material Culture."

42. Vergil, *Aeneid*, book 1, lines 267–71. In this passage, Jupiter explains to Venus that all will be well; Aeneas will survive, and so will his son. Note the use of *imperio* and *transferet* in the following verse (emphasis added): "At puer Ascanius, cui nunc cognomen Iulo / additur (Ilus erat, dum res stetit Ilia regno), / triginta magnos volvendis mensibus orbis / *imperio* explebit, regnumque ab sede Lavini / *transferet*, et Longam multa vi muniet Albam."

43. Pocock, *Barbarism and Religion*, 127–50. Pocock offers a useful overview in the chapter "The Historiography of *Translatio Imperii*."

44. For examples, see Akbari, *Idols in the East*, 5.

45. Sgarbi, *"Translatio Studiorum,"* 67–108. The three medieval chapters offer the most recent overview of the medieval tradition.

46. Nederman, "Empire and the Historiography of European Political Thought." Marsiglio's writing contains a fairly straightforward account of how the empire moved from the emperors of Rome to Pepin and the Carolingians, and then to the Germans.

47. *Reg.*, 7:203.

48. Macrides, "New Constantine."

49. See Abulafia, *Frederick II*, 247–48, for an example of relic translation and German politics.

50. Demus, *Church of San Marco*, 56–58 and notes.

51. Durand, "La translation des reliques," discusses the theme of the new Jerusalem (37–41) and includes editions of many documents recording the translation (44–51).

52. Angold, *Fourth Crusade*, 237–39. For Heraclius's legend as recorded in the Middle Ages, see Jacobus de Voragine, *Golden Legend*, 544–46.

53. Boutet, "De la *translatio imperii* à la *finis saeculi."*

54. Durand, "La translation des reliques," 37–41.

55. Pincus, "Venice and the Two Romes," 109. Pincus writes, "Venice, Florence, Milan, Padua—to name a number of centers—all become 'Second Romes.' The concept of Second Rome is a topos for the city states of Italy as they develop self-sufficiency and search for individual identity. What is particular about Venice is the distinctiveness of the *two* strands that make up its image and the stage-managing."

56. Angold, *Fourth Crusade*, 240.

57. Monk of St. George, "Translatio corporis Beatissimi Pauli Martyris," 142. Cracco, "Chiesa e istituzioni," 17, briefly discusses the justifications for the crusade in this text. He views the period following the Fourth Crusade as the moment when church and state came together in Venice, in defiance of papal criticism and other threats. Madden, *Enrico Dandolo*, 31–38, has shown that the real church-state crisis occurred earlier, during the conflict between Patriarch Enrico Dandolo (the uncle of Doge Enrico Dandolo) and Doge Pietro Polani in 1147, also known as the "Venetian investiture controversy."

58. Ms Gerli 26, 71r. There was no relevant iniquity between father and son, but rather fraternal conflict between Isaac Angelos and Alexius III. Whether the author was confused or speaking metaphorically about interfamilial strife is unclear.

59. Monk of St. George, "Translatio corporis Beatissimi Pauli Martyris," 141.

60. Madden, *Enrico Dandolo*, 200 and 268n31–32.

61. For example, the "Translatio Symonensis" begins with a paean for his wisdom; MS Gerli 26, fol. 71v. So does the "Translatio Pauli"; see Monk of St. George, "Translatio corporis Beatissimi Pauli Martyris," 141.

62. Madden, *Enrico Dandolo*, 196 and 266n145.

63. Madden, "Venetian Version."

64. Carile's *La cronachistica veneziana* remains the seminal work on the Venetian chronicles. More recently, Şerban Marin has reconsidered a number of issues in the chronicles; see his essay "Between Justification and Glory." Carile has identified more than one thousand separate chronicles written in Venice from the mid-thirteenth century to well into the seventeenth century. Many families produced their own accounts; they borrowed from one another without evident rhyme or reason.

65. Constantine IX Monomachos (r. 1042–55). It was actually the forces of Michael IV (1010–1041) that captured the relics of the virgin martyrs during Byzantium's battle with

Sicilian Muslims in 1039. Niero, "Reliquie e corpi di santi," 198. See also Musolino, *Santa Lucia a Venezia*, 41.

66. Andrea Dandolo, *Chronica*, 280: "Devoti etiam principes sanctorum occultatas reliquias tamdem inveniunt; et obtinuit dux mirisicam Crucem auro inclusam, quam post inventionem matris Constantinus in bellis secum detulerat et ampullam Sanguinis miraculosi Iesu Christ, et brachium sancti Georgii martyris cum parte capitis Sancti Iohannis Baptiste, quas dux mittens Venetias in sua capella collocari iussit. . . . Inventis similiter corporibus sanctarum Agathe et Lucie virginis, que Basilius et Constantinus Augustus de Sicilia deferri Constantinopolim fecerant, dux obtentum corpus sancta Lucie Venetias, in monasterio Sancti Georgii mandavit, quod in ecclesia eius nomini dedicate repositum est. Corpus vero beate Agathe quibusdam Siculis peregrines concessum est."

67. Ibid., 284. For the office of procurator, see Müeller, "Procurators of San Marco." See also Demus, *Church of San Marco*, 52–54.

68. Andrea Dandolo, *Chronica*, 280, 285, 287, 289, 297, 308, 310.

69. Ibid., 280.

70. Ibid., 289.

71. Biblioteca Nazionale Marciana, Venice, Marc. Codex Lat. LX (a. cc. 234–39).

72. Poncelet, "Le légendier de Pierre Calò," 30–34; Petrus Calò, *Legendae Sancti Dominici*, 129–30.

73. Petrus Calò, *Legendae Sancti Dominici*, 158–59.

74. The Monastery of San Daniele was founded in 1138. Bishop Giovanni Polani of Castello gave the parish church of San Daniele to a group of Fruttuarian monks, whose reform movement was not unlike that of the Cistercians in theology, though, according to Madden, it was more willing to operate under the oversight of a bishop. These monks had built a religious house near the church, took over the new site after Polani's gift, and thrived during the twelfth and thirteenth centuries. See Madden, *Enrico Dandolo*, 26–27 and 216n60, and Spinelli, "I monasteri Benedettini," 113–14. See also the preface to Elisabeth Santschi's edition of *Benedettini in S. Daniele (1046–1198)*, vii–lvi. It is not credible that this Marco Zorzi, who gave such a rich gift to San Daniele, was the same Marco Zorzi who was abbot of San Giorgio Maggiore at the time. The Zorzi were an important Venetian family, however, so it is likely that they were related.

75. *ESC*, 1:cviii.

76. Petrus Calò, "Translatio S. Ioannis Alexandrini."

77. Ibid., 181: "Involvit illum in sindone munda."

78. Ibid.

79. Andrea Dandolo, *Chronica*, 285.

80. Biblioteca Nazionale Marciana, Venice, Marc. Codex Zanetti Lat., 360 (=1809).

81. Riant, in *ESC*, 1:cix, writes, "Celle de Sainte Lucie . . . n'a pas été compose plus tard que la fin du XVe siècle, ainsi que le prouve l'écriture du manuscript auquel je l'ai empruntée."

82. If one considers "the city" to be only the Golden Horn, the section behind the walls of Theodosius, then the expanded Venetian quarter is about half. Jacoby, "Venetian Quarter," 154.

83. "Corporis beate virginis ac martiris Lucie," 185.

84. Ibid. This is the only source I have found that specifically credits Baldwin with giving a relic to Enrico Dandolo. The attribution to Baldwin is credible, given his general pattern of diplomatic use of relics.

85. Damerini, *L'isola e il cenobio*, 91.

86. Polacco, *Della triplicata traslazione*. The church dedicated to St. Lucia was destroyed to make room for a train station (although it still bears her name—Ferrovia Santa Lucia), so the relics have now endured four translations. Her body now shares a church with San Geremiaso (St. Jeremy) a few blocks away from the train station. In 1617, there was a particularly large celebration of the relics of Venice. Polacco's pamphlet was presumably produced as part of a larger local hagiographical effort.

87. These crises were not limited to the many issues brought about by the Fourth Crusade, but also included the conflicts with Byzantium in the 1170s, internal reform, the murder of a doge, and the re-creation of the Venetian polity. See Madden, *Enrico Dandolo*, 43–62.

Chapter 6

1. Martino da Canal, *Les estoires de Venise*, 40; Fasoli, "La chronique des Veniciens," 53–61; Limentani, "Martin Da Canal."

2. Perry, "St. Mark's Trophies."

3. Petrus Calò, "Translatio S. Barbare." There is also a seventeenth-century pamphlet on the subject housed in the Marciana Library in Venice: Palmieri, *Historia della translatione del glorioso corpo della Beata Vergine*.

4. *ESC*, 1:186–88.

5. Ibid., 2:37–38.

6. This is the same saint whose head Peter Capuano brought to Gaeta around 1210. See chapter 4 and Anonymous of Gaeta, "Qualiter caput S. Theodori."

7. Anonymous of Venice, "Translatio corporis Beatissimi Theodori Martyris." See also Niero, "Reliquie e corpi di santi," 200–201.

8. Anonymous of Venice, "Translatio corporis Beatissimi Theodori Martyris," 159.

9. Demus, *Church of San Marco*, 19–22. Constantinople more or less gave St. Theodore to the Byzantine/Italian refugees from the Lombard invasion. As Greek influence waned, Marcian devotion increased over the first few centuries of Venice's history.

10. Demus, *Church of San Marco*, 19–22. St. Theodore was a fourth-century Roman soldier (and hence is known as Theodore Tyro, the title given to recruits) who was burned to death in 306, thus making him both warrior and martyr.

11. Perry, "St. George."

12. Demus, *Church of San Marco*, 19–22 and 22n75. The columns were erected after 1172, but the statues came much later. The statue of St. Theodore today is a composite, although there is an earlier Theodore warrior in the museum of the Palazzo Ducale.

13. Demus, *Church of San Marco*, 125–37, presents a full discussion of each of the icons. See figs. 2–5 for the relevant icons.

14. Ibid., 137. Demus writes, "This decorative character, this elegance of composition and line is, indeed, the most important element to have grown out of the interplay of Byzantine and late Romanesque tendencies on Venetian soil. It is, in fact, the new ingredient which the Venetians added to the 'imported' qualities, an ingredient which, to a large extent, was to shape the development of relief sculpture in Venice."

15. Ibid. Demus guesses that the first Heracles relief was made about 1230 and the second one as much as a decade later, but lacks solid evidence. Our terminus date is based on da Canal's description of the icons as of 1267, but they seem to have originated earlier. Martino da Canal, *Les estoires de Venise*, 290.

16. *George Akropolites: History*, 239.

17. Robert of Clari, *Conquest of Constantinople*, 127. Robert of Clari, *Li estoires*, 107–8: "Or gesoit li cors monseigneur saint Dimitre en le chité, qui ne vaut onques soufrir que se

chités fust prise par forche; si decouroit si grans plentés d'oille de chu cors saint que ch'estoit une fine merveille. Si avint, si comme Jehans li Blaks se gesoit une matinee en se tente, que mesires sains Dimitres vint, si le feri d'une lanche parmi le cors, si l'ochist."

18. Perry, "St. George."

19. Ibid.; Riley-Smith, *First Crusaders*, 151–52 and 151n52; "Narratio quomodo relliquiae martyris Georgii."

20. Demus, *Church of San Marco*, 134.

21. Ibid., 134 and 134nn56–57.

22. Ibid., 126–27.

23. Ibid., 135.

24. Perry, "St. George."

25. Klein, "Refashioning Byzantium in Venice," 209–10.

26. Pincus, "Christian Relics." The hallway is now closed to tourists (as the entrance to the church and the palazzo are regulated separately). I am grateful to the Office of the Patriarchate of Venice at San Marco for allowing me access to the hallway and granting me permission to photograph the plaque.

27. Ibid., 39.

28. Andrea Dandolo, *Chronica*, 280.

29. Pincus, "Christian Relics," 42; Hahnloser and Volbach, *Tesoro di San Marco*, 139–41.

30. Pincus, "Christian Relics," 46n39. See also Kaufmann, *Eucharistic Vessels*.

31. Pincus, "Christian Relics," 46.

32. Ibid.

33. Pomorisac, *Les émaux byzantins de la Pala d'oro*, 25, cited in Pincus, "Christian Relics," 57n28. See also Volback, "Gli smalti della Pala d'oro," 6–10.

34. Pincus, "Christian Relics," 46–47nn47–52. Although focused on a later period, Kedar, "Noms de saints et mentalité populaire à Gênes," offers an excellent comparative model.

35. Jacobus de Voragine, *Legenda aurea*, 925; Jacobus de Voragine, *Iacopo da Varagine e la sua Cronaca di Genova*, esp. 1:127–31. The latter volume contains the *Istoria sive legenda translationis beatissimi Johannis Baptiste*. One should also see Thompson, *Cities of God*, 309–14, for the ritual importance of the Baptist, baptism, and baptisteries among the Italian city-states.

36. Nicol, *Last Centuries of Byzantium*, 34.

37. On Genoa and Venice, see Kedar, *Merchants in Crisis*.

38. Beyond overt military activity, see Katele, "Piracy and the Venetian State," 865–89.

39. Nicol, *Last Centuries of Byzantium*, 34.

40. Gill, *Byzantium and the Papacy*, 39.

41. Pincus, "Christian Relics," 46.

42. For arm reliquaries, see Hahn, "Voices of Saints," 21–27. The arm was meant to convey an action of some sort to the viewers of the relic, whether blessing or supplication or, I argue, the military strength of Christendom's foremost soldier-saint. See Perry, "St. George."

43. Nicol, *Last Centuries of Byzantium*, 30–37, 60–63.

44. Crouzet-Pavan, *Venice Triumphant*, 71.

45. See Kedar, *Merchants in Crisis*.

46. Crouzet-Pavan, *Venice Triumphant*, 71–74. The main episodes of violence occurred in 1294–99, 1351–55, and 1374–81, when the Genoese penetrated all the way to Chioggia. See also Katele, "Piracy."

47. Pincus has included an edition of the letter in her appendix to "Christian Relics." The original letter is enrolled in the Archivio di Stato, Venice, *Commemoriali*, Reg. 24

(1573–84), cc. 173–74. The Latin reads, "Et qualiter Dominis noster Jesus Christus ipsas in Civitate Venetiarum cum corpore beati Marci, Evangelisti sui, voluit collocari."

48. Niero, "Reliquie e corpi di santi," 201–4. The fourteenth-century purchase and use of relics has received some scholarly attention, but the fifteenth-century military acquisition of relics ahead of the Turkish advance has not. For the former, see Cutler, "From Loot to Scholarship"; Hetherington, "Purchase of Byzantine Relics and Reliquaries"; and Klein, "Refashioning Byzantium in Venice," 222–24. For a concise list of relics taken by Venetians from Latin Constantinople, see Demus, *Church of San Marco*, 17n60.

49. Perry, "Material Culture," 21–24.

50. Muir, *Civic Ritual*, 119.

51. Demus, *Mosaic Decoration*, 231.

52. Muir, *Civic Ritual*, 119–20; Martino da Canal, *Les estoires de Venise*, 250. Muir writes, "By 1267, when Martin da Canal described the ceremony, a *desponsatio*, or matrimonial covenant, between the doge and the sea had been grafted onto the *benedictio*, creating a composite rite and establishing the rudiments for the marriage of the sea, or the Sensa festival. This significant transformation was probably a response to the heightened concern for Venice's own imperial image that followed the conquest of Constantinople in 1204" (120).

53. Perry, "*Translatio Symonensis*," 112.

54. Crouzet-Pavan, "Ecological Understanding of the Myth of Venice"; Crouzet-Pavan, "*Sopra le acque salse*"; *Venice Triumphant*, esp. 46–50. See also Tenenti, *Venezia e il senso del mare*.

55. Monk of the Lido, "Historia," 260: "Sancte Pater! Venetia, filia tua."

56. Crouzet-Pavan, *Venice Triumphant*, 46–50.

57. Benzoni, "Venezia, la città di Nettuno." A fine example of this imagery can be found in the Minneapolis Institute of Arts. The artists Jacopo Bassano and his son Francesco painted *The Element of Water* in Venice in 1576–77. The background contains a dark classical cityscape merging into a subterranean view. Neptune rides triumphantly through the clouds. In the foreground, people are engaged in the buying and selling of fish. Anyone familiar with the fish of the Adriatic will recognize the catch as typical of the region, including the ubiquitous *sarde* (large sardines), meaty *branzini* (sea bass), *orata* (sea bream), mollusks, scampi, perhaps eels, and a large *San Giuseppe* (John Dory), an odd-looking flat fish. The Venetian qualities of this scene are unmistakable.

58. Muir, *Civic Ritual*, 103n1; Pietro de'Natali, *Il poemetto di Pietro de' Natali*.

59. Luke 22:38.

60. Perry, "1308 and 1177," 125–28.

61. Dale, "Inventing a Sacred Past," 89n174.

62. Demus, *Church of San Marco*, 9–10.

63. See Dale, "Inventing a Sacred Past," 85–86; Martino da Canal, *Les estoires de Venise*, 219.

64. Pincus, "Venice and the Two Romes," 112n14; Buchthal, *Historia Troiana*, 58.

65. Pincus, "Venice and the Two Romes," 105. See also Marin, "Venice and *Translatio Imperii*," 45–50.

66. Pertusi, "Le profezie sulla presa di Costantinopoli."

67. See Marin's "Between Justification and Glory," "'Dominus quartae partis,'" "Precedent to the Fourth Crusade," "Venetian 'Empire' in the East," and "Venetian and Non-Venetian Crusaders," 111–71.

68. In 1124, the Venetians crushed an Egyptian fleet and gained a street and other concessions in every city in the Kingdom of Jerusalem, as well as a third of Tyre. After

that, they raided Rhodes and wintered in Chios, where they allegedly acquired the relic of St. Isidore of Chios. They then raided Greeks and Hungarians over the next two years before John II Comnenus acquiesced. See Madden, *Enrico Dandolo*, 15–18, and Riley-Smith, "Venetian Crusade of 1122–1124."

69. Marin, "Precedent to the Fourth Crusade," 246. The appendixes contain editions of relevant passages from twenty-seven different chronicles.

70. For Dandolo's larger relic project, see Klein, "Refashioning Byzantium in Venice," 196–209; Pincus, "Venice and Its Doge"; Thiriet, "Byzance et les Byzantins"; and Lazzarini, "'Dux ille Danduleus.'"

71. These ceremonials, dating from the sixteenth century in their extant form, have been published in Saccardo, *La cappella di S. Isidoro*, 8–13. Saccardo has included both a facsimile of the handwritten documents and a typed edition.

72. The translatio is contained within a large, bound fourteenth-century codex: Biblioteca Nazionale Marciana, Venice, Marc. Codex Lat. LX (a. cc. 234–39). It was also published in Cerbano Cerbani, "Translatio Isidori." I have not been able to locate any twelfth-century versions of this story and am increasingly suspicious of its veracity. Of importance here is its fourteenth-century memorialization.

73. Andrea Dandolo, *Chronica*, 233–36; Cerbano Cerbani, "Translatio Isidori," 321–24.

74. Demus, *Church of San Marco*, 17.

75. Wolff, *Later Crusades*, 12, 59–68; Nicol, *Byzantium and Venice*, 260–70.

76. Demus, *Mosaics of San Marco*, 2 (text): 192–93.

77. Hetherington, "Purchase of Byzantine Relics and Reliquaries."

78. Niero, "Reliquie e corpi di santi," 202–4.

79. Vergaro, *Racconto dell'apparato et solennità* (1617); Thiepolo Primicerio, *Trattato delle santissime* (1617).

80. The emergence of the Venetian arengo paralleled the development of "communal" government in many other city-states of Italy, a subject that has been vastly studied. For a general survey, including an excellent bibliography, see Jones, *Italian City-State*. See also Mundy, "Philip Jones and the Medieval City-State." Coleman published a review article entitled "The Italian Communes," though he excluded Venice (as is typical of scholars of the rest of Italy). For the development of the arengo in terms of Venetian law, see the somewhat dated, but still seminal, Maranini, *La costituzione di Venezia*, and Cassandro, "Concetto caratteri e struttura dello stato veneziano."

81. Madden, *Enrico Dandolo*, 56, 227nn94–96.

82. Ibid., 136–38.

83. Madden, "Venetian Version," 326, suggests that Venetians believed their own stories for at least the first century after the conquest.

84. For the organization of Venetian daily existence, see Crouzet-Pavan, *Venice Triumphant*, 138–82. There remains much scholarly work to be done on parish life, governance, and identity.

85. Madden, *Enrico Dandolo*, 6–7.

86. Crouzet-Pavan, *Venice Triumphant*, 14–17.

87. Madden, *Enrico Dandolo*, 1.

88. Monk of St. George, "Translatio corporis Beatissimi Pauli Martyris," 144.

Epilogue

1. Gratian, *De consecratione, corpus iuris canonici*, 1:263–64. C. XXXVII: Quando alicui corpora sanctorum de loco ad locum transferre non licet: "Item ex Concilio Maguntiensi,

[I.] c. 51. Corpora sanctorum de loco ad locum nullus transferre presumat sine consilio principis, uel episcoporum sanctaeque sinodi licentia." C. XXXVI: Quibus ex causis loca sanctorum mutanda sint: "Item Augustinus. IX. Pars. Tribus ex causis loca sanctorum transmutanda sunt. Prima, cum necessitas persecutorum loca eorum grauauerit. Secunda, cum difficultas locorum fuerit. Tercia, cum malorum societate grauantur." See also Dooley, *Church Law on Sacred Relics*, 10–11, 28–29.

2. Bolton, "Show with a Meaning," 54–57.

3. Ibid., 55–61.

4. *Decrees of the Ecumenical Councils*, 263–64.

5. Kuttner and García y García, "New Eyewitness Account." García y García discovered the text in 1961, and he and Kuttner both worked on the description and evaluation of it. Kuttner produced the commentary and appendixes.

6. Bolton, "Show with a Meaning," 63.

7. Kuttner and García y García, "New Eyewitness Account," 128–29.

8. Ibid., 128: "Nona hora diei esset."

9. Bolton, "Show with a Meaning," 63–64.

10. Frolow, *La relique de la Vraie Croix*, 494–95: "HIC CONTINETUR LIGNUM VIVIFICE CRUCIS DE CONSTANTINOPOLI TRANSLATUM AD URBEM TEMPORE OMINI INNOCENTII PP. TERTII."

11. Kuttner and García y García, "New Eyewitness Account," 128: "Magnam partem de lingo sancte crucis de Constantinopoli allato omnibus demonstravit."

12. Bolton, "Show with a Meaning," 63.

13. Kuttner and García y García, "New Eyewitness Account," 165.

14. Ibid.

15. Ibid.

16. Ibid.

17. Ibid.

18. Gallo, "Reliquie e reliquiari veneziani," 187.

19. Durand, *Le trésor de la Sainte-Chapelle*.

20. Andrea, "What Remains to Be Said About Relic Thievery."

21. "St. Lucy Vanishes Without Trace," *Catholic Herald*, November 13, 1981, 2, http://archive.catholicherald.co.uk/article/13th-november-1981/2/st-lucy-vanishes-without-trace.

22. "St. Lucy's Relics Found Intact," *Catholic Herald*, December 18, 1981, 1, http://archive.catholicherald.co.uk/article/18th-december-1981/1/st-lucys-relics-found-intact.

BIBLIOGRAPHY

Primary Sources

Unpublished

Archivio di Stato, Venice
  Cancelleria Inferiore
    B. 1
    B. 8
    B. 30
    B. 106
    Codice diplomatico veneziano
    N. 4284
    Commemoriali, Reg. 24 (1573–84), cc. 173–74
Biblioteca Nazionale Braidense, Milan
  MS Gerli 26, 71r–74v
Biblioteca Nazionale Marciana, Venice
  Marc. Codex Lat. LX (a. cc. 234–39)
  Marc. Codex Zanetti Lat., 360 (=1809)

Published

Andrea, Alfred J. *Contemporary Sources for the Fourth Crusade.* Boston: Brill, 2000.
———. "The *Devastatio Constantinopolitana*: A Special Perspective on the Fourth Crusade: An Analysis, New Edition, and Translation." *Historical Reflections / Reflexions Historiques* 19, no. 1 (1993): 110–60.
Andrea, Alfred J., and Paul Rachlin. "Holy War, Holy Relics, Holy Theft: The Anonymous of Soisson's *De terra Iherosolimitana*: An Analysis, Edition, and Translation." *Historical Reflections / Reflexions Historiques* 18, no. 1 (1992): 147–75.
Andrea Dandolo. *Chronica per extensum descripta.* In *Rerum italicarum scriptores*, vol. 12, pt. 1, edited by Ester Pastorello, 1–327. Bologna: Nicola Zanichelli, 1938.
Annali Genovesi di Caffaro e de' suoi continuari dal MCLXXIV al MCCXXIV. Edited by L. T. Belgrano and C. Imperiale. Vols. 1–2. Genoa: Tipografia del R. Istituto Sordo-Muti, 1901.
Anonymous of Gaeta. "Qualiter caput S. Theodori ad Caietam translatum est." In *Exuviae sacrae Constantinopolitanae*, 1:150–55.
Anonymous of Halberstadt. "De peregrinatione in Grecia & adventu reliquiarum de Grecia libellus." In *Exuviae sacrae Constantinopolitanae*, 1:10–21.
Anonymous of Venice. "Translatio corporis Beatissimi Theodori Martyris, cum multis miraculis." In *Exuviae sacrae Constantinopolitanae*, 1:156–63.

Benedettini in S. Daniele (1046–1198). Edited by Elisabeth Santschi. Venice: Il Comitato Editore, 1989.

Biblia sacra vulgatae editionis. Edited by V. Loch. 9th ed. Rome, 1592–93.

Burchard of Ursperg. *Chronicon*. Edited by O. Abel and L. Weiland. In *Monumenta Germaniae Historica*, vol. 23. Hannover: Hahnsche Buchhandlung, 1916.

Canon of Langres. "Historia translationum reliquiarum S. Mamantis." In *Exuviae sacrae Constantinopolitanae*, 1:22–34.

Cerbano Cerbani. "Translatio Isidori. Cerbani Cerbani, clerici Veneti, translatio mirifici Martyris Isidori a Chio insula in civitatem Venetam (Jun. 1125)." In *Recueil des historiens des croisades: Historiens occidentaux*, 5:321–34. Paris: Imprimerie royale, 1895.

Conciliorum oecumenicorum decreta. Edited by Giuseppe Alberigo et al. Bologna: Instituto per le Scienze Religiose, 1973.

Corner, Flaminio. *Notizie storiche delle chiese e monastery di Venezia e di Torcello*. Padua, 1758; repr., Venice: Arnaldo Forni Editore, 1990.

"Corporis beate virginis ac martiris Lucie, Venetias ex Constantinopli urbe, translatio." In *Exuviae sacrae Constantinopolitanae*, 1:184–86.

Decrees of the Ecumenical Councils. Edited by N. Tanner. Vol. 1. London: Sheed and Ward, 1990.

Decretum magistri Gratiani. Edited by Emil Friedberg. Leipzig: Bernhardi Tauchnitz, 1879. Available at http://geschichte.digitale-sammlungen.de/decretum-gratiani/ online /angebot (accessed May 24, 2014).

The Deeds of Pope Innocent III: By an Anonymous Author. Translated and edited by J. M. Powell. Washington, D.C.: Catholic University of America Press, 2004.

Exuviae sacrae Constantinopolitanae. Vols. 1–2. Edited by Paul Riant. Paris: E. Leroux, 1877–78. Republished with a preface by Jannic Durand. Paris: Éditions du Comité des travaux historiques et scientifiques, 2004.

Geoffrey of Villehardouin. *La conquête de Constantinople*. Edited by Edmond Faral. 2 vols. Paris: Société d'édition "Les Belles Lettres," 1938.

———. *Joinville and Villehardouin: Chronicles of the Crusades*. Translated by Caroline Smith. London: Penguin Books, 2008.

George Akropolites: The History. Edited by Ruth Macrides. Oxford: Oxford University Press, 2007.

Gesta Innocentii III. Translated by David R. Gress-Wright. In "The *Gesta Innocentii III*: Text, Introduction, and Commentary." Ph.D. diss., Bryn Mawr College, 1981.

Gratian. *De consecratione, corpus iuris canonici*. Vol. 1. Edited by Emil Friedberg. Leipzig: B. Tauchnitz, 1879.

Guiot de Provins. *Les œuvres de Guiot de Provins, poète lyrique et satirique*. Edited by J. Orr. Manchester: Imprimerie de l'université, 1915.

Gunther of Pairis. *The Capture of Constantinople: The "Hystoria Constantinopolitana" of Gunther of Pairis*. Edited and translated by Alfred Andrea. Philadelphia: University of Pennsylvania Press, 1997.

The History of the Albigensian Crusade. Peter of les Vaux-de-Cernay's Historia Albigensis. Translated by W. A. Sibly and M. D. Sibly. Woodbridge: Boydell Press, 1998.

Jacobus de Voragine. *The Golden Legend*. Translated by G. Ryan and H. Ripperger. New York: Arno Press, 1969.

———. *Iacopo da Varagine e la sua Cronaca di Genova dalle origini al MCCXCVII*. Edited by G. Monleone. 3 vols. Rome: Tipografia del Senato, 1941.

———. *Legenda aurea: Vulgo historia Lombardica dicta*. Edited by J. G. Th. Graesse. Melle: Wagener Edition, 2003.

Martino da Canal. *Les estoires de Venise*. Edited by A. Limentani. Florence: L. S. Olschki, 1972.

———. *Les estoires de Venise*. Translated by Laura Morreale. Archivo del litorale Adriatico 12. Padova: Unipress, 2009.

Matthew of Amalfi. "Translatio corporis S. Andree de Constantinopoli in Amalphiam." In *Exuviae sacrae Constantinopolitanae*, 1:165–78.

McCleary, Nelson. "Note storiche ed archeologiche sul testo della translatio Sancti Marci." Translated by C. Cecchelli. *Memorie Storiche Forogiuliesi* 27–29 (1931–33): 223–64.

Monk of Saint George. "Translatio corporis Beatissimi Pauli Martyris, de Constantinopoli Venetias." In *Exuviae sacrae Constantinopolitanae*, 1:141–49.

Monk of the Lido. "Historia de translatione Magni Nicolai." In *Recueil des historiens des croisades: Historiens occidentaux*, 5:253–92. Paris: Imprimerie royale, 1895.

"Narratio quomodo relliquiae martyris Georgii ad nos Aquicinenses pervenerunt." In *Recueil des historiens des croisades: Historiens occidentaux*, 5:248–52. Paris: Imprimerie royale, 1895.

Niketas Choniates. *Historia*. Edited by I. Bekker. Bonn: Weber, 1835.

———. *O City of Byzantium*. Translated by H. Magoulias. Detroit: Wayne State University Press, 1984.

Oliver of Paderborn. *Die Schriften des Kölner Domscholasters, späteren Bischofs von Paderborn und Kardinal-Bischofs von S. Sabina, Oliverus*. Edited by H. Hoogeweg. Tübingen: Litterarischer Verein in Stuttgart, 1894.

Patrologia Latina. Edited by Jacques-Paul Migne. Rome, 1844–55 and 1862–65.

Petrus Calò. *Legendae Sancti Dominici*. Edited by Simon Tugwell. Rome: Apud Institutum Historicum Ordinis Fratrum Praedictatorum, 1997.

———. "Translatio S. Barbare." In *Exuviae sacrae Constantinopolitanae*, 1:182–83.

———. "Translatio S. Ioannis Alexandrini." In *Exuviae sacrae Constantinopolitanae*, 1:179–81.

Pietro de'Natali. *Il poemetto di Pietro de' Natali sulla pace di Venezia tra Alessandro III e Federico Barbarossa*. Edited by O. Zenatti. Rome: Forzani, 1905.

Polacco, D. Giorgio. *Della triplicata traslazione del corpo della gloriosa Vergine, & martire S. Lucia*. Venezia: Barezzo Barezzi, 1617.

Die Register Innocenz' III. Edited by Othmar Hageneder et al. Vols. 1, 2, 5, 6, 7, 8 (by register year). Graz: H. Boöhlaus Nachf., 1964, 1979, 1993, 1995, 1997, 2001.

Ricardus de Gerboredo. "De capta et direpta a Latinis Constantinopoli, et quomodo Walo caput S. Iohannis Baptiste invenit et ad Ambianum deportavit." In *Exuviae sacrae Constantinopolitanae*, 1:35–44.

Robert of Auxerre. *Chronicon*. Edited by Oswald Holder-Egger. In *Monumenta Germaniae Historica, Series Scriptores*, vol. 26. Hanover, 1882.

Robert of Clari. *The Conquest of Constantinople*. Translated by E. McNeal. New York: Columbia University Press, 2005.

———. *Li estoires de chiaus qui conquisent Coustantinoble*. Edited by Philippe Lauer. Paris: Eì. Champion, 1924.

Rostang of Cluny. "Narratio exceptionis apud Cluniacum capitis Beati Clementis, ex ore Dalmacii de Serciaco, militis, excepta." In *Exuviae sacrae Constantinopolitanae*, 1:127–40.

Saint Augustine. *De doctrina Christiana libri quatuor*. In *Patrologiae Latinae*, edited by J. P. Migne, vol. 34. Paris, 1845. Available at http://www.augustinus.it/latino/pl_34.htm (accessed September 20, 2013).

San Giorgio Maggiore. Edited by L. Lanfranchi. 2 vols. Venice: Comitato per la Pubblica-zione delle Fonte Relative alla Storia di Venezia, 1968 and 1986.

Sulpicius Severus. *Writings*. Translated by B. M. Peebles. Washington, D.C.: Catholic University of America Press, 1949.

Thiepolo Primicerio, G. *Trattato delle santissime reliquie ultimamente retrovate nel santuario della Chiesa di San Marco*. Venice: Pinelli, Stampator Ducale, 1617.

Vergaro, Giulio. *Racconto dell'apparato et solennità fatta nella ducal Chiesa de San Marco di Venetia: Con l'occasione dell'inventione, & espositione del sangue pretiosissimo del costato di Christo, del latte della Beata Vergine, con altre santissime reliquie*. Venice: Pinelli, Stampator Ducale, 1617.

Vergil. *Aeneid*. Wauconda, Ill.: Bolchazy-Carducci, 1999.

Secondary Sources

Abulafia, David. *Frederick II: A Medieval Emperor*. London: Penguin, 1988.

Akbari, Suzanne Conklin. *Idols in the East: European Representations of Islam and the Orient, 1100–1450*. Ithaca: Cornell University Press, 2009.

Andrea, Alfred J. "The Anonymous Chronicler of Halberstadt's Account of the Fourth Crusade: Popular Religiosity in the Early Thirteenth Century." *Historical Reflections / Reflexions Historiques* 22, no. 2 (1996): 447–77.

———. "Cistercian Accounts of the Fourth Crusade: Were They Anti-Venetian?" *Analecta Cisterciensia* 41 (1985): 3–41.

———. "Conrad of Krosigk: Bishop of Halberstadt, Crusader, and Monk of Sittichenback; His Ecclesiastical Career, 1184–1225." *Analecta Cisterciensia* 43 (1987): 11–91.

———. "The *Historia Constantinopolitana*: An Early Thirteenth-Century Cistercian Looks at Byzantium." *Analecta Cisterciensia* 36 (1980): 267–302.

———. "What Remains to Be Said About Relic Thievery and the Fourth Crusade?" Public lecture, 39th International Congress on Medieval Studies, Kalamazoo, Mich., May 6–9, 2004.

Angold, Michael. *The Byzantine Empire, 1025–1204: A Political History*. London: Longman, 1997.

———. *The Fourth Crusade*. New York: Pearson-Longman, 2003.

Barry, Fabio. "*Disiecta Membra*: Ranieri Zeno, the Imitation of Constantinople, the *Spolia* Style, and Justice at San Marco." In *San Marco, Byzantium, and the Myths of Venice*, edited by Henry Maguire and Robert S. Nelson, 7–62. Washington, D.C.: Dumbarton Oaks Research Library and Collection, 2010.

Benzoni, Gino. "Venezia, la città di Nettuno." *Studi Veneziani*, n.s., 24 (1995): 91–102.

———. "Venezia: Tra mito e realità." *Studi Veneziani*, n.s., 45 (2003): 15–26.

Bolton, Brenda. "A Show with a Meaning: Innocent III's Approach to the Fourth Lateran Council, 1215." *Medieval History* 1 (1991): 53–67.

Boutet, Dominique. "De la *translatio imperii* à la *finis saeculi*: Progrès et décadence dans la pensée de l'histoire au Moyen Age." In *Progrès, réaction, décadence dans l'Occident médiéval*, edited by Emmanuèle Baumgartner and Laurence Harf-Lancner, 37–48. Geneva: Librairie Droz S.A., 2003.

Brown, Elizabeth. "The Cistercians in the Latin Empire of Constantinople and Greece, 1204–1276." *Traditio* 14 (1958): 63–120.

Buc, Philippe. "Conversion of Objects." *Viator* 28 (1997): 99–143.

Buchthal, Hugo. *Historia Troiana: Studies in the History of Mediaeval Secular Illustration*. London: Warburg Institute, 1971.

Carile, Antonio. *La cronachistica veneziana (secoli XIII–XVI) di fronte alla spartizione della Romania nel 1204.* Florence: Leo S. Olschki, 1969.

———. "Le origini di Venezia nella tradizione storiografica." In *Storia della cultura Veneta,* edited by Girolamo Arnaldi and Manlio Pastore Stocchi, 1:136–66. Vicenza: Neri Pozza, 1976.

———. "Partitio terrarum imperii Romanie." *Studi Veneziani* 7 (1965): 125–305.

Carruthers, Mary. *The Book of Memory: A Study of Memory in Medieval Culture.* Cambridge: Cambridge University Press, 1990.

Cassandro, Giovanni. "Concetto caratteri e struttura dello stato veneziano." *Bergomum* 38, no. 2 (1964): 33–55.

Chiesa, Paolo. "Ladri di reliquie a Costantinopoli durante la quarta crociata: La traslazione a Venezia del corpo di Simeone profeta." *Studi Medievali* 36, no. 1 (1995): 431–59.

———. "Santità d'importazione a Venezia tra reliquie e racconti." In *Oriente cristiano e santità: Figure e storie di santi tra Bisanzio e l'Occidente,* edited by Sebastiano Gentile, 107–15. Milan: Centro Tibaldi, 1998.

Claudon, Ferdinand. *Histoire de Langres et de ses institutions municipales jusqu'au commencement du XVIᵉ siècle.* Dijon: Association bourguignonne des sociétés savantes and the Société historique et archéologique de Langres, 1954.

Coleman, Edward. "The Italian Communes: Recent Work and Current Trends." *Journal of Medieval History* 25, no. 4 (1999): 373–97.

Constable, Giles. "The Disputed Election at Langres in 1138." *Traditio* 13 (1957): 119–52.

———. "Troyes, Constantinople, and the Relics of St. Helen in the Thirteenth Century." In *Mélanges offerts à René Crozet,* edited by P. Gallais and Y. Riou, 2:1035–42. Poitiers: Société d'études médiévales, 1966.

Cracco, Giorgio. "Chiesa e istituzioni civili nel secolo della quarta crociata." In *La Chiesa di Venezia nei secoli XI–XIII,* edited by Franco Tonon, 11–30. Venice: Edizioni Studium Cattolico Veneziano, 1988.

———. "I testi agiografici: Religione e politica nella Venezia del Mille." In *Storia di Venezia,* vol. 1, *Origini–Età Ducale,* edited by L. C. Ruggini, G. Cracco, and G. Ortalli, 923–61. Rome: Instituto della Enciclopedia Italiana, 1992.

Crouzet-Pavan, Elisabeth. *"Sopra le acque salse": Espaces, pouvoir et société à Venise à la fin du Moyen Âge.* 2 vols. Rome: École française, 1992.

———. "Toward an Ecological Understanding of the Myth of Venice." In *Venice Reconsidered: The History and Civilization of an Italian City-State, 1297–1797,* edited by John Martin and Dennis Romano, 39–66. Baltimore: Johns Hopkins University Press, 2000.

———. *Venice Triumphant: The Horizons of a Myth.* Translated by Lydia G. Cochrane. Baltimore: Johns Hopkins University Press, 2002.

Cutler, Anthony. "From Loot to Scholarship: Changing Modes in the Italian Response to Byzantine Artifacts, ca. 1200–1750." *Dumbarton Oaks Papers* 49 (1995): 237–67.

Daguin, Arthur. "Les évêques de Langres." *Bulletin de la Société Historique et Archeologique de Langres* 3 (1901): 22–30.

Dale, Thomas E. A. "Cultural Hybridity in Medieval Venice: Reinventing the East at San Marco After the Fourth Crusade." In *San Marco, Byzantium, and the Myths of Venice,* edited by Henry Maguire and Robert S. Nelson, 151–92. Washington, D.C.: Dumbarton Oaks Research Library and Collection, 2010.

———. "Inventing a Sacred Past: Pictorial Narratives of St. Mark the Evangelist in Aquileia and Venice, ca. 1000–1300." *Dumbarton Oaks Papers* 48 (1994): 53–104.

Damerini, Gino. *L'isola e il cenobio di San Giorgio Maggiore*. Venice: Fondazione Giorgio Cini, 1969.

Del Treppo, Mario, and Alfonso Leone. *Amalfi medioevale*. Naples: Giannini Editore, 1977.

Demus, Otto. *The Church of San Marco in Venice: History, Architecture, Sculpture*. With Ferdinando Forlati. Washington, D.C.: Dumbarton Oaks Research Library and Collection, 1960.

———. *The Mosaic Decoration of San Marco, Venice*. Chicago: University of Chicago Press, 1988.

———. *The Mosaics of San Marco in Venice*. Pt. 1, *The Eleventh and Twelfth Centuries*. 2 vols. Chicago: University of Chicago Press, 1984.

Didier, J. "La pluralité des archidiacres au diocèse de Langres." *Bulletin de la Société Historique et Archéologique de Langres* 12, no. 152 (1951): 269–76.

Dooley, E. "Church Law on Sacred Relics." Ph.D. diss., Catholic University of America, 1931.

Durand, Jannic. "La translation des reliques imperials de Constantinople à Paris." In *Le trésor de la Sainte-Chapelle*, edited by Jannic Durand, 37–51. Paris: Réunion des musées nationaux, 2001.

———. *Le trésor de la Sainte-Chapelle*. Edited by Jannic Durand. Paris: Réunion des musées nationaux, 2001.

Durand, Zuletzt M. "Les fragments des reliques byzantines de sainte Hélène d'Athyra retrouvés au trésor de la cathédrale de Troyes." *Cahiers Archéologiques* 46 (1998): 169–82.

Dvornik, Francis. *The Idea of Apostolicity in Byzantium and the Legend of the Apostle Andrew*. Cambridge: Harvard University Press, 1958.

Edbury, Peter. "The Lyon *Eracles* and the Old French Continuations." In *Montjoie: Studies in Crusade History in Honour of Hans Eberhard Mayer*, edited by H. E. Mayer et al., 139–52. Aldershot, U.K.: Variorum, 1997.

Fasoli, Gina. "La chronique des Veniciens di Martino da Canale." *Studi Medievali* 3, no. 2 (1961): 42–74.

———. "Nascita di un mito." In *Studi storici in onore di Gioacchino Volpe*, 1:445–79. Florence: Sansoni, 1958.

Fentress, James, and Chris Wickham. *Social Memory*. Oxford: Blackwell, 1992.

Fiengo, Giuseppe. *Gaeta: Monumenti e storia urbanistica*. Naples: Edizioni Scientifiche Italiane, 1971.

Fotheringham, John. "Genoa and the Fourth Crusade." *English Historical Review* 25 (1910): 26–57.

———. *Marco Sanudo: Conqueror of the Archipelago*. Oxford: Clarendon Press, 1915.

Frolow, Anatole. *La relique de la Vraie Croix*. Paris: Institut francais d'etudes byzantines, 1961.

Gabriele, Matthew. *An Empire of Memory: The Legend of Charlemagne, the Franks, and Jerusalem Before the First Crusade*. Oxford: Oxford University Press, 2011.

Gallo, Rodolfo. "Reliquie c reliquiari veneziani." *Rivista Mensile della Città Venezia* 13 (1934): 187–214.

Gaposchkin, M. Cecilia. *The Making of Saint Louis: Kingship, Sanctity, and Crusade in the Later Middle Ages*. Ithaca: Cornell University Press, 2008.

Geary, Patrick. *Furta Sacra: Thefts of Relics in the Central Middle Ages*. Princeton: Princeton University Press, 1978.

————. "Sacred Commodities: The Circulation of Medieval Relics." In *Living with the Dead in the Middle Ages*, 194–220. Ithaca: Cornell University Press, 1994.

————. "St. Helen of Athyra and the Cathedral of Troyes in the Thirteenth Century." In *Living with the Dead in the Middle Ages*, 221–42. Ithaca: Cornell University Press, 1994.

Gerland, Ernst. *Geschichte des lateinischen Kaiserreiches von Konstantinopel*. Pt. 1, *Geschichte der Kaiser Baldwin und Heinrich, 1204–1216*. Darmstadt: Wissenschaftliche Buchgesellschaft, 1966.

Gill, Joseph. *Byzantium and the Papacy: 1198–1400*. New Brunswick: Rutgers University Press, 1979.

Grubb, James. "When Myths Lose Power: Four Decades of Venetian Historiography." *Journal of Modern History* 58, no. 1 (1986): 43–94.

Hahn, Cynthia. *Strange Beauty: Issues in the Making and Meaning of Reliquaries, 400–Circa 1204*. University Park: Pennsylvania State University Press, 2012.

————. "The Voices of Saints: Speaking Reliquaries." *Gesta* 36, no. 1 (1997): 20–31.

Hahnloser, Hans, and Wolfgang Volbach. *Il tesoro di San Marco*. Florence: Sansoni, 1965.

Hamilton, Bernard. "The Latin Church in the Crusader States." In *East and West in the Crusader States: Context, Contacts, Confrontations*, edited by K. Ciggaar et al., 1–20. Leuven: Peeters, 1996.

Harper, J. "Turks as Trojans; Trojans as Turks: Visual Imagery of the Trojan War and the Politics of Cultural Identity in Fifteenth-Century Europe." In *Postcolonial Approaches to the European Middle Ages—Translating Cultures*, edited by A. Kabir and D. Williams, 151–82. Cambridge: Cambridge University Press, 2005.

Harris, Jonathan. "Distortion, Divine Providence, and Genre in Nicetas Choniates' Account of the Collapse of Byzantium, 1180–1204." *Journal of Medieval History* 26, no. 1 (2000): 19–31.

Heinzelmann, Martin. *Translationsberichte und andere Quellen des Reliquienkultes*. Turnhout: Brepols, 1979.

Hetherington, Paul. "A Purchase of Byzantine Relics and Reliquaries in Fourteenth-Century Venice." *Arte Veneta: Rivista di Storia dell'Arte* 37 (1983): 9–30.

Jacoby, David. "The Latin Empire of Constantinople and the Frankish States in Greece." In *The New Cambridge Medieval History*, vol. 5, *c. 1198–c. 1300*, edited by David Abulafia, 525–42. Cambridge: Cambridge University Press, 1999.

————. "The Venetian Quarter of Constantinople from 1082 to 1261: Topographical Considerations." In *Novum Millenium: Studies on Byzantine History and Culture Dedicated to Paul Speck*, edited by C. Sode and S. Takács, 153–70. Aldershot, U.K.: Ashgate, 2001.

Janin, Raymond. *La géographie ecclésiastique de l'Empire byzantin*. Pt. 1, *Le siege de Constantinople et le Patriarcat œcuménique*. Vol. 3, *Les églises et les monastères*. Paris: Centre national de la recherche scientifique, 1953.

————. "Les sanctuaires de Byzance sous la domination Latine." *Études Byzantines* 2 (1944): 39–176.

Jones, Graham. "Constantinople, 1204, Renewal of Interest in Imperial and Other Byzantine Cults in the West, and the Growth of New Traditions." In *Niš and Byzantium III: 800 Years After the Fall of Constantinople (1204–2004); Collection of Scientific Works*, edited by Miša Rakocija, 29–47. Niš, 2005.

Jones, Philip. *The Italian City-State: From Commune to Signoria*. Oxford: Clarendon Press, 1997.

Joranson, Einar. "The Problem of the Spurious Letter of Emperor Alexius to the Court of Flanders." *American Historical Review* 55, no. 4 (1950): 811–32.

Katele, Irene. "Piracy and the Venetian State: The Dilemma of Maritime Defense in the Fourteenth Century." *Speculum* 63, no. 4 (1988): 865–89.

Kaufmann, Heidi, ed. *Eucharistic Vessels of the Middle Ages*. Cambridge, Mass.: Busch-Reisinger Museum, 1975.

Kedar, Benjamin. "The Fourth Crusade's Second Front." In *Urbs Capta: The Fourth Crusade and Its Consequences*, edited by Angeliki Laiou, 89–110. Paris: Lethielleux, 2005.

———. *Merchants in Crisis: Genoese and Venetian Men of Affairs and the Fourteenth-Century Depression*. New Haven: Yale University Press, 1976.

———. "Noms de saints et mentalité populaire à Gênes, au XIVᵉ siècle." *Le Moyen Âge: Revue d'Histoire et de Philologie* 73 (1967): 431–46.

Klein, Holger A. "Eastern Objects and Western Desires: Relics and Reliquaries Between Byzantium and the West." *Dumbarton Oaks Papers* 58 (2004): 283–314.

———. "Refashioning Byzantium in Venice, ca. 1200–1400." In *San Marco, Byzantium, and the Myths of Venice*, edited by Henry Maguire and Robert S. Nelson, 193–226. Washington, D.C.: Dumbarton Oaks Research Library and Collection, 2010.

Krosigk, Konrad von. *Urkundenbuch der Familie von Krosigk: Eine Sammlung von Regesten, Urkunden und sonstigen Nachrichten zur Geschichte der Herren von Krosigk und ihrer Besitzungen*. Vol. 1. Halle: S. Schmidt, 1882.

Kuttner, Stephan, and Antonio García y García. "A New Eyewitness Account of the Fourth Lateran Council." *Traditio* 20 (1964): 115–78.

Lazzarini, Vittorio. " 'Dux ille Danduleus': Andrea Dandolo e la cultura a metà del Trecento." In *Convegno di studi su Petrarca, Venezia, e il Veneto*, edited by G. Padoan, 123–56. Florence: L. S. Olschki, 1976.

———. "I titoli dei dogi di Venezia." *Nuovo Archivio Veneto*, n.s., 5 (1903): 271–313.

Limentani, Alberto. "Martin Da Canal e 'Les estoires de Venise.' " In *Storia della cultura Veneta*, edited by G. Folena, 1:590–601. Vicenza: Neri Pozzi, 1976.

Lock, Peter. *The Franks in the Aegean, 1204–1500*. London: Longman, 1995.

Longnon, Jean. *Les compagnons de Villehardouin: Recherches sur les croisés de la quatrième croisade*. Geneva: Droz, 1978.

MacClannan, Anne. "Bulgarini's Assumption with Doubting Thomas: Art, Trade, and Faith in Post-Plague Siena." In *A Faithful Sea: The Religious Cultures of the Mediterranean, 1200–1700*, edited by A. Husain et al., 65–78. Oxford: Oneworld, 2007.

Macrides, Ruth. "The New Constantine and the New Constantinople—1261?" *Byzantine and Modern Greek Studies* 6 (1980): 13–41.

Madden, Thomas. *Enrico Dandolo and the Rise of Venice*. Baltimore: Johns Hopkins University Press, 2003.

———. "Outside and Inside the Fourth Crusade." *International History Review* 17 (November 1995): 726–43.

———. "The Venetian Version of the Fourth Crusade: Memory and the Conquest of Constantinople in Medieval Venice." *Speculum* 87 (2012): 311–44.

———. "Vows and Contracts in the Fourth Crusade: The Treaty of Zara and the Attack on Constantinople in 1204." *International History Review* 15, no. 5 (1993): 441–68.

Magdalino, Paul. *The Empire of Manuel I Komnenos, 1143–1180*. Cambridge: Cambridge University Press, 1993.

Maguire, Henry, and Robert S. Nelson, eds. *San Marco, Byzantium, and the Myths of Venice*. Washington, D.C.: Dumbarton Oaks Research Library and Collection, 2010.

Majeska, George. "The Relics of Constantinople After 1204." In *Byzance et les reliques du Christ*, edited by J. Durand and B. Flusin, 183–90. Paris: Association des amis du Centre d'histoire et civilisation de Byzance, 2004.

———. "St. Sophia in the Fourteenth and Fifteenth Centuries: The Russian Travelers on the Relics." *Dumbarton Oaks Papers* 27 (1973): 69–87.

Maleczek, Werner. *Pietro Capuano: Patrizio amalfitano, cardinale, legato alla quarta crociata, teologo*. Translated by Fulvio Delle Donne. Amalfi: Presso la Sede del Centro, 1997.

Mango, Cyril. "Notes on Byzantine Monuments: Frescoes in the Octagon of St. Mary Chalkoprateia." *Dumbarton Oaks Papers* 23–24 (1969–70): 369–72.

Maranini, Giuseppe. *La costituzione di Venezia dalle origini alla serrata del Maggior Consiglio*. Venice, 1927; repr., Florence: La Nuova Italia, 1974.

Marin, Şerban. "Between Justification and Glory: The Venetian Chronicles' View of the Fourth Crusade." In *The Fourth Crusade: Event, Aftermath, and Perceptions*, edited by Thomas Madden, 113–22. Aldershot, U.K.: Ashgate, 2008.

———. "'Dominus quartae partis et dimidiae totius Imperii Romaniae': The Fourth Crusade and the Dogal Title in the Venetian Chronicles' Representation." *Quaderni della Casa Romena* 3 (2004): 119–50.

———. "A Precedent to the Fourth Crusade: The Anti-Byzantine Campaign of Doge Domenico Michiel in 1122–1126 According to the Venetian Chronicles." *Annuario: Istituto Romeno di Cultura e Ricerca Umanistica di Venezia* 6–7 (2004–5): 239–66.

———. "Venetian and Non-Venetian Crusaders in the Fourth Crusade, According to the Venetian Chronicles' Tradition." *Annuario: Istituto Romeno di Cultura e Ricerca Umanistica di Venezia* 4 (2002): 111–71.

———. "The Venetian 'Empire' in the East: The Imperial Elections in Constantinople on 1204 in the Venetian Chronicles' Representation." *Annuario: Istituto Romeno di Cultura e Ricerca Umanistica di Venezia* 5 (2003): 185–245.

———. "Venice and *Translatio Imperii*: The Relevance of the 1171 Event in the Venetian Chronicles' Tradition." *Annuario: Istituto Romeno di Cultura e Ricerca Umanistica di Venezia* 3 (2001): 45–103.

Martin, John, and Dennis Romano. "Reconsidering Venice." In *Venice Reconsidered: The History and Civilization of an Italian City-State, 1297–1797*, edited by John Martin and Dennis Romano, 1–38. Baltimore: Johns Hopkins University Press, 2000.

Matthews, Thomas. *The Byzantine Churches of Istanbul: A Photographic Survey*. University Park: Pennsylvania State University Press, 1976.

McCormick, Michael. *Eternal Victory: Triumphal Rulership in Late Antiquity, Byzantium, and the Early Medieval West*. Cambridge: Cambridge University Press, 1986.

Mercuri, Chiara. *Corona di Cristo corona di re: La monarchia francese e la corona di spine nel Medioevo*. Rome: Edizioni di Storia e Letteratura, 2004.

Morris, Colin. "Policy and Visions: The Case of the Holy Lance at Antioch." In *War and Government in the Middle Ages: Essays in Honour of J. O. Prestwich*, edited by J. Gillingham and J. C. Holt, 33–45. Totowa, N.J.: Barnes and Noble Books, 1984.

Most, Glenn. *Doubting Thomas*. Cambridge: Harvard University Press, 2005.

Müeller, Reinhold. "The Procurators of San Marco in the Thirteenth and Fourteenth Centuries: A Study of the Office as a Financial and Trust Institution." *Studi Veneziani* 13 (1973): 105–220.

Muir, Edward. *Civic Ritual in Renaissance Venice*. Princeton: Princeton University Press, 1981.

Mundy, J. H. "Philip Jones and the Medieval City-State." *Journal of European Economic History* 28, no. 1 (1999): 185–200.

Murray, Alan. "'Mighty Against the Enemies of Christ': The Relic of the True Cross and the Armies of the Kingdom of Jerusalem." In *The Crusades and Their Sources: Essays Presented to Bernard Hamilton*, edited by J. France and W. G. Zajac, 217–38. Aldershot, U.K.: Ashgate, 1998.

Musolino, Giovanni. *Santa Lucia a Venezia: Storia, culto, arte*. Venice: Stamperia di Venezia, 1987.

Nederman, Cary. "Empire and the Historiography of European Political Thought: Marsiglio of Padua, Nicholas of Cusa, and the Medieval/Modern Divide." *Journal of the History of Ideas* 66, no. 1 (2005): 1–15.

Nicol, Donald. *Byzantium and Venice: A Study in Diplomatic and Cultural Relations*. Cambridge: Cambridge University Press, 1988.

———. *The Last Centuries of Byzantium, 1261–1453*. London: Hart-Davis, 1972.

Niero, Antonio. "Questioni agiografiche su San Marco." *Studi Veneziani* 12 (1970): 3–27.

———. "Reliquie e corpi di santi." In *Culto dei santi a Venezia*, edited by Silvio Tramontin, 181–208. Venice: Edizioni Studium Cattolico Veneziano, 1965.

Nitti, Francesco. "La leggenda della traslazione di S. Nicola da Mira a Bari." *Iapigia* 8 (1937): 265–74.

Otter, Monika. "*Prolixitas Temporum*: Futurity in Medieval History Narratives." In *Reading Medieval Culture: Essays in Honor of Robert W. Hanning*, edited by Robert M. Stein and Sandra Pierson Prior, 45–67. Notre Dame: Notre Dame University Press, 2005.

Ousterhout, Robert. "Some Notes on the Construction of Christos Ho Pantepotes (Eski Imaret Camii) in Istanbul." *Christanike Archaiologike Hetaireia* 16 (1991–92): 47–56.

Palmieri, Matheo. *Historia della translatione del glorioso corpo della Beata Vergine, e martire Santa Barbara di Nicomedia, portato à Venetia: Da Constantinopoli dal Nobil'homo Sier Raffael Baseggio l'anno 1258 & riposto nella Chiesa di Santa Maria de Padri Crociferi*. Il Criuellari: Padua, 1642.

Paul, Nicholas, and Suzanne Yeager. "Introduction: Crusading and the Work of Memory, Past and Present." In *Remembering the Crusades: Myth, Image, and Identity*, edited by Nicholas Paul and Suzanne Yeager, 1–25. Baltimore: Johns Hopkins University Press, 2012.

Perocco, G., ed. *The Horses of San Marco, Venice*. Milan: Olivetti, 1979.

Perry, David. "The Material Culture of Medieval Venetian Identity." In *Mediterranean Identities in the Premodern Era: Entrepôts, Islands, Empires*, edited by Kathryn Reyerson and John Watkins, 15–34. Aldershot, U.K.: Ashgate, 2014.

———. "Paul the Martyr and Venetian Memories of the Fourth Crusade." In *Remembering the Crusades: Myth, Image, and Identity*, edited by Nicholas Paul and Suzanne Yeager, 215–32. Baltimore: Johns Hopkins University Press, 2012.

———. "St. George and Venice." In *Matter of Faith: An Interdisciplinary Study of Relics and Relic Veneration in the Medieval Period*, edited by James Robinson and Anna Harnden, 15–22. London: British Museum Press, 2014.

———. "1308 and 1177: Venice and the Papacy in Real and Imaginary Crusades." In *La Papauté et les croisades / The Papacy and the Crusades*, edited by Michel Balard, 117–30. Aldershot, U.K.: Ashgate, 2012.

———. "The *Translatio Symonensis* and the Seven Thieves: A Venetian Fourth Crusade *Furta Sacra* Narrative and the Looting of Constantinople." In *The Fourth Crusade:*

Event, Aftermath, and Perceptions, edited by Thomas Madden, 89–112. Aldershot, U.K.: Ashgate, 2008.

Perry, Marilyn. "St. Mark's Trophies: Legend, Superstition, and Archaeology in Renaissance Venice." *Journal of the Warburg and Courtauld Institutes* 40 (1977): 27–49.

Pertusi, Agostino. "Ai confini tra religione e politica: La contesa per le reliquie di S. Nicola tra Bari, Venezia e Genova." *Quaderni Medievali* 5 (1978): 6–56.

———. "Le profezie sulla presa di Costantinopoli (1204) nel cronista veneziano Marco (c. 1292) e le loro fonti bizantine (Pseudo-Costantino Magno, Pseudo Daniele, Pseudo-Leone il Saggio)." *Studi Veneziani*, n.s., 3 (1979): 13–47.

———. "Venezia e Bisanzio: 1000–1204." *Dumbarton Oaks Papers* 33 (1979): 1–22.

Pincus, Debra. "Andrea Dandolo and the Construction of the Ruler in Fourteenth-Century Venice." In *Venice Reconsidered: The History and Civilization of an Italian City-State, 1297–1797*, edited by J. Martin and D. Romano, 89–137. Baltimore: Johns Hopkins University Press, 2000.

———. "Christian Relics and the Body Politic: A Thirteenth-Century Relief Plaque in the Church of San Marco." In *Interpretazioni veneziane: Studi di storia dell'arte in onore di Michelangelo Muraro*, edited by D. Rosand, 39–57. Venice: Arsenale Editrice, 1984.

———. "Venice and Its Doge in the Grand Design: Andrea Dandolo and the Fourteenth-Century Mosaics of the Baptistry." In *San Marco, Byzantium, and the Myths of Venice*, edited by Henry Maguire and Robert S. Nelson, 245–72. Washington, D.C.: Dumbarton Oaks Research Library and Collection, 2010.

———. "Venice and the Two Romes: Byzantium and Rome as a Double Heritage in Venetian Cultural Politics." *Artibus et Historiae* 13, no. 26 (1992): 101–14.

Pocock, John. *Barbarism and Religion*. Vol. 3. Cambridge: Cambridge University Press, 2003.

Pomorisac, J. De Luigi. *Les émaux byzantins de la Pala d'oro de l'Eglise de Saint Marc à Venise*. Zurich: P. G. Keller, 1966.

Poncelet, Albert. "Le légendier de Pierre Calò." *Analecta Bollandiana* 29 (1910): 5–116.

Powell, James. *Anatomy of a Crusade*. Philadelphia: University of Pennsylvania Press, 1986.

Pryor, John. "The *Eracles* and William of Tyre: An Interim Report." In *The Horns of Hattin*, edited by Benjamin Kedar, 270–93. Aldershot, U.K.: Variorum, 1992.

———. "Transportation of Horses by Sea During the Era of the Crusades: Eighth Century to 1285 A.D." *Mariner's Mirror* 68 (1982): 9–30.

Queller, Donald, Thomas Compton, and Donald Campbell. "The Fourth Crusade: The Neglected Majority." *Speculum* 49, no. 3 (1974): 441–65.

Queller, Donald, and Thomas Madden. *The Fourth Crusade: The Conquest of Constantinople*. Philadelphia: University of Pennsylvania Press, 1997.

———. "Some Further Arguments in Defense of the Venetians on the Fourth Crusade." *Byzantion* 62 (1992): 433–73.

Remensnyder, Amy. "Legendary Treasure at Conques: Reliquaries and Imaginative Memory." *Speculum* 71, no. 4 (1996): 884–906.

Reynolds, Susan. *Kingdoms and Communities in Western Europe, 900–1300*. Oxford: Oxford University Press, 1997.

Riant, Paul. "Dépouilles religieuses à Constantinople au XIIIᵉ siècle et des documents historuqes nés de leur transport en Occident." *Mémoires de la Société Nationale des Antiquaires de France*, 4th ser., 6 (1875): 1–241.

Richard, Jean. "The Latin Church in Constantinople (1204–27)." In *Latins and Greeks in the Eastern Mediterranean After 1204*, edited by Benjamin Arbel et al., 45–62. London: Frank Cass, 1989.

Riley-Smith, Jonathan. *The First Crusade and the Idea of Crusading.* London: Athlone Press, 1986.

———. *The First Crusaders, 1095–1131.* Cambridge: Cambridge University Press, 1997.

———. "The Venetian Crusade of 1122–1124." In *I comuni italiani nel regno crociato di Gerusalemme*, edited by G. Airaldi and B. Kedar, 339–50. Genoa: University of Genoa, Instituto di Medievistica, 1986.

Robbert, Louise. "Venetian Participation in the Crusade of Damietta." *Studi Veneziani*, n.s., 30 (1995): 15–34.

Rousseau, Constance. "A Papal Matchmaker: Principle and Pragmatism During Innocent III's Pontificate." *Journal of Medieval History* 24, no. 3 (1998): 259–71.

Rubenstein, Nicolai. "Italian Reactions to the Terraferma Expansion in the Fifteenth Century." In *Renaissance Venice*, edited by J. R. Hale, 197–217. London: Faber and Faber, 1973.

Runciman, Steven. *A History of the Crusades.* Vol. 3. Cambridge: Cambridge University Press, 1954.

Saccardo, Pietro. *La cappella di S. Isidoro nella Basilica di San Marco.* Venice: La Procuratoria di San Marco, 1987.

Schmandt, Raymond. "The Fourth Crusade and the Just War Theory." *Catholic History Review* 61 (1975): 191–221.

Schulz, Juergen. "La piazza medievale di San Marco." *Annali di Architettura* 4/5 (1992–93): 134–56.

Ševcenko, Nancy. "The Limburg Staurothek and Its Relics." In *Thyiniama ste mneine tes Laskarinas Boura*, edited by M. Vassilaki et al., 1–13. Athens: Benaki Museum, 1994.

Sgarbi, Marco, ed. *"Translatio Studiorum": Ancient, Medieval, and Modern Bearers of Intellectual History.* Leiden: Brill, 2012.

Siberry, Elizabeth. *Criticism of Crusading, 1095–1274.* Oxford: Oxford University Press, 1985.

Simpson, Alicia. "Before and After 1204: The Versions of Niketas Choniates' 'Historia.'" *Dumbarton Oaks Papers* 60 (2006): 189–221.

Skinner, Patricia. *Family Power in Southern Italy: The Duchy of Gaeta and Its Neighbours, 850–1139.* Cambridge: Cambridge University Press, 1995.

Spiegel, Gabrielle M. *The Past as Text: The Theory and Practice of Medieval Historiography.* Baltimore: Johns Hopkins University Press, 1999.

Spinelli, Giovanni. "I monasteri Benedettini fra il 1000 ed il 1300." In *La Chiesa di Venezia nei secoli XI–XIII*, edited by Franco Tonon, 108–34. Venice: Edizioni Studium Cattolico Veneziano, 1988.

Swietek, Francis. "Gunther of Pairis and the *Historia Constantinopolitana*." *Speculum* 53 (January 1978): 49–79.

Tassini, Dionisio. *La questione storico giuridica del patriarcato di Venezia (Aquileia).* Genoa: G. Bacchi-Palazzi, 1906.

Tenenti, Alberto. *Venezia e il senso del mare: Storia di un prisma culturale dal XIII al XVIII secolo.* Naples: Istituto Italiano per gli Studi Filosofici, 1999.

Thiriet, Freddy. "Byzance et les Byzantins vus par le Vénitien Andrea Dandolo." *Revue des Études Sud-Est Européennes* 10, no. 1 (1972): 5–15.

———. *La Romanie vénitienne au Moyen Age: Le developpement et l'exploitation du domaine colonial vénetien (XII–XV siècles).* Paris: E. De Boccard, 1959.

Thompson, Augustine. *Cities of God: The Religion of the Italian Communes, 1125–1325.* University Park: Pennsylvania State University Press, 2005.

Throop, Palmer. *Criticism of the Crusade: A Study of Public Opinion and Propaganda.* Amsterdam: N. V. Swets & Zeitlinger, Boekhandel en Uitgeversmaatschappij, 1940.

Tobler, Titus, and Augustus Molinier. *Itinera Hierosolymitana et descriptiones Terrae Sanctae.* Vol. 1. Geneva: J.-G. Fick, 1879.

Tramontin, Silvio. "Realtà e leggenda nei racconti marciani veneti." *Studi Veneziani* 12 (1970): 35–58.

Vincent, Nicholas. *The Holy Blood: King Henry III and the Westminster Blood Relic.* Cambridge: Cambridge University Press, 2001.

Volback, Wolfgang. "Gli smalti della Pala d'oro." In *La Pala d'oro,* edited by H. R. Hahnloser and R. Polacco, 3–74. Venice: Canal & Stamperia, 1994.

Whalen, Brett. "The Discovery of the Holy Patriarchs: Relics, Ecclesiastical Politics, and Sacred History in Twelfth-Century Crusader Palestine." *Historical Reflections / Reflexions Historiques* 27, no. 1 (2001): 139–76.

———. *Dominion of God: Christendom and Apocalypse in the Middle Ages.* Cambridge: Harvard University Press, 2009.

———. "Joachim of Fiore and the Division of Christendom." *Viator* 34 (2003): 89–108.

Winkelmann, Eduard. *Philipp von Schwaben und Otto IV von Braunschweig.* Vols. 1–2. Darmstadt: Wissenschaftliche Buchgesellschaft, 1963.

Wolff, Robert. *The Later Crusades: A History of the Crusades.* Vol. 2. Madison: University of Wisconsin Press, 1969.

———. "A New Document from the Period of the Latin Empire of Constantinople: The Oath of the Venetian Podestà." In *Annuaire de l'Institut de philologie et d'histoire orientales et slaves XII: Mélanges Grégoire,* 4:539–73. Brussels: Secrétariat de l'Institut, 1953.

———. "The Organization of the Latin Patriarchate of Constantinople, 1204–1261: Social and Administrative Consequences of the Latin Conquest." *Traditio* 6 (1948): 33–60.

———. "Politics in the Latin Patriarchate of Constantinople, 1204–1261." *Dumbarton Oaks Papers* 8 (1954): 225–303.

Wormald, Francis. "The Rood of Bromholm." *Journal of the Warburg Institute* 1 (July 1937): 31–45.

Wortley, John. "The Marian Relics at Constantinople." *Greek, Roman, and Byzantine Studies* 45 (2005): 171–87.

———. Review of *Exuviae sacrae Constantinopolitanae,* by Comte Paul Riant. *Revue de l'Histoire des Religions* 3 (2006). http://rhr.revues.org/5176.

INDEX

Page numbers in *italics* refer to illustrations.

Mamluks, 167

Manuel Comnenus, Emperor, 78, 92–93, 95, 160

March Pact: division of church property, 17, 30, 52–54, 59–62, 69–70; organizing churches, 27, 30; papal response, 47, 49, 50–60; ratification of, 49, 50, 54, 63; terms of, 13, 16–19, 47–48, 52–54

Marciana Library (Venice), 155–57

Marco Nicola, 147

Marin, Serban, 204n64

Mark, Saint, 140–41, 142, 146, 171, 173, 184

Mark the Evangelist, Saint, 101, 140–48, 157, 164, 168, 203n21

Marsiglio of Padua, 204n46

Martin, Abbot of Pairis, 24, 27–30, 44, 86, 195n43, 199n145, 201n31; See also *Historia Constantinopolitana*

Martin of Tours, Saint, 80, 107, 123–24, 200n149

Martin of Troyes, Saint, 34–35

martyrs, chants for, 196n49

Mary Chalkoprateia, Saint, 119

Matthew of Amalfi, 95–96, 197n86

Matthias, Saint, 39

medieval imagination: divine power, 113–17; power of relics, 112, 126–27. *See also* miracles

memorializing constructs, 111–34; background, 111–13; communal ratification, 6–7, 126–29; conflict over meaning of Fourth Crusade, 121; Constantinople, 151–52; digression, 117–21; direct address, 121–26; Fourth Crusade, 47, 54–57, 64, 72–73, 84, 110–17, 184; image/counterimage, 138; localization, 116–17, 126–29, 137, 146–47, 152, 154–57, 172, 176–77; monastic interpretations, 125; myths/anti-myths, 138, 143–44; providential history, 113–17; relic translation, 77, 120, 154–57, 179; retrospective prophecy, 129–30, 133, 149. *See also* miracles

Mesarites, John and Nicholas, 21

Michael VI, emperor, 204n65

Michael VIII Palaiologos, emperor, 45, 149–50, 166–67

miracles: authorizing relic thefts, 78–82, 89, 98–99, 108, 120, 130–34, 147–48; key miracles, 129, 149; localization, 83, 96, 111, 113, 130, 132–33, 171; in medieval imagination, 112, 130–33, 146; miraculous voyage

themes, 91–92, 95; on-site intercession, 85–87, 133, 142, 171; positive and negative tropes, 132; post-translation, 160; redemptive power of, 111; universalizing, 130. *See also* divine favor; sea voyages as trope; *translatio* (transported relics) narratives, *and specific saints*

Monte Cassino Abbey and Monastery, 38, 94

Mont Saint-Quentin Abbey, 33

Morosini, Thomas, Patriarch of Constantinople, 57–59, 67–68, 100, 144

Mourtzouphlos. *See* Alexius V Doukas Mourtzouphlos

Muslims, 49, 64, 65, 72, 156, 168, 180, 183

Napoleon, 184

"Narratio exceptionis apud Cluniacum capitis beati Clementis," 37–38, 102–5, 126, 179, 198n119

negative (smiting) miracles, 132

Neptune, Venice as city of, 170, 208n57

Nero, 149

New Jerusalem, 204n51

"New Rome," 150, 167

Nicholas Hydruntinus, 25

Nicholas, Saint, 42, 142, 143, 144, 147, 157, 170, 203n21

Nicol, Donald, 166

Niketas Choniates, 14–15, 19, 20–21, 24, 44, 69, 95, 108

Nivelon de Chérisy, Bishop of Soissons, 26–27; biographical data, 194n12, 195n19; diversion to Constantinople, 194n8; *Paradiso*, 1, 132; relic acquisition and distribution, 29, 33, 39–40, 80–84, 127, 145. *See also* "Land of Jerusalem"

numerology, 118

Orgerio Pane, Genoese chronicle of, 32

Orthodox church property. *See* Greek church property

Ottoman Turks, 174, 183

Otto of Brunswick, 85, 86

Pairis, 105–10, 111, 114, 130, 133. See also *Historia Constantinopolitana*

Pala d'Oro, 165

Palazzo Ducale, 164–66, 175–76, 206n12, 207n26

Pantocrator, 20, 28, 108

papal legates, 34–40, 66–69